CLASSIC GOLF STORIES

CLASSIC GOLF STORIES

Twenty-Six Incredible Tales from the Links

EDITED WITH AN INTRODUCTION BY

JEFF SILVERMAN

Skyhorse Publishing

Skyhorse Publishing books may be purchased in bulk at special discounts for sales promotion, corporate gifts, fund-raising, or educational purposes. Special editions can also be created to specifications. For details, contact the Special Sales Department, Skyhorse Publishing, 307 West 36th Street, 11th Floor, New York, NY 10018 or info@skyhorsepublishing.com.

Skyhorse® and Skyhorse Publishing® are registered trademarks of Skyhorse Publishing, Inc.®, a Delaware corporation.

Visit our website at www.skyhorsepublishing.com.

10 9 8 7 6 5 4 3 2 1

Library of Congress Cataloging-in-Publication Data is available on file

ISBN: 978-1-61608-381-6

Printed in China

For Guy Cary,
the most classic golf story I know

CONTENTS

Why Golf is Art and Art is Golf
We have not far to seek—
So much depends upon the lie,
So much upon the cleek.

—Rudyard Kipling
From "Verses on Games"

INTRODUCTION

E ssentially, every time we set out to play golf, we set out in search of untold stories. Not every one will be a classic, of course, unless we can expand our fairways to include absurdity, burlesque, and all the other insanely hysterical things we human beings are capable of inflicting on a golf ball. Still, regardless of how well or not so well we play the game, a round of golf is plot in a nutshell with a surlyn cover. It begins, as stories do, with infinite possibilities and hopes for a happy ending. Then, along the way, all hell's likely to break loose. Nature taunts us. Luck rewards—or kills—us, the difference determined by silly millimeters. Hazards await us. Penalties are exacted on us. Despair moves in. Elation moves it out. Despair moves back in again. Character is tested. *True* character is revealed.

I remember, in college lit classes, the way professors would proudly march out the observation somewhere in a lecture that "In literature, as in life . . ." I would zone out immediately. The two are pretty much the same, I thought; after all, what's literature if not life—or at least a few pieces of it—recorded on a page in the symbols we use to communicate? And what's golf, then, if not the most maddening endeavor ever devised by evil Druids to play out everything life can throw at us over eighteen holes of varying length and difficulty? Golf and literature go hand in hand.

It's the very nature of the game—how we handle what golf confronts us with—that's led so many superb writers over so long a time to wade into it, and retrieve so many splendid stories. Some of which—to suit the demands of the title attached to this collection—are, indeed, "classic."

So what makes a golf story a *classic* golf story? A number of things, really, but, ultimately, I think, it comes down to this: Even if the language is a bit thick or floral by contemporary standards, even if certain aspects of the game seem a little arcane, even if the manners are as dead as the dodo and the atmosphere seems somewhat out of whack with ours, they can hold up a mirror that still offers a true reflection of who we are—as men, as women, and as golfers. In short, they stand the test of time—all in this volume have been standing for at least eighty years, with several still upright into their third century—and they continue to speak to us.

According to the Oxford English Dictionary, the word "golf" was originally teed up in the written language in the 1450s, and by the mid-seventeenth century, it had bounced its way into poetry. The game's first appearance in fiction came in 1771, with a brief aside on the diversion "called Golf" in "the fields called the Links" of Edinburgh in Tobias Smollett's novel *The Expedition of Humphry Clinker*. By the second half of the nineteenth century, as the game really took off through the British Isles, and sports became more fit subject matter for popular journals directed toward the moneyed, leisure class, golf, quite naturally, began developing a literature—both fiction and non—of its own. In essence, the game, and writing about the game, began to grow up together.

With golf's arrival on American shores just before the twentieth century, American writers began getting in on the fun—playing the game, and writing about it, too. As did their transplanted brethren. In 1892, when golf was still very much a novelty in the New World, Rudyard Kipling, a confirmed hacker, settled in for a few years on an estate in Vermont. One of the first things he did was establish a small course on the property.

Summer and winter alike, he'd take his whacks on this makeshift layout of indeterminate par that extended from the meadow beyond his front door right to the edge of the Connecticut River. The Nobel Prize winner's sojourn was wonderfully productive. Not only did he write *Captains Courageous* and the Jungle Books in Vermont, he also invented the red golf ball, allowing him to soldier on with his passion—and keep track of his shots—even through the North American snow cover.

What's so enjoyable for me about reading these stories from the shank of the nineteenth century and the beginnings of the twentieth is the window they provide in what *hasn't* changed about golf and golfers. The questions Canadian belletrist Arnold Haultain asks in "The Mystery of Golf" are the same ones we ask ourselves today. We continue to play the game for the same reasons W. G. Simpson played it in the 1880s, and we still navigate the course with the same aspect and mien Horace Hutchinson advocated in 1890. A. A. Milne (certainly more at home in Pooh Corner than Amen Corner), H. Rider Haggard, F. Scott Fitzgerald, Owen Johnson, Charles E. Van Loan, Bernard Darwin, and P. G. Wodehouse—to name a few of the scratch writers you'll walk the land with in the following pages—all tap into the same emotions, the same frustrations, and even the same occasional joys we still tap into whenever we tee one up and see nothing but open fairway ahead. In golf, past is always prologue.

Sure, clubs now come in space-age metals, and the new balls have nuclear reactors in their core, but what brings us to the game, what we take from the game, and even what we give back to it, remains—refreshingly—akin to what our long line of forebears on the links experienced in their plus fours and wool jackets. Then, as now, the game finds fascinating ways to engage us, instruct us, cajole us, tease us, entertain us, enrage us, and, unless our given name happens to be Eldrick, regularly defeat us.

Which is why we keep coming back for more. We golfers are a gluttonous bunch, on the course, and on the page. And as the classics coming up make clear, we've been that way for longer than any golfer alive can now remember.

Jeff Silverman

THE PRAISE AND ORIGIN OF GOLF

SIR W. G. SIMPSON

I

There are so many good points about the royal and ancient game of golf that its comparative obscurity, rather than its increasing popularity, is matter for wonder. It is apparently yet unknown to the Medical Faculty. The golfer does not find it in the list of exercises recommended by doctors to persons engaged in warfare with the results of sedentary habits. He is moved to pity British subjects compelled to stir their livers by walking, horse-riding, or cycling. He knows how monotonous it is following one's nose, or flogging a horse and following it, compared with flogging and following a ball. For the wearied and bent cyclist, who prides himself on making his journey in as short a time as possible, he has a pitying word. Men who assume that the sooner the journey is over the greater the pleasure, evidently do not love their pursuit for its own sake.

With any other sport or pastime golf compares favourably.

With cricket? The golfer has nothing to say against that game, if you are a good player. But it is a pastime for the few. The rest have to hang about the pavilion, and see the runs made. With the golfer it is different. He does not require to be even a second-class player, in order to get into matches. Again, the skilful cricketer has to retire when he gets up in years. He might exclaim with Wolsey: 'Had I served my golf as I have served my cricket, she would not thus have deserted me in my old age.' How different it is with golf! It is a game for the many. It suits all sorts and conditions of men. The strong and the weak, the halt and the maimed, the octogenarian and the boy, the rich and the poor, the clergyman and the infidel, may play every day, except Sunday. The late riser can play comfortably, and be back for his rubber in the afternoon; the sanguine man can measure himself against those who will beat him; the half-crown seeker can find victims, the gambler can bet, the man of high principle, by playing for nothing, may enjoy himself, and yet feel good. You can brag, and lose matches; depreciate yourself, and win them. Unlike the other Scotch game of whisky-drinking, excess in it is not injurious to the health.

Better than fishing, shooting, and hunting? Certainly. These can only be indulged in at certain seasons. They let you die of dyspepsia during the rest of the year. Besides, hunting, you are dependent on horses and foxes for sport; shooting, on birds; fishing, on the hunger of a scaly but fastidious animal. The pleasures of sport are extracted from the sufferings of dumb animals. If horses, grouse, or fish could squeal, sports would be distressful rather than amusing.

Golf has some drawbacks. It is possible, by too much of it, to destroy the mind; a man with a Roman nose and a high forehead may play away his profile. That peculiar mental condition called 'Fifish' probably had its origin in the east of the Kingdom. For the golfer, Nature loses her significance. Larks, the casts of worms, the buzzing of bees, and even children, are hateful to him. I have seen a golfer very angry at getting into a bunker by killing a bird, and rewards of as much as ten shillings have been offered for boys maimed on the links. Rain comes to be regarded solely in its relation to the putting greens; the daisy is detested, botanical specimens are but 'hazards,' twigs 'break clubs.' Winds cease to be east, south, west, or north. They are ahead, behind, or sideways, and the sky is bright or dark, according to the state of the game.

A cause of the comparative obscurity of golf is that the subject cannot easily be treated by the novelist. Golf has no Hawley Smart. Its Whyte Melville did not write, but played. You can ride at a stone wall for love and the lady, but what part can she take in driving at a bunker? It is natural that Lady Diana should fall in love with Nimrod when she finds him in the plough, stunned, broken-legged, the brush, which he had wrested from the fox as he fell, firm in his lifeless grasp. But if beauty found us prone on the putting green, a 27½ imbedded in our gory locks, she might send us home to be trepanned; but nothing could come of it, a red coat notwithstanding. No! at golf ladies are simply in the road. Riding to hounds and opening five-barred gates, soft nothings may be whispered, but it is impossible at the same moment to putt and to cast languishing glances. If the dear one be near you at the tee, she may get her teeth knocked out, and even between the shots arms dare not steal round waists, lest the party behind should call out 'fore!' I have seen a golfing novel indeed; but it was in manuscript, the publishers having rejected it. The scene was St. Andrews. He was a soldier, a statesman, an orator, but only a seventh-class golfer. She, being St. Andrews born, naturally preferred a rising player. Whichever of the two made the best medal score was to have her hand. The soldier employed a lad to kick his adversary's ball into bunkers, to tramp it into mud, to lose it, and he won; but the lady would not give her hand to a score of 130. Six months passed, during which the soldier studied the game morning, noon, and night, but to little purpose. Next medal-day arrived, and he was face to face with the fact that his golf, unbacked by his statesmanship, would avail him nothing. He hired and disguised a professional in his own clothes. The ruse was successful; but, alas! the professional broke down. The soldier, disguised as a marker, however, cheated, and brought him in with 83. A three for the long hole roused suspicion, and led to inquiry. He was found out, dismissed from the club, rejected by the lady (who afterwards made an unhappy marriage with a left-handed player), and sent back in disgrace to his statesmanship and oratory. It was as good a romance as could be made on the subject, but very improbable.

Although unsuited to the novelist, golf lends itself readily to the dreaming of scenes of which the dreamer is the hero. Unless he is an exceptionally good rider, or can afford 300 guinea mounts, a man cannot expect to be the hero of the hunting-field. The sportsman knows what sort of shot he is, and the fisher has no illusions; but every moderately good golfer, on the morning of the medal-day may lie abed and count up a perfect score for himself. He easily recalls how at different times and often he has done each hole in par figures. Why not this day, and all the holes consecutively? It seems so easy. The more he thinks of it the easier it seems, even allowing for a few mistakes. Every competitor who is awake soon enough sees the necessity for preparing a speech against the contingency of the medal being presented to him in the evening. Nor is any one much crashed when all is over, and he has not won. If he does well, it was but that putt, that bad lie, that bunker. If his score is bad, what of it ? Even the best are off their game occasionally. Next time it will be different. Meanwhile his score will be taken as a criterion of his game, and he is sure to win many half-crowns from unwary adversaries who underrate him.

The game of golf is full of consolation. The long driver who is beaten feels that he has a soul above putting. All those who cannot drive thirty yards suppose themselves to be good putters. Your hashy player piques himself on his power of recovery. The duffer is a duffer merely because every second shot is missed. Time or care will eliminate the misses, and then! Or perhaps there is something persistently wrong in driving, putting, or approaching. He will discover the fault, and then! Golf is not one of those occupations in which you soon learn your level. There is no shape nor size of body, no awkwardness nor ungainliness, which puts good golf beyond one's reach. There are good golfers with spectacles, with one eye, with one leg, even with one arm. None but the absolutely blind need despair. It is not the youthful tyro alone who has cause to hope. Beginners in middle age have become great, and, more wonderful still, after years of patient duffering, there may be a rift in the clouds. Some pet vice which has been clung to as a virtue may be abandoned, and the fifth-class player burst upon the world as a medal-winner. In golf, whilst there is life there is hope.

It is generally agreed that the keenest pleasure of the game is derived from long driving. When the golfer is preparing to hit a far clean straight shot, he feels the joy of the strong man that rejoiceth to run a race; that is to say, the joy we have authority for believing that the Jewish runner felt. The modern sprinter experiences none. On the contrary, there is the anticipation, through fatigue, of as much pain as if he were ringing the dentist's door-bell. For the golfer in the exercise of his strength there is neither pain nor fatigue. He has the combined pleasures of an onlooker and a performer. The blow once delivered, he can stand at ease and be admired whilst the ball makes the running.

There is no such being as a golfer uninterested in his driving. The really strong player seems to value his least; but this is merely because so many of his shots are good that they do not surprise him. Let it, however, be suggested that some other is a longer driver than he, and the mask of apathy will at once fall from his face, his tongue will be loosened, and he will proceed to boast. Even when a man cannot feel that he drives quite as far as the best, his pride in his own frame is not necessarily destroyed, as by most other sports. The runner, the jumper, the lifter of weights, even the oarsman, is crushed down into his true place by the brutal rudeness of competitive facts. Not so the golfer. A. says, 'I drive with a very light club, therefore admire my strength.' B. smiles complacently, whilst you marvel at the heaviness of his—a brawny muscular smile. Little C.'s club is nearly as long as himself. The inference is that little C.'s garments cover the limbs of a pocket Hercules. D. can drive as far with a cleek as common men with a club. D. is evidently a Goliath. The inferences may be all wrong. A. may be a scrag, C. a weed, D. merely beefy. On the other hand, each may be what he supposes himself. This is one of the glorious uncertainties of the game.

To some minds the great field which golf opens up for exaggeration is its chief attraction. Lying about the length of one's drives has this advan-

tage over most forms of falsehood, that it can scarcely be detected. Your audience may doubt your veracity, but they cannot prove your falsity. Even when some rude person proves your shot to be impossibly long, you are not cornered. You admit to an exceptional loft, to a skid off a paling, or, as a last appeal to the father of lies, you may rather think that a dog lifted your ball. 'Anyhow,' you add conclusively, 'that is where we found it when we came up to it.'

II

Golf, besides being a royal game, is also a very ancient one. Although it cannot be determined when it was first played, there seems little doubt that it had its origin in the present geological period, golf links being, we are informed, of Pleistocene formation.

Confining ourselves to Scotland, no golfer can fail to be struck with the resemblance to a niblick of the so-called spectacle ornament of our sculptured stones.

Many antiquarians are of opinion that the game did not become popular till about the middle of the 15th century. This seems extremely probable, as in earlier and more lawless times a journey so far from home as the far-hole at St. Andrews would have been exceedingly dangerous for an unarmed man.

It is not likely that future research will unearth the discoverer of golf. Most probably a game so simple and natural in its essentials suggested itself gradually and spontaneously to the bucolic mind. A shepherd tending his sheep would often chance upon a round pebble, and, having his crook in his hand, he would strike it away; for it is as inevitable that a man with a stick in his hand should aim a blow at any loose object lying in his path as that he should breathe.

On pastures green this led to nothing: but once on a time (probably) a shepherd, feeding his sheep on a links—perhaps those of St. Andrews— rolled one of these stones into a rabbit scrape. 'Marry' he quoth, 'I could not do that if I tried'—a thought (so instinctive is ambition) which nerved him to the attempt. But man cannot long persevere alone in any arduous undertaking, so our shepherd hailed another, who was hard by, to witness his endeavour. 'Forsooth, that is easy,' said the friend, and trying failed. They now searched in the gorse for as round stones as possible, and, to their surprise, each found an old golf ball, which, as the reader knows, are to be found there in considerable quantity even to this day. Having deepened the rabbit scrape so that the balls might not jump out of it, they set themselves to practicing putting. The stronger but less skilful shepherd, finding himself worsted at this amusement, protested that it was a fairer test of skill to play for the hole from a considerable distance. This being arranged, the game was found to be much more varied and interesting. They had at first called it 'putty,' because the immediate object was to putt or put the ball into the hole or scrape, but at the longer distance what we call driving was the chief interest, so the name was changed to 'go off,' or 'golf.' The sheep having meantime strayed, our shepherds had to go after them. This proving an exceedingly irksome interruption, they hit upon the ingenious device of making a circular course of holes, which enabled them to play and herd at the same time. The holes being now many and far apart, it became necessary to mark their whereabouts, which was easily done by means of a tag of wool from a sheep, attached to a stick, a primitive kind of flag still used on many greens almost in its original form.

Since these early days the essentials of the game have altered but little. Even the styme must have been of early invention. It would naturally occur as a quibble to a golfer who was having the worst of the match, and the adversary, in the confidence of three or four up, would not strenuously oppose it.

That golf was taken up with keen interest by the Scottish people from an early day is evidenced by laws directed against those who preferred it to archery and church-going. This state of feeling has changed but little. Some historians are, however, of opinion that during the seventeenth century golf lost some of its popularity. We know that the great Montrose was at one time devoted to it, and that he gave it up for what would now be considered the inferior sport of Covenanter-hunting. It is also an historical fact that Charles I. actually stopped in the middle of a game on Leith Links, because, forsooth, he learned that a rebellion had broken out in Ireland. Some, however, are of opinion that he acted on this occasion with his usual cunning—that at the time the news arrived he was being beaten, and that he hurried away to save his half-crown rather than his crown. Whatever the truth may be, it is certain that any one who in the present day abandoned a game because the stakes were not sufficiently high would be considered unworthy of the name of a golfer.

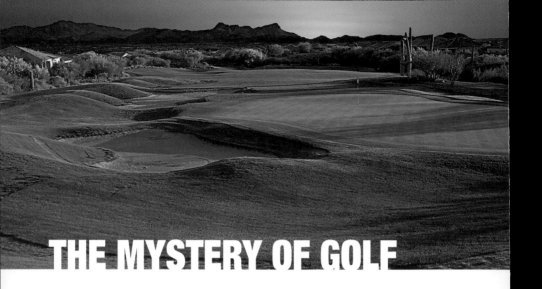

THE MYSTERY OF GOLF

ARNOLD HAULTAIN

PROEM

Three things there are as unfathomable as they are fascinating to the masculine mind: metaphysics; golf; and the feminine heart. The Germans, I believe, pretend to have solved some of the riddles of the first, and the French to have unravelled some of the intricacies of the last; will someone tell us wherein lies the extraordinary fascination of golf?

I have just come home from my Club. We played till we could not see the flag; the caddies were sent ahead to find the balls by the thud of their fall; and a low large moon threw whispering shadows on the dew-wet grass or ere we trode the home-green. At dinner the talk was of golf; and for three mortal hours after dinner the talk was—of golf. Yet the talkers were neither idiots, fools, nor monomaniacs. On the contrary many of them were grave men of the world. At all events the most monomaniacal of the lot was a prosperous man of affairs, worth I do not know how many thousands, which thousands he had made by the same mental faculties by which this evening he was trying to probe or to elucidate the profundities and complexities of this so-called "game." Will some one tell us wherein lies its mystery?

* * *

I am a recent convert to golf. But it is the recent convert who most closely scrutinizes his creed—as certainly it is the recent convert who most zealously avows it. The old hand is more concerned about how he plays than about why he plays; the duffer is puzzled at the extraordinary fascination which his new-found pass-time exercises over him. He came to scoff; he remains to play; he inwardly wonders how it was that he was so long a heretic; and, if he is a proselyte given to Higher Criticism, he seeks reasons for the hope that is in him.

Well, I know a man, whether in the flesh or out of the flesh I cannot tell, I know such an one who some years ago joined a golf club, but did not play. The reasons for so extraordinary a proceeding were simple. The members (of course) were jolly good fellows; the comfort was assured; the links—the landscape, he called it—were beautiful. But he did not play. What fun was to be derived from knocking an insignificant-looking little white ball about the open country he did not see. Much less did he see why several hundred pounds a year should be expended in rolling and cutting and watering certain patches of this country, while in others artfully-contrived obstacles should be equally expensively constructed and maintained. Least of all could he understand (he was young then, and given to more violent games) how grown-up men could go to the trouble of travelling far, and of putting on flannels, hob-nailed boots, and red coats, for the simple and apparently effortless purpose of hitting a ball as seldom as possible with no one in the world to oppose his strength or his skill to their hitting; and it seemed to him not a little childish to erect an elaborate club-house, with dressing-rooms, dining-rooms, smoking-rooms, shower-baths, lockers, verandas, and what not, for so simple a recreation, and one requiring so little exertion. Surely marbles would be infinitely more

diverting than that. If it were football, now, or even tennis—and he once had the temerity to venture to suggest that a small portion of the links might be set apart for a court—the turf about the home-hole was very tempting. The dead silence with which this innocent proposition was received gave him pause. (He sees now that an onlooker might as well have requested from a whist party the loan of a few cards out of the pack to play card-tricks withal.)

Yet it is neither incomprehensible nor irrational, this misconception on the part of the layman of the royal and antient game of golf. To the uninitiated, what is there in golf to be seen? A ball driven of a club; that is all. There is no exhibition of skill opposed to skill or of strength contending with strength; there is apparently no prowess, no strategy, no tactics—no pitting of muscle and brain against muscle and brain. At least, so it seems to the layman. When the layman has caught the infection, he thinks—and knows—better.

But, as a matter of fact, contempt could be poured upon any game by anyone unacquainted with that game. We know with what apathetic contempt Subadar Chinniah or Jemadar Mohamed Khan looks on while Tommy Atkins swelters as he bowls or bats or fields under a broiling Indian sun, or Tommy's subalterns kick up the maidan's dust with their polo-ponies' hoofs. And what could be more senseless to a being wholly ignorant of cards than the sight of four grey-headed men gravely seating themselves before dinner to arrange in certain artificial combinations certain uncouth pictures of kings and queens and knaves and certain spots of red and black? Not until such a being recognizes the infinite combinations of chance and skill possible in that queen of sedentary games does he comprehend the fascination of whist. And so it is with golf. All that is requisite in golf, so it seems to the onlooker, is to hit; and than a "hit" nothing, surely, can be simpler or easier—so simple and easy that to have a dozen sticks to hit with, and to hire a boy to carry them, is not so much a sign of pitiable insanity as of wilful stupidity. The puerility of the proceeding is enough to make the spectator irate. Especially as, owing to the silence and the seriousness with which the golfer plays, and his reticence as to the secret of the game—for none knows better than the golfer that the game renders up its secret only to the golfer, if even to him—this quiet, red-coated individual is surrounded with a sort of halo of superiority, a halo not made by himself. No wonder the onlooker's anger is aroused. That expertness in puerility of this sort should of itself exalt a man, make him possessed of that which obviously, yet unintentionally, raises him above the intelligent yet indignant onlooker—there is something in this past finding out. Nor does he find it out till he himself is converted. Golf is like faith: it is the substance of things hoped for, the evidence of things not seen; and not until it is personally experienced does the unbelieving change from the imprecatory to the precatory attitude.

However, the erstwhile aforesaid nonplaying member of the golf club in question, the suppleness of his epiphyses, it may be, becoming (perhaps not quite imperceptibly) unequal to the activity and agility demanded of them by more ardent games, purchased, first one club, then another, then a sheaf, and betook himself to the task of finding out *a posteriori*, by the experimental method, what there was in the confounded game that brought the players there by scores to play.—And to talk of their play. For it should be added that the talk at that club puzzled him as much as the play. It was not enough that keen King's Counsel, grave judges, erudite men of letters, statesmen, and shrewd men of business should play as if the end of life were to hole a ball; but they talked as if the way a ball should be holed were the only knowledge worth possessing. Well, he played; or, to be more precise, he attempted to play, and, fortunately for him, he persevered in the attempt. Then indeed did the scales fall from his eyes. He discovered that there was more in golf than met the eye—much more.

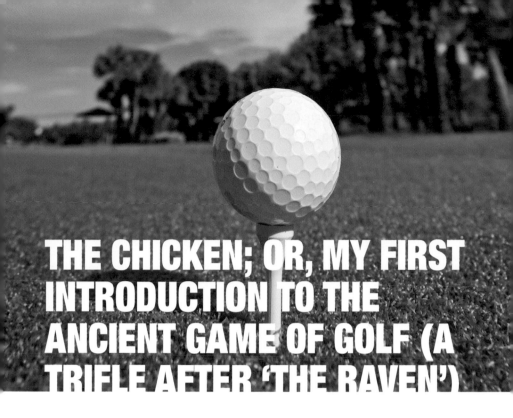

THE CHICKEN; OR, MY FIRST INTRODUCTION TO THE ANCIENT GAME OF GOLF (A TRIFLE AFTER 'THE RAVEN')

S. F. OUTWOOD

Once upon a day most dreary, I was wandering weak and weary,
Thinking I had very seldom seen so drear a looking moor;
For the stillness was unbroken by a single sign or token,
That a voice had ever spoken; when I felt upon my jaw
Something hit me without warning, nearly breaking through my jaw,
  And from pain I knew no more.

Ah, distinctly I remember, that it was a chill November
When I stood thus watching faintly, divers sparks to Heaven soar;
Then two awful men came stealing, while with pain I still was reeling,
Plainly I recall the feeling, as they kept on shouting 'Fore!'

But I moved not in my horror, while they still kept shouting 'Fore!'
   Feeling pain and nothing more.

But fierce danger still was pending, for I still with anguish bending
Heard the sound of ether rending, as an object through it tore,
And beside me there alighted something that was round and whited,
Looking like a star affrighted, that had shone in days of yore,
There it lay, a grim and ghastly whitewashed wreck of days of yore.
   Round and white and nothing more.

Presently my soul grew stronger, hesitating then no longer,
'Sirs,' said I to these two strangers, 'tell me this I do implore,
By the red coats ye are wearing, by the weapons ye are bearing,
Know ye whence these things came tearing—are they meteoric ore?
One has wounded me severely, and seems hard as any ore.'
   But they laughed and nothing more.

Then, into their faces peering, long I stood there wondering, fearing;
Fighting frantic fears no mortal ever had to fight before;
They had laughed when I had spoken, and I guessed by this same token
They were idiots who had broken, doubtless, through the asylum door,
Idiots who'd escaped from Earlswood, having broken through the door.
   This alas! and nothing more.

But while I, half bent on flying, still within my mind was trying,
To think out how them in safety to their home I might restore;
One man broke the pause by saying that 'twas 'cussed nonsense playing
If fools would continue staying even when they halloed "Fore!"
Staying mooning on the hazard while four lungs were bellowing "Fore!"'
   Then he swore and said no more.

Now through all my mind came stealing quite a different kind of feeling,
As I thought I'd heard some speaking of a game like this before;

So, by way of explanation, I delivered an oration
Of a suitable duration, which I think they thought a bore;
And I said, 'I'll watch your playing,' but they muttered, 'Cussed bore!'
    Just these words and nothing more.

Then I seemed to see quite plainly, two boys near in clothes ungainly,
Waiting by us bearing weapons—such a curious, endless store!
And I said, 'You'll be agreeing that no earthly, living being
Ever yet was blessed by seeing such queer things as these before?
Hooks and crooks of all descriptions such as ne'er were seen before.'
    'Clubs be they, and nothing more.'

Thus spoke one they called a caddie, though he spoke more like a Paddy,
And I said whilst slowly following, 'Tell their names I do implore!'
Then these words he seemed to utter in a most uncivil mutter,
'Driver, cleek, spoon, brassey, putter,' till he reached about a score,
Muttering thus he still continued, till he reached at least a score,
    Or may be a trifle more.

Soon the boy, when some one halloed, went ahead while still I followed,
Wondering much to see how quickly he across the bracken tore:
Faster still he flew and faster to his most unhappy master,
Who had met with some disaster, which he seemed to much deplore,
For his ball was in a cart-rut, this alone he did deplore,
    Only this and nothing more.

Here he cried, 'Do try and be quick! don't you see I want my niblick?
Curse these deep and muddy places which one's balls will quite immure.'
Then the mud so fierce did lash he, that his garments soon were splashy
And he called out for his mashie and he very loudly swore,
Mashing, splashing, did not aid him, nor did all the oaths he swore,
    The ball sank in and nothing more.

Whilst I was engaged in thinking how deep down the thing was sinking,
Listening to the flow of language that from out his lips did pour;
Suddenly he dived and sought it, and from out the mud he brought it,
Tossed it to the boy who caught it, then he counted up his score,
Said if he at first had tee'd it, he'd have saved quite half his score,
    Now he'd try the hole no more.

So I thought the game was ended, but their talk was so much blended
With a language unfamiliar which I had not heard before;
For in argument quite stormy they disputed about 'dormie,'

And the word it clean did floor me, though I thought it deeply o'er.
Tried to sift its derivation, but while still I thought it o'er
    It perplexed me more and more.

'Players,' said I, 'sure I'm dying just to send that ball a-flying,
Let me show you how I'd make it up into the heavens soar!'
And one answered 'Come and try it! we should like to see you sky it!
Here's a club, six bob will buy it, I have plenty at the store.'
'Twas the man who teaches golfing, and who keeps clubs in a store,
    Just himself and nothing more.

Then the other, who was playing, said he did not mind delaying
Just to see me make a something, of a record of a score,
So unto the Tee they led me, and of six good bob they bled me,
And with flattery they fed me, but the ball it would not soar;
So they said I must 'address' it, but no language made it soar,
    It just rolled and nothing more.

'Ball,' I said, 'thou thing of evil! Emblem of a slippery devil!
White thou seemest, yet I reckon thou art black right to the core;
On thy side I see a token of the truth that I have spoken,
And a gash, that I have broken, shows thee to be whitened o'er;
Shows thy true self 'neath the varnish with which thou art covered o'er,
    Only black and nothing more!

Then with rage I took my driver, smiting at this foul survivor
Of the devil very fiercely, but the turf, alas, I tore,
And an awful crash resounding as of splintered timber sounding
Heard I, as the head went bounding, and my club broke to the core;
Just a stick I held all broken, broken right across the core,
    But a stick and nothing more.

And the ball, no thought of flitting, still was sitting, still was sitting,
Quietly on its little sandheap, just as it had sat of yore;
I was greatly aggravated and I very plainly stated
That the game was overrated, as I've heard men say before;
So I'd swore I'd chuck the game up, as some others have before,
    And would play it never more!

MISS CARRINGTON'S PROFESSIONAL

M. GERTRUDE CUNDILL

For the end of September the morning was wonderfully warm, and the links were deserted. Young Hilyard sat in the front of the Professional's workshop and polished a mashie, occasionally calling to Thompson, the instructor, in no gentle voice to hurry up. He had come early to practice, and had found a desired club not yet complete. Hence his impatience.

Though, in general, a young man who dressed well, this morning was the exception that proved the rule. His heavy boots were dusty and his coat and collar had been discarded. A corn-cob pipe and a faded college cap completed his costume.

The 10:30 tram whizzed past, and Hilyard was idly speculating as to the chances of some men arriving, when the gate clicked, and a girl came along the pathway. For a moment he felt inclined to retreat as he surveyed the neat figure in spotless piqué. He had not expected such a visitor and felt he was hardly fit to be seen by such a one, but, on second thoughts, what was the good? If she meant to play she would see him sooner or later. And he gave a finishing rub to a club.

By this time the young lady had cut across the grass, and was only a yard or two away from him.

"Good morning," she said briskly.

Hilyard glanced over his shoulder to see if the professional instructor was visible.

"I want you to give me a lesson this morning, please."

Evidently she was addressing himself, and he faced about.

It was an exceedingly pretty girl who confronted him and she carried a bag of the latest pattern, full of new clubs.

The young man rose and lifted his cap. This was non-committal. It might mean to allow her to pass, or it might be in respectful acquiescence to her desire.

"Miss Dawson," she went on, "told me you preferred giving lessons in the morning, and I should like to begin at once."

The die was cast. Hilyard reflected that Thompson was busy in the workshop on the favorite club. He himself was as competent as Thompson, and it was awkward to enlighten her now; besides, it would take Thompson off the much-desired club.

"Certainly—er—miss—one moment, please," he stammered. Then he dashed into the workshop.

"Here, Thompson, there's a lady outside who wants a lesson. You go on with my club; I will take her in hand, and she can pay you just the same."

"Yes, Mr. Hilyard, quite so, sir," assented Thompson, agreeably.

Coaching beginners was no sinecure.

"I am very anxious to get on well," said the girl as he emerged again, "and I want you to teach me all the correct positions for different shots. A few lessons, I think, put one in the right way, and one has nothing to unlearn afterward. Don't you think so?"

"Yes, miss, I do. The ladies here would be all the better off for some."

Then he summoned a caddie and led the way to "Tee No. 1." Thereupon his pupil drew from her pocket an enormous red and white paper "tee" and proffered it.

"Good heavens! where did you—" began Hilyard, but her astonished face stopped him, and he proceeded. "I don't advise your using such a high one, miss. It's better to make your own tee," and he took a little sand, and showed her how to place her ball.

She was as obstinate as most novices as to the way of holding her club, and Hilyard had to restrain himself as he explained why the thumb of the right hand must come round, not down the shaft, and her eye must be fixed on the ball, not its destination.

However, after hurting her thumb, and expending great vigor in beating the air, she came round to his way of thinking, and adopted his suggestions in other small particulars.

The first hole was not reached until the ball had traversed most of the surrounding country. By that time its form was barely recognizable, having been subjected to sudden "toppings" and severe poundings.

Amusing as the situation was, Hilyard wished he had met his pupil under more favorable auspices. It was quite impossible in his present role to be as nice as he well knew how to be. And this was somewhat of a privation.

He picked up the patent bag from its grasshopper-like position, gave it to the caddie, and prepared to follow the last erratic stroke. On the little silver plate the name "G. Carrington" met his eye. Why, the crack golfer who had lately come to reside near must be her father! And he wondered if it was permissible to ask her about it, but he decided that under the circumstances it was not.

"It is funny," said Miss Carrington, as he again showed her the position to drive from, "that Miss Dawson does not stand a bit like that to address her ball."

"Oh," said Hilyard, "no two people teach in the same style."

"Yes, but you taught her."

Hilyard was cornered.

"Well, you see one must let some people do as they can. It's no good following the teacher exactly if the style does not suit the pupil."

"Oh, I see. But Miss Dawson said she liked your style immensely. It was so simple—"

Never having, that he remembered, seen the lady in question, Hilyard had nothing to say, but he wished he had studied Thompson's attitudes more particularly.

And it struck him that the heat was becoming intense.

"Confound it all, I wish I'd introduced myself and offered to help her a bit. It is a waste of time following such a pretty girl as mute as an oyster," he thought, as he trudged toward the second hole, having driven for her.

She used her iron through the green with great effect, and ran after her ball, in the pleasure of really having sent it some distance.

"I am improving, am I not, Thompson? Miss Dawson was sure I would play well."

"That's a good lie," remarked her instructor, coming upon the ball at the same moment.

Miss Carrington's face was a study.

"Really Thompson, I think you're forgetting—"

And Hilyard, for a moment puzzled, almost forgot his respectful mien, and only just checked his laughter as he explained that he was referring to the position of her ball and not to her remark.

"Now, miss, you can play a nice approach shot. I would take your iron."

She played. Then, as she tried for the hole under his instructions—

"You are a Londoner, aren't you, Thompson?" inquired Miss Carrington.

"Yes, I came from there originally," Hilyard ingenuously replied.

"I thought Miss Dawson said so."

"Oh, bother Miss Dawson," thought Hilyard. "I'll begin to think she is my fate."

"But I notice," she continued, "you have not at all a cockney accent. It is so ugly. Still, I suppose the Board Schools have helped to do away with that."

"Yes, miss, no doubt," Hilyard replied, demurely. He could hardly repress a chuckle, however. A good public school and Cambridge after, perhaps, had assisted him in placing "H" correctly. But he was perfectly grave as he turned his attention to her putting.

The third drive was not an unqualified success, although the pupil addressed her ball for nearly five minutes, swung around on one toe, dropped the left shoulder and went through several wonderful preparations which mystified Hilyard until reminded they were due to Miss Dawson.

A chat with Thompson and a little putting would have been a more profitable way of spending the morning.

Then he recollected what fun it would be when subsequently some fellow introduced him as one of the best players the club could boast. For Mr. Hilyard did not undervalue himself altogether. Of course, she would be angry at first; then she would see the amusing side of it, and it would put them on a very friendly footing.

He tried to persuade her to confine herself to what he called "the lazy man's course" and play back over the first few holes. But nothing would deter her from playing across the brook, and a good half hour was spent in trying to induce her balls to go over, not into, the water. After six new ones had valiantly taken a plunge, three only of which were recovered, Hilyard ventured his opinion.

"Your lesson will be over, miss, before we half finish the course, and you said you wanted to do the nine holes."

"Have you anybody else this morning?" she inquired.

"No, not until three o'clock."

"Oh, then, it is all right. I don't lunch till half-past one," and whack, went still another ball, while Hilyard groaned.

Finally she gave up, with tears in her eyes.

"I can't see what I do wrong," she said. "Oh, I detest this stupid game—and I haven't used my mashie or niblick or brassey yet!"

She threw down her club, and her instructor seized it and lifted the ball across.

"Now you can play a nice shot. Take your mashie, if you like; the grass is long. You play quite nicely through the green."

Miss Carrington brightened up.

"And I really don't put badly, do I?"

Hilyard thought ruefully of the six strokes it had required to put the ball in from a yard distant, but politeness is the role of the instructor, and a little ambiguity comes easily.

"Remarkably well for a beginner," he rejoined.

"But I must not be discouraged if I play worse to-morrow, must I?" she asked. "I know beginners generally do well, so I must not be too elated."

Worse to-morrow! Hilyard thought of the morose Thompson, and wondered if he would survive the round.

And then Miss Carrington declared herself tired, and, climbing onto the stone wall, sat down and fanned herself with her hat. Hilyard surveyed her lazily from his recumbent position on the grass, not quite sure whether he ought not to stand respectfully.

Evidently she was a young lady accustomed to being agreeable to her subordinates, for, after a moment's silence, she began:

"I suppose they don't require you here in winter, do they?"

Hilyard thought of the links in mid-winter, and shivered. "No, miss—" How that word always stuck.

"Well, then, when you are out of employment—do you make clubs?" Had she asked did he frequent them, it would have been more to the point.

"Not many. But there is the new curling club. I'm in hopes—" He paused before such an astounding prevarication.

"Oh, that they will make you caretaker. That will be nice."

She scanned the surrounding country, and her eyes fell upon the flock of ever-nibbling sheep, not far distant.

"I really think, do you know, it's rather cruel to have those sheep for—oh, obstacles, is it?"

"For what?" asked Hilyard, raising himself on one elbow and dropping the grass he was biting.

Miss Carrington reddened a little.

"Well, perhaps that is not the word. I mean what they have to make play more difficult. Sometimes they are heaps of stones, I think, or sand-pits, or something—"

Hilyard saw daylight. "Oh, bunkers, you mean, or hazards of any kind. But what has that to do with sheep?"

"Well, aren't they 'hazards.' Every time I play they get in my way, and I thought they'd be more—"

But at the sight of the face before her, crimson in the effort to refrain from laughter, she stopped, and then laughed herself, as it was explained to her that their use was in keeping the grass short.

"I am very stupid," she ejaculated. "I'm always finding myself out in such stupid mistakes."

"There's a fine prospect of discovering another shortly," thought Hilyard, and nearly laughed again.

Play was resumed after a little by the undaunted lady.

"I wish you would play, too," she said, "for I should like to know how to score when I am playing with anybody."

So, helping himself to her driver, Hilyard drove in his best style, secretly pleased at a chance to distinguish himself. And the distance at which the ball dropped was a phenomenal one.

"How easily you play," said the girl behind him. "I have to take so much trouble, and my very best did not go so far."

And then she got mixed up with the scoring of the strokes. "I don't see what you mean. The like?—like what?"

"Oh, nothing. I mean it is your play. Now you'll have to play the odd. You are behind me still."

"I don't see anything odd. It is only natural I should be—"

She hit hard and badly.

"Play two more. Now I play one off two."

"Oh, dear, it's quite hopeless. No, I don't see a bit, and when I play with anybody I don't know what I'm doing. I never know whether I'm winning or losing. Can't you explain better?"

Hilyard was not, as a rule, "slow to anger," and what he would have blamed in a man he forgave in a pretty girl, though he marveled to himself, somewhat, at his painstaking explanation.

Some distant convent bell was ringing two o'clock, when he touched his cap and was about to retire to the workshop. "Half-past ten to-morrow morning, then, please," said Miss Carrington, smiling pleasantly. "I am very pleased with the way you teach. Shall I—pay you to-morrow or now?"

"To-morrow, if you please. Good morning, miss."

Hilyard went in to have a "shower," in a very complex frame of mind. He felt rather guilty as regards his deception, and furthermore, wondered if the amount of pleasure derived thereby counterbalanced the morning's work and a pump-like feeling in the top of his head. The sun was frequently too much for him.

To-morrow morning would certainly find him quietly at home, and the proper Thompson in the field.

But by the time he was sitting at lunch in the cool dining-room, with an extra good salad before him, and a huge glass containing one of Hawkins' best concoctions and lots of cracked ice, his mood changed. Now and then a faint smile passed over his face. And as he raised his glass to his lips he bowed, as though drinking a health.

"To our next merry meeting, whatever capacity I am in," he said aloud. "And if the meetings continue I know in what capacity I'll hope to be," he added as an afterthought.

Of course, by to-morrow she might have found out her mistake. If so, his services, he thought ruefully, would be dispensed with. If not, the chance must not be lost of meeting her again.

Before he left the links, he ran into Thompson's. "Look here," he said, "I want you to keep out of the way to-morrow about half-past ten, in case I should be late. If that young lady should see you first, tell her you are only the assistant. It is just for tomorrow morning," and he made for his tram. And Thompson, as he felt in his pocket something that had not been there before, hoped the day might come when he would be rich enough to do other people's work and pay for the privilege.

The next day dawned bright and clear, and Hilyard was up betimes and out to the links on his wheel. He had considered the advisability of an improvement in his costume. Surely even a Professional might indulge in a fresh colored shirt. He had discovered in the glass that a sweater, after all, was not conducive to beauty.

So when Miss Carrington came along the gallery from the ladies' room, she found him in the same position as the day before, looking a trifle more presentable. "Dear me," she thought, "he'd really look quite like a gentleman if he were only properly dressed."

Which somehow seems to disprove the old adage of "the coat not making the gentleman."

Fortunately, for the second time, there was no one about. At the second hole a foursome of ladies could be seen, but Hilyard had watched the start, and, as none of them was known to him, they were likely to cause him no inconvenience.

"I hope it doesn't matter, miss," he said, "but I can't give you any time after twelve. I am expecting a party (this sounded professional) then."

By lunch time there were sure to be lots of men and girls about, and he did not mean to have it made awkward for both of them. "Oh, twelve will do nicely," replied Miss Carrington. "I made myself too tired yesterday."

To give a beginner her due, Miss Carrington certainly did better. At all events, the difference was a marked one in Hilyard's eyes. With sincerest flattery she imitated his style in every stroke, and very gracefully, too.

Somehow the line between the lady of leisure and the Professional became less strictly drawn. Conversation seemed to come more naturally, though it was, perforce, confined to local topics.

As Hilyard holed out, when they were half-way round the links, he made some remark that fell a little strangely from the lips of a Thompson.

Miss Carrington looked up quickly. Then, as he replaced the flag:

"Have you never been anything better than—" she hesitated; "at least, have you always been in the position you are now?" she asked, rather shyly.

"Always," was the quick assent—"neither better nor worse."

Truthfully, his life had been singularly free from ups and downs.

"Oh!"—It was a disappointed "Oh"—"I thought, perhaps—" But she evidently decided to leave the thought unspoken, and she teed her ball quite expertly and drove a fairly clean shot.

And Hilyard found it imperative to dally over the putting, and showed her many different tricks. Also, it must be confessed, the humble and inferior Thompson would have rendered his position an insecure one had he dared to look so often and so pleasantly upon a pupil, no matter what might be her charms.

They played the last hole, which was before the door. Two of Hilyard's chums had just set off from tee No. 1, but they were too far off to recognize him.

No one was on the gallery though voices and laughter drifted out from the club-room. Feeling such luck was more than he should have expected, Hilyard dismissed himself as speedily as possible, and made his way to the workshop. It was a realistic touch that would have been better omitted. As he sallied from the door with some new balls, Miss Carrington sped across the grass to meet him.

"You went without my paying you, Thompson," she said, breathlessly. She held a five-dollar bill, and Hilyard saw a loophole.

"I haven't any change," he began; then the gate opened suddenly.

Miss Carrington turned and bowed smilingly in response to a cheery greeting, and Hilyard felt a bang on the back.

"Hello, Hilyard, old man, haven't seen you for an age! So glad you and Miss Carrington have met. I have been trying to get hold of you to give you the pleasure," said "that ass Elmore."

Hilyard, speechless, waited for results, and in the perceptibly drawn-up figure and cold, expressionless face read his death-blow.

"We have not met," she said stiffly. "I was merely obliged to speak on a matter of business. You are lunching with father later, are you not, Mr. Elmore? I'll see you in a few moments," and she returned to the club-house.

Elmore looked after her retreating form and then at his friend's dejected face.

"What on earth have you been doing, Hilyard?" he asked. "I never saw Miss Carrington so furious."

"What have you done, you mean," said Hilyard, sulkily. Then he told his tale.

"Upon my word," exclaimed Elmore, as the recital ended, "for pure, unadulterated cheek! Really, Hil, I can't believe it. And to Grace Carrington of all people!

"I'll do my best for you," in answer to an appeal, "but it will make a poor showing, I am afraid. You'd better lunch elsewhere if you wish to enjoy yourself," and he departed.

Hilyard's inward communings belong to the category of those things better left unsaid.

So the would-be Professional for several days felt far from happy in his mind. His susceptibilities had been worked upon in an incredibly short time. He was also unused to being denied anything that might add to his pleasure. Besides, it was not specially agreeable to keep continually coming upon his ex-pupil evidently doing excellent work with driver and cleek, and have to pass by while the genuine Thompson studiously turned his head away to hide his smiles. And he concluded he was more sinned against than sinning.

Elmore's reports, too, were unfavorable.

"It's no use talking to her, Hil; she's ripping. She told me never to refer to the subject again. And she says, apart from any other annoyance, it has been very provoking to be obliged to unlearn all you taught her."

This was the most cruel thrust of all. Hilyard almost made up his mind not to think of her again.

Golf being the uppermost thought in everybody's mind that season, Hilyard was not surprised to receive an invitation to a "golf dinner" from the wife of the Golf Club president. Most of the guests were to be elderly, but a golf dinner without Hilyard would have had as much point to it as a links devoid of holes.

Accordingly he put on his scarlet coat and set off, thankful that golf was not a drawing-room accomplishment, and therefore no exhibition of his talent would be expected after dinner.

He was late in arriving and everybody was ready to go into the dining-room. Mrs. Granton was talking to a girl by the deep window-seat, and Hilyard recognized Miss Carrington, with a slight tremor of excitement.

Mrs. Granton greeted him with a playful remonstrance as to his lack of eagerness to join them. She was a woman who always had a little joke or smart saying in readiness, and fired it off whether or not the occasion was suitable.

Hilyard forgot to smile, but muttered some excuse, and found himself bowing, with heightened color, to the young lady he was to take in. She was self-possession personified, for in youth it is never acquired in half measures.

So the procession wended its way to dinner, and Hilyard wondered vaguely how long the corridor really was. They seemed to traverse miles, and not a remark was volunteered by the possessor of the small gloved hand that barely rested on his arm.

Mrs. Granton had worked nobly to introduce an atmosphere of golf. In the center of the table a miniature links was laid out in as detailed a fashion as space would permit. Even some tiny sheep grazed in one corner. The flowers and ribbons were of the club colors, scarlet and white. The dinner-cards were spirited little paintings of players in action; the menus fairly bristled with appropriate quotations—in fact, at a first glance they seemed to cater more to intellectual than bodily wants. The dinner-rolls were ball shaped, and the ices later were cunning imitations of the same. Everything of a golfing nature that could be made in confectionery was there.

Miss Carrington was having an animated discussion with her other neighbor, a gentleman of society. At least she looked animated and listened attentively, though the speaker was neither very able nor rapid.

Hilyard sat in silence, and resolved it was too late in life to learn to countenance being thus absolutely ignored.

He leaned forward.

"Miss Carrington," he began. She turned slightly.

"I'm sorry to bother you, but do you think it would be possible for us to address each other once during each course? I don't wish to make our hostess feel more uncomfortable than necessary. Couldn't you pretend we were utter strangers meeting for the first time?"

"I am afraid I am not very good at pretending anything, Mr.—Hilyard."

"Oh, I think everybody has some instincts of the actor; don't you?" He helped himself to some entrée, the chief merit of which lay in its wonderful resemblance to balls on tees. "I wonder," he continued easily, "why we were not asked to eat our food with small cleeks or mashies, after the chopstick method. It would have been the essence of realism."

Miss Carrington barely allowed herself to smile.

"I think this dinner is a most charming idea."

"Yes, so do I. Originality in any form is delightful, even if carried to excess. Though I fancy the 'Etiquette of Entertaining' or some such volume is responsible for most of this."

There was a pause for some minutes, and both the young people seemed engrossed in the course set before them.

Miss Carrington suddenly straightened as if steeling herself to something unpleasant. "I wonder, Mr. Hilyard—and I can't help telling you that I am a little surprised—that you seem to think any apology quite unnecessary."

Hilyard was a bit of a judge. He knew better than to play the abject penitent in this case. So he looked up slowly at the blue eyes fixed upon him, and said in a deliberate tone:

"Really, Miss Carrington, I assure you I depended on Elmore to express my regret more trustworthily than he evidently has done. But I don't mind admitting to you that I have been a little astonished that you—well, you know, a fellow is not highly complimented at being taken for the Professional, and you can't deny the originality of the idea was due to you. I merely assisted in carrying it out."

Miss Carrington broke her bread nervously. Their eyes met and they both laughed.

"But you could have easily explained my mistake."

"Then I couldn't have gone round with you!"

The blue eyes dropped. Hilyard noted afresh the length of the lashes.

"Wouldn't it have been more prudent to have gone without your cake and waited for another that would have lasted longer?"

"It takes a very big cake to satisfy me. But still, I have hopes."

The conversation then became general. With dessert came a lull, and Hilyard, noticing Miss Carrington and the talkative old gentleman seemed destitute of ideas, ventured again to turn the conversation to personalities by observing, in an apparently easy-going way: "By the bye, Miss Carrington, has Thompson shown you when to use a niblick yet? I remember—"

"Thompson has shown me everything," she somewhat tartly responded. "I know the use of every club, from a driving cleek to a bulger brassey. Oh," with enthusiasm, "*how well he plays!*"

"Indeed. Well, I hope he will get you thoroughly grounded before the new man comes. It will be a pity," with emphasis, "to be obliged to unlearn all he has taught you."

Miss Carrington tried to look unconscious of the hit.

"He is a remarkably nice man," she retorted, "and he does not expect to be taken any notice of."

"Seen better days, I expect," rejoined Hilyard; "and then, you know, the Board Schools," he added.

Miss Carrington's chair was pushed out from the table with rather too much vehemence. And she followed in the wake of the other ladies.

Hilyard, left alone with the men, was the life of the party. He told his own new jokes and laughed as heartily at the Captain's three-year-olds.

On returning to the drawing-room he devoted himself to the oldest lady in the room, apparently ignorant of the fact that the youngest one was being bored to distraction by the golfing anecdotes of her host.

Truly, he was a master of finesse.

As the party broke up he found himself side by side with somebody who would have looked demure enough if her eyes had not contradicted it, and a low voice said:

"Thompson is obliged to be in town to-morrow, Mr. Hilyard. So I shan't get a lesson unless—"

She received no encouragement.

"Perhaps you wouldn't mind showing me that three-quarter swing with the niblick you spoke of."

It is astonishing how easily a novice adopts the correct phrases.

"Shall I have to call you 'Miss' every second word, and carry all the clubs, and not speak until spoken to?"

"No; you can do anything you please."

"Then may I call for you at ten? I feel I am entitled to some little return for giving over to Thompson my most promising and only pupil. Don't you think so, too?"

Miss Carrington evidently did.

So, after that, Hilyard's friends found he was useless in a foursome, and, in fact, impossible to fix any engagement with, unless the party happened to include—But, after all, that is neither here nor there.

Suffice it to add that the two days' golf Professional plays his new part quite as well as his first one—at least, if one can judge from the success with which the new venture, not an athletic one, is crowned.

AN INLAND VOYAGE

A. A. MILNE

Thomas took a day off last Monday in order to play golf with me. For that day the Admiralty had to get along without Thomas. I tremble to think what would have happened if war had broken out on Monday. Could a Thomasless Admiralty have coped with it! I trow not. Even as it was, battleships grounded, crews mutinied, and several awkward questions in the House of Commons had to be postponed till Tuesday

Something—some premonition of this, no doubt—seemed to be weighing on him all day.

"Rotten weather," he growled, as he came up the steps of the club.

"I'm very sorry," I said. "I keep on complaining to the secretary about it. He does his best."

"What's that?"

"He taps the barometer every morning, and says it will clear up in the afternoon. Shall we go out now, or shall we give it a chance to stop?"

Thomas looked at the rain and decided to let it stop. I made him as comfortable as I could. I gave him a drink, a cigarette, and "Mistakes with the Mashie." On the table at his elbow I had in reserve "Faulty Play with the Brassy" and a West Middlesex Directory. For myself, I wandered about restlessly, pausing now and again to read enviously a notice which said that C. D. Topping's handicap was reduced from twenty-four to twenty-two. Lucky man!

At about half-past eleven the rain stopped for a moment, and we hurried out.

"The course is a little wet," I said, apologetically, as we stood on the first tee, "but with your naval experience you won't mind that. By the way, I ought to warn you that this isn't all casual water. Some of it is river."

"How do you know which is which?"

"You'll soon find out. The river is much deeper. Go on—your drive."

Thomas won the first hole very easily. We both took four to the green, Thomas in addition having five splashes of mud on his face while I only had three. Unfortunately the immediate neighbourhood of the hole was under water. Thomas, the bounder, had a small heavy ball, which he managed to sink in nine. My own, being lighter, refused to go into the tin at all, and floated above the hole in the most exasperating way.

"I expect there's a rule about it," I said, "if we only knew, which gives me the match. However, until we find that out, I suppose you must call yourself one up."

"I shall want some dry socks for lunch," he muttered as he sploshed off to the tee.

"Anything you want for lunch you can have, my dear Thomas. I promise you that you shall not be stinted. The next green is below sea-level altogether, I'm afraid. The first in the water wins."

Honours, it turned out, were divided. I lost the hole, and Thomas lost his ball. The third tee having disappeared, we moved on to the fourth.

"There's rather a nasty place along here," I said. "The secretary was sucked in the other day, and only rescued by the hair."

Thomas drove a good one. I topped mine badly, and it settled down in the mud fifty yards off. "Excuse me," I shouted as I ran quickly after it, and I got my niblick on to it just as it was disappearing. It was a very close thing.

"Well," said Thomas, as he reached his ball, "that's not what I call a brassy lie."

"It's what we call a corkscrew lie down here," I explained. "If you haven't got a corkscrew, you'd better dig round it with something, and then when the position is thoroughly undermined—Oh, good shot!"

Thomas had got out of the fairway in one, but he still seemed unhappy.

"My eye," he said, bending down in agony; "I've got about half Middlesex in it."

He walked round in circles saying strange nautical things, and my suggestions, that he should (1) rub the other eye, and (2) blow his nose suddenly, were received ungenerously.

"Anything you'd like me to do with my ears?" he asked, bitterly. "If you'd come and take some mud out for me, instead of talking rot—"

I approached with my handkerchief and examined the eye carefully.

"See anything?" asked Thomas.

"My dear Thomas, it's *full* of turf. We mustn't forget to replace this if we can get it out. What the secretary would say—There! How's that?"

"Worse than ever."

"Try not to think about it. Keep the *other* eye on the ball as much as possible. This is my hole, by the way. Your ball is lost."

"How do you know?"

"I saw it losing itself. It went into the bad place I told you about. It's gone to join the secretary. Oh, no, we got him out, of course; I keep forgetting. Anyhow, it's my hole."

"I think I shall turn my trousers up again," said Thomas, bending down to do so. "Is there a local rule about it?"

"No; it is left entirely to the discretion and good taste of the members. Naturally a little extra license is allowed on a very muddy day. Of course, if—Oh, I see! You meant a local rule about losing your ball in the mud? No, I don't know of one—unless it comes under the heading of casual land. Be a sportsman, Thomas, and don't begrudge me the hole."

The game proceeded, and we reached the twelfth tee without any further contretemps; save that I accidentally lost the sixth, ninth, and tenth holes, and that Thomas lost his iron at the eighth. He had carelessly laid it down for a moment while he got out of a hole with his niblick, and when he turned round for it the thing was gone.

At the twelfth tee it was raining harder than ever. We pounded along with our coat-collars up and reached the green absolutely wet through.

"How about it?" said Thomas.

"My hole, I think; and that makes us all square."

"I mean how about the rain? And it's just one o'clock."

"Just as you like. Well, I suppose it is rather wet. All right, let's have lunch."

We had lunch. Thomas had it in the only dry things he had brought with him—an ulster and a pair of Vardon cuffs, and sat as near the fire as possible. It was still raining in torrents after lunch, and Thomas, who is not what I call keen about golf, preferred to remain before the fire. Perhaps he was right. I raked up an old copy of "Stumers with the Niblick" for him, and read bits of the "Telephone Directory" out aloud.

After tea his proper clothes were dry enough in places to put on, and as it was still raining hard, and he seemed disinclined to come out again, I ordered a cab for us both.

"It's really rotten luck," said Thomas, as we prepared to leave, "that on the one day when I take a holiday it should be so beastly."

"Beastly, Thomas?" I said in amazement. "The *one* day? I'm afraid you don't play inland golf much?"

"I hardly ever play round London."

"I thought not. Then let me tell you that today's was the best day's golf I've had for three weeks."

"Golly!" said Thomas.

A METHOD OF PLAY

J. H. TAYLOR

It is a patent fact that every golfer must be possessed of a method of some kind. As I have already said, it is useless attacking the game in a haphazard, go-as-you-please kind of style, Micawber–like, waiting for something to turn up. When playing, my paramount idea is that each individual hole should be set down as possessing a par value, just as a security is possessed of a certain value in pounds, shillings, or pence. Hence you say to yourself, "I should be able to do this hole in four, this one in five, this in three," and so on, hole by hole, until you reach the end of the round.

This means to an end is just an imaginary Colonel Bogey, only upon a very high scale. In your own mind you set up a certain standard, you are aware of what should be done and what you are doing, and you know what there is remaining to be faced.

Method, however, is one thing, theory is another; but practice, constant use and intelligent application, is quite as important. A player cannot in fairness hope to acquit himself well unless he is prepared to devote ample time to and to go unreservedly for the game. The greater the amount of practice he gets through, the steadier will be the game he will play. He knows what he is capable of, he does not find it at all necessary to strain after effect, and he is able to control himself when faced by anything that may crop up at an unexpected moment.

A player who wishes to be successful must never allow himself to think of what he has already done. That has gone, never to return; idle regrets are useless; he must concentrate the whole of his attention upon what he has in front of him. He must not allow a bad or an unfortunate stroke to put him off his game; he must think only of what is to come, what yet remains to be accomplished.

The ordinary player might be thrown out of his stride after making a poor shot, perhaps, but he must educate himself up to the point of feeling no regret for what has already occurred.

Accidents will occasionally happen, I am fully aware, but a careful player is one who will not accept any risks when he knows in exactly how many strokes he should be able to reach the hole he is playing to. In medal competitions (or in any other, as far as that goes) you cannot afford to play a bad stroke, and that is the long and short of it.

Nothing is easier than to set up, as I have suggested, this par value for the various holes, no matter what course they may be upon. Should the medal competition be upon the links attached to the club of which the player is a member, he is fully aware of what he can do, and has done, under ordinary conditions. Even in the Championships the course is thrown open during the week prior to their decision, and in playing round the golfer discovers what difficulties are likely to beset his path. After that the method I have referred to should not be a hard matter.

But, and I would like strongly to impress this upon all players, don't get into the habit of carefully preserving the scores you may have made before the all-important day. It is a bad plan to do this, and I will explain why this is the case.

Very possibly you may have played a round of extraordinary excellence, and naturally feel elated at your performance. You check the round, hole by hole, but you overlook the possible explanation that it may have happened when you played far above your average form. Then, when the real test comes along, something happens, or you discover you are not doing nearly so well. This knowledge of your present failure to equal the past is calculated to annoy you, and the chances are all in favour of its affecting your play. Now this is a thing that must be carefully guarded against. You must devote the whole of your attention to the task in hand, and must not allow yourself to be distracted by any side issues.

Mr. C. B. Fry has told us how he once failed to win a sprint race by wondering how the other man was getting on. It is just the same in golf; and once you allow your mind to wander and to begin wondering about the why and the wherefore, it is a difficult matter to get back into your stride again.

Many of the players in medal competitions, I have noticed, go at the game in just a happy-go-lucky style, trusting they may be fortunate enough to pull through—somehow. Such a practice is really of no use at all. I cannot lay down too strongly that the great secret of success is the absolute concentration of thought. Never allow yourself to wander, and never play to the gallery. It is the steady game that brings the player to the fore.

Especially is this the case when you have reached the green and the hole is smiling at you from a distance of, say, ten yards. When I am faced with a putt of that length my rule invariably is to try and make certain of the hole in 2. I never diverge from that. I never allow the possibility of getting down in 1 to sway my balance of thought and certainty of intention; but very frequently you will find that as you attempt to lay the ball dead it will suddenly disappear from view into the hole.

On the other hand, if you attempt to hole such a putt as I have described in 1, the chances are all in favour of your miscalculating your strength and distance, and it may, as a result, render the playing of 3 a necessity, this meaning the loss of a stroke that caution would have rendered superfluous. The proper amount of caution upon the green means everything to the player, for it is there that the scores are made or spoilt.

When a return is made to the pavilion, and the players have gathered for a cigar and a chat, you may hear of drives that have been topped, but not very frequently. A golfer will much oftener talk about the putts he has missed, and for these failures he blames his ill fortune, conveniently and persistently overlooking the fact that by overstraining himself in the effort to reach the possible he has missed, like the dog in the fable, the absolute certainty.

Poor putting, it may be said without fear, is the cause of a player's downfall in the majority of instances. As I have just explained, the addition of an extra stroke is quite an easy matter; and should you make this addition at all frequently, the difference it makes to the aggregate may be readily imagined.

Score playing, however, is one of the most nerve trying of any contest in the world of athletics. Many players repeatedly fail to do themselves justice on account of their feeling of nervousness, for never yet has there been a man possessed of absolutely no nerves. "The invisible man" we have had, but the nerveless man—oh, no!

Despite my many years of close connection with the game, I admit that I never enter upon a medal round without feeling a tremor run through my nerves. But by concentration of thought upon the business in hand I am enabled to conquer that feeling of nervousness and to finally wear it down.

Every man is beyond doubt affected in a similar manner; but he must cultivate the will power necessary to grapple with these attacks of nerves. He must, I repeat; for unless he is capable of doing so he will find his play affected in a wonderful degree. This self-control, though, cannot be gained at once; but the mere fact of playing on and on and trying to think out the strokes, and that alone, renders the task, as he goes on, an easier one.

The player improves as the time and practice go on. He does not feel too much cast down and disheartened over one particular failure, or too elated over the accomplishment of a big performance. The real secret of success is this concentration. You must make yourself capable, like a batsman or a footballer, of playing yourself into form, and guard against going off with a rush and a big flourish of trumpets at the start, going up like a rocket and coming down like the proverbial stick.

The golfer of scant experience is far too apt to try for a great deal too much as soon as he commences playing, and the result is just as natural—utter and complete disaster. He makes a bad stroke, and then he broods over it, refusing to cast it aside and try and hope for better things to come, as they will do, in the future.

Can you wonder at his non-success under these circumstances? I think not, for concentration of thought on the game ahead is an absolute necessity.

EVEN THREES

OWEN JOHNSON

I

Ever since the historic day when a visiting clergyman accomplished the feat of pulling a ball from the tenth tee at an angle of two hundred and twenty-five degrees into the river that is the rightful receptacle for the eighth tee, the Stockbridge golf course has had seventeen out of eighteen holes that are punctuated with water hazards. The charming course itself lies in the flat of the sunken meadows which the Housatonic, in the few thousand years which are necessary for the proper preparation of a golf course, has obligingly eaten out of the high accompanying bluffs. The river, which goes wriggling on its way as though convulsed with merriment, is garnished with luxurious elms and willows, which occasionally deflect to the difficult putting greens the random slices of certain notorious amateurs.

From the spectacular bluffs of the educated village of Stockbridge nothing can be imagined more charming than the panorama that the course presents on a busy day. Across the soft green stretches, diminutive caddies may be seen scampering with long buckling nets, while from the riverbanks numerous recklessly exposed legs wave in the air as the more socially presentable portions hang frantically over the swirling current. Occasionally an enthusiastic golfer, driving from the eighth or ninth tees, may be seen to start immediately in headlong pursuit of a diverted ball, the swing of the club and the intuitive leap of the legs forward forming so continuous a movement that the main purpose of the game often becomes obscured to the mere spectator. Nearer, in the numerous languid swales that nature has generously provided to protect the interests of the manufacturers, or in the rippling patches of unmown grass, that in the later hours will be populated by enthusiastic caddies, desperate groups linger in botanizing attitudes.

Every morning lawyers who are neglecting their clients, doctors who have forgotten their patients, businessmen who have sacrificed their affairs, even ministers of the gospel who have forsaken their churches gather in the noisy dressing room and listen with servile attention while some unscrubbed boy who goes around under eighty imparts a little of his miraculous knowledge.

Two hours later, for every ten that have gone out so blithely, two return crushed and despondent, denouncing and renouncing the game, once and for all, absolutely and finally, until the afternoon, when they return like thieves in the night and venture out in a desperate hope; two more come stamping back in even more offensive enthusiasm; and the remainder straggle home moody and disillusioned, reviving their sunken spirits by impossible tales of past accomplishments.

There is something about these twilight gatherings that suggests the degeneracy of a rugged race; nor is the contamination of merely local significance. There are those who lie consciously, with a certain frank, commendable, wholehearted plunge into iniquity. Such men return to their worldly callings with intellectual vigor unimpaired and a natural reaction toward the decalogue. Others of more casuistical temperament, unable all at once to throw over the traditions of a New England conscience to the exigencies of the game, do not at once burst into falsehood, but by a confusing process weaken their memories and corrupt their imaginations. They never lie of the events of the day. Rather they return to some jumbled happening of the week before and delude themselves with only a lingering qualm, until from habit they can create what is really a form of paranoia, the delusion of greatness, or the exaggerated ego. Such men, inoculated with self-deception, return to the outer world to deceive others, lower the standards of business morality, contaminate politics, and threaten the vigor of the republic.

R. N. Booverman, the treasurer, and Theobald Pickings, the unenvied secretary of an unenvied board, arrived at the first tee at precisely ten o'clock on a certain favorable morning in early August to begin the thirty-six holes which six times a week, six months of the year, they played together as sympathetic and well-matched adversaries. Their intimacy had arisen primarily from the fact that Pickings was the only man willing to listen to Booverman's restless dissertations on the malignant fates which seemed to pursue him even to the neglect of their international duties, while Booverman, in fair exchange, suffered Pickings to enlarge *ad libitum* on his theory of the rolling versus the flat putting greens.

Pickings was one of those correctly fashioned and punctilious golfers whose stance was modeled on classic lines, whose drive, though it averaged only twenty-five yards over the hundred, was always a well-oiled and graceful exhibition of the Royal St. Andrew's swing, the left sole thrown up, the eyeballs bulging with the last muscular tension, the club carried back until the whole body was contorted into the first position of the traditional hoop snake preparing to descend a hill. He used the interlocking grip, carried a bag with a spoon driver, an aluminum cleek, had three abnormal putters, and wore one chamois glove with air holes on the back. He never accomplished the course in less than eighty-five and never exceeded ninety-four, but, having aimed to set a correct example rather than to strive vulgarly for professional records, was always in a state of offensive optimism due to a complete sartorial satisfaction.

Booverman, on the contrary, had been hailed in his first years as a coming champion. With three holes eliminated, he could turn in a card distinguished for its fours and threes; but unfortunately these sad lapses inevitably occurred. As Booverman himself admitted, his appearance on the golf links was the signal for the capricious imps of chance who stir up politicians to indiscreet truths and keep the Balkan pot of discord bubbling, to forsake immediately these prime duties, and enjoy a little relaxation at his expense.

Now, for the first three years Booverman responded in a manner to delight imp and devil. When, standing thirty-four for the first six holes, he sliced into the jungle, and, after twenty minutes of frantic beating of the bush, was forced to acknowledge a lost ball and no score, he promptly sat down, tore large clutches of grass from the sod, and expressed himself to the admiring delight of the caddies, who favorably compared his flow of impulsive expletives to the choice moments of their own home life. At other times he would take an offending club firmly in his big hands and break it into four pieces, which he would drive into the ground, hurling the head itself, with a last diabolical gesture, into the Housatonic River, which, as may be repeated, wriggled its way through the course as though convulsed with merriment.

There were certain trees into which he inevitably drove, certain waggish bends of the river where, no matter how he might face, he was sure to arrive. There was a space of exactly ten inches under the clubhouse where his balls alone could disappear. He never ran down a long putt, but always hung on the rim of the cup. It was his adversary who executed phenomenal shots, approaches of eighty yards that dribbled home, sliced drives that hit a fence and bounded back to the course. Nothing of this agreeable sort had ever happened or could ever happen to him. Finally the conviction of a certain predestined damnation settled upon him. He no longer struggled; his once rollicking spirits settled into a moody despair. Nothing encouraged him or could trick him into a display of hope. If he achieved a four and two twos on the first holes, he would say vindictively:

"What's the use? I'll lose my ball on the fifth."

And when this happened, he no longer swore, but said gloomily with even a sense of satisfaction: "You can't get me excited. Didn't I know it would happen?"

Once in a while he had broken out,

"If ever my luck changes, if it comes all at once—"

But he never ended the sentence, ashamed, as it were, to have indulged in such a childish fancy. Yet, as Providence moves in a mysterious way its wonders to perform, it was just this invincible pessimism that alone could have permitted Booverman to accomplish the incredible experience that befell him.

II

Topics of engrossing mental interest are bad form on the golf links, since they leave a disturbing memory in the mind to divert it from that absolute intellectual concentration which the game demands. Therefore Pickings and Booverman, as they started toward the crowded first tee, remarked *de rigueur*:

"Good weather."

"A bit of a breeze."

"Not strong enough to affect the drives."

"The greens have baked out."

"Fast as I've seen them."

"Well, it won't help me."

"How do you know?" said Pickings politely, for the hundredth time. "Perhaps this is the day you'll get your score."

Booverman ignored the remark, laying his ball on the rack, where two predecessors were waiting, and settled beside Pickings at the foot of the elm which later, he knew, would rob him of a four on the home green.

Wessels and Pollock, literary representatives, were preparing to drive. They were converts of the summer, each sacrificing their season's output in a frantic effort to surpass the other. Pickings, the purist, did not approve of them in the least. They brought to the royal and ancient game a spirit of Bohemian irreverence and banter that offended his serious enthusiasm.

When Wessels made a convulsive stab at his ball and luckily achieved good distance, Pollock remarked behind his hand, "A good shot, damn it!"

Wessels stationed himself in a hopefully deprecatory attitude and watched Pollock build a monument of sand, balance his ball, and whistling nervously through his teeth, lunge successfully down. Whereupon, in defiance of etiquette, he swore with equal fervor, and they started off.

Pickings glanced at Booverman in a superior and critical way, but at this moment a thin dyspeptic man with undisciplined whiskers broke in serenely without waiting for the answers to the questions he propounded:

"Ideal weather, eh? Came over from Norfolk this morning; ran over at fifty miles an hour. Some going, eh? They tell me you've quite a course here; record around seventy-one, isn't it? Good deal of water to keep out of? You gentlemen some of the cracks? Course pretty fast with all this dry weather? What do you think of the one-piece driver? My friend, Judge Weatherup. My name's Yancy—Cyrus P."

A ponderous person who looked as though he had been pumped up for the journey gravely saluted, while his feverish companion rolled on:

"Your course's rather short, isn't it? Imagine it's rather easy for a straight driver. What's your record? Seventy-one amateur? Rather high, isn't it? Do you get many cracks around here? Caddies seem scarce. Did either of you gentlemen ever reflect how surprising it is that better scores aren't made at this game? Now, take seventy-one; that's only one under fours, and I venture to say at least six of your holes are possible twos, and all the rest, sometime or other, have been made in three. Yet you never hear of phenomenal scores, do you, like a run of luck at roulette or poker? You get my idea?"

"I believe it is your turn, sir," said Pickings, both crushing and parliamentary. "There are several waiting."

Judge Weatherup drove a perfect ball into the long grass, where successful searches averaged ten minutes, while his voluble companion, with an immense expenditure of force, foozled into the swale to the left, which was both damp and retentive.

"Shall we play through?" said Pickings with formal preciseness. He teed his ball, took exactly eight full practice swings, and drove one hundred and fifty yards as usual directly in the middle of the course.

"Well, it's straight; that's all can be said for it," he said, as he would say at the next seventeen tees.

Booverman rarely employed that slogan. That straight and narrow path was not in his religious practice. He drove a long ball, and he drove a great many that did not return in his bag. He glanced resentfully to the right, where Judge Weatherup was straddling the fence, and to the left, where Yancy was annoying the bullfrogs.

"Darn them!" he said to himself. "Of course now I'll follow suit."

But whether or not the malignant force of suggestion was neutralized by the attraction in opposite directions, his drive went straight and far, a beautiful two hundred and forty yards.

"Fine shot, Mr. Booverman," said Frank, the professional, nodding his head, "free and easy, plenty of follow-through."

"You're on your drive today," said Pickings, cheerfully.

"Sure! When I get a good drive off the first tee," said Booverman, discouraged, "I mess up all the rest. You'll see."

"Oh, come now," said Pickings, as a matter of form. He played his shot, which came methodically to the edge of the green.

Booverman took his mashy for the short running-up stroke to the pin, which seemed so near.

"I suppose I've tried this shot a thousand times," he said savagely. "Anyone else would get a three once in five times—anyone but Jonah's favorite brother."

He swung carelessly, and watched with a tolerant interest the white ball roll on to the green straight for the flag. All at once Wessels and Pollock, who were ahead, sprang into the air and began agitating their hats.

"By George! It's in!" said Pickings. "You've run it down. First hole in two! Well, what do you think of that?"

Booverman, unconvinced, approached the hole with suspicion, gingerly removing the pin. At the bottom, sure enough, lay his ball for a phenomenal two.

"That's the first bit of luck that has ever happened to me," he said furiously, "absolutely the first time in my whole career."

"I say, old man," said Pickings in remonstrance, "you're not angry about it, are you?"

"Well, I don't know whether I am or not," said Booverman obstinately. In fact, he felt rather defrauded. The integrity of his record was attacked. "See here, I play thirty-six holes a day, two hundred and sixteen a week, a thousand a month, six thousand a year; ten years, sixty thousand holes; and this is the first time a bit of luck has ever happened to me—once in sixty thousand times."

Pickings drew out a handkerchief and wiped his forehead.

"It may come all at once," he said faintly.

This mild hope only infuriated Booverman. He had already teed his ball for the second hole, which was poised on a rolling hill one hundred and thirty-five yards away. It is considered rather easy as golf holes go. The only dangers are a matted wilderness of long grass in front of the tee, the certainty of landing out of bounds on the slightest slice, and of rolling down hill into a soggy substance on a pull. Also there is a tree to be hit and a sand pit to be sampled.

"Now watch my little friend the apple tree," said Booverman. "I'm going to play for it, because, if I slice, I lose my ball, and that knocks my whole game higher than a kite." He added between his teeth: "All I ask is to get around to the eighth hole before I lose my ball. I know I'll lose it there."

Due to the fact that his two on the first brought him not the slightest thrill of nervous joy, he made a perfect shot, the ball carrying the green straight and true.

"This is your day, all right," said Pickings, stepping to the tee.

"Oh, there's never been anything the matter with my irons," said Booverman darkly, "Just wait till we strike the fourth and fifth holes."

When they climbed the hill, Booverman's ball lay within three feet of the cup, which he easily putted out.

"Two down," said Pickings inaudibly. "By George! What a glorious start!"

"Once in sixty thousand times," said Booverman to himself. The third hole lay two hundred and five yards below; backed by the road and trapped by ditches, where at that moment Pollock, true to his traditions as a war correspondent, was laboring in the trenches, to the unrestrained delight of Wessels, who had passed beyond.

"Theobald," said Booverman, selecting his cleek and speaking with inspired conviction, "I will tell you exactly what is going to happen. I will smite this little homeopathic pill, and it will land just where I want it. I will probably put out for another two. Three holes in twos would probably excite any other human being on the face of this globe. It doesn't excite me. I know too well what will follow on the fourth or fifth watch."

"Straight to the pin," said Pickings in a loud whisper. "You've got a dead line on every shot today. Marvelous! When you get one of your streaks, there's certainly no use in my playing."

"Streak's the word," said Booverman, with a short, barking laugh. "Thank heaven, though, Pickings, I know it! Five years ago I'd have been shaking like a leaf. Now it only disgusts me. I've been fooled too often; I don't bite again."

In this same profoundly melancholy mood he approached his ball, which lay on the green, hole high, and put down a difficult putt, a good three yards for his third two.

Pickings, despite all his classic conservatism, was so overcome with excitement that he twice putted over the hole for a shameful five.

Booverman's face as he walked to the fourth tee was as joyous as a London fog. He placed his ball carelessly, selected his driver, and turned on the fidgety Pickings with the gloomy solemnity of a father about to indulge in corporal punishment.

"Once in sixty thousand times, Picky. Do you realize what a start like this—three twos—would mean to a professional like Frank or even an amateur that hadn't offended every busy little fate and fury in the whole hoodooing business? Why the blooming record would be knocked into the middle of next week."

"You'll do it," said Pickings in a loud whisper. "Play carefully."

Booverman glanced down the four-hundred-yard straightaway and murmured to himself:

"I wonder, little ball, whither will you fly?
I wonder, little ball, have I bid you good-by?
Will it be 'mid the prairies in the regions to the west?
Will it be in the marshes where the pollywogs nest?
Oh, tell me, little ball, is it ta-ta or good-by?"

He pronounced the last word with a settled conviction, and drove another long, straight drive. Pickings, thrilled at the possibility of another miracle, sliced badly.

"This is one of the most truly delightful holes of a picturesque course," said Booverman, taking out an approaching cleek for his second shot. "Nothing is more artistic than the tiny little patch of putting green under the shaggy branches of the willows. The receptive graveyard to the right gives a certain pathos to it, a splendid, quiet note in contrast to the feeling of the swift, hungry river to the left, which will now receive and carry from my outstretched hand this little white floater that will float away from me. No matter; I say again the fourth green is a thing of ravishing beauty."

His second shot, low and long, rolled up in the same unvarying line.

"On the green," said Pickings.

"Short," said Booverman, who found to his satisfaction that he was right by a yard.

"Take your time," said Pickings, biting his nails.

"Rats! I'll play it for a five," said Booverman.

His approach ran up on the line, caught the rim of the cup, hesitated, and passed on a couple of feet.

"A four, anyway," said Pickings with relief.

"I should have had a three," said Booverman doggedly. "Any one else would have had a three, straight on the cup. You'd have had a three, Picky; you know you would."

Pickings did not answer. He was slowly going to pieces, forgetting the invincible stoicism that is the pride of the true golfer.

"I say, take your time, old chap," he said, his voice no longer under control. "Go slow! Go slow!"

"Picky, for the first four years I played this course," said Booverman angrily, "I never got better than a six on this simple three hundred-and-fifty-yard hole. I lost my ball five times out of seven. There is something irresistibly alluring to me in the mosquito patches to my right. I think it is the fond hope that when I lose this nice new ball I may step inadvertently on one of its hundred brothers, which I may then bring home and give decent burial."

Pickings, who felt a mad and ungolfish desire to entreat him to caution, walked away to fight down his emotion.

"Well?" he said, after the click of the club had sounded.

"Well," said Booverman without joy, "that ball is lying about two hundred and forty yards straight up the course, and by this time it has come quietly to a little cozy home in a nice, deep hoof track, just as I found it yesterday afternoon. Then I will have the exquisite pleasure of taking my niblick, and whanging it out for the loss of a stroke. That'll infuriate me, and I'll slice or pull. The best thing to do, I suppose, would be to play for a conservative six."

When, after four butchered shots. Pickings had advanced to where Booverman had driven, the ball lay in clear position just beyond the bumps and rills that ordinarily welcome a long shot. Booverman played a perfect mashy which dropped clear on the green, and ran down a moderate putt for a three.

They then crossed the road and arrived by a planked walk at a dirt mound in the midst of a swamp. Before them the oozy marsh lay stagnant ahead and then sloped to the right in the figure of a boomerang, making for those who fancied a slice a delightful little carry of one hundred and fifty yards. To the left was a procession of trees, while beyond, on the course, for those who drove a long ball, a giant willow had fallen the year before in order to add a new perplexity and foster the enthusiasm for luxury that was beginning among the caddies.

"I have a feeling," said Booverman, as though puzzled but not duped by what had happened—"I have a strange feeling that I'm not going to get into trouble here. That would be too obvious. It's at the seventh or eighth holes that something is lurking around for me. Well, I won't waste time."

He slapped down his ball, took a full swing, and carried the far-off bank with a low, shooting drive that continued bounding on.

"That ought to roll forever," said Pickings, red with excitement.

"The course is fast—dry as a rock," said Booverman deprecatingly.

Pickings put three balls precisely into the bubbling water, and drew alongside on his eighth shot. Booverman's drive had skimmed over the dried plain for a fair two hundred and seventy-five yards. His second shot, a full brassy, rolled directly on the green.

"If he makes a four here," said Pickings to himself, "he'll be playing five under four—no, by thunder! Seven under four!" Suddenly he stopped, overwhelmed. "Why, he's actually around threes—two under three now. Heavens! if he ever suspects it, he'll go into a thousand pieces."

As a result, he missed his own ball completely, and then topped it for a bare fifty yards.

"I've never seen you play so badly," said Booverman in a grumbling tone. "You'll end up by throwing me off."

When they arrived at the green, Booverman's ball lay about thirty feet from the flag.

"It's a four, a sure four," said Pickings under his breath.

Suddenly Booverman burst into an exclamation,

"Picky, come here. Look—look at that!"

The tone was furious. Pickings approached.

"Do you see that?" said Booverman, pointing to a freshly laid circle of sod ten inches from his ball. "That, my boy, was where the cup was yesterday. If they hadn't moved the flag two hours ago, I'd have had a three. Now, what do you think of that for rotten luck?"

"Lay it dead," said Pickings anxiously, shaking his head sympathetically. "The green's a bit fast."

The putt ran slowly up to the hole, and stopped four inches short.

"By heavens! Why didn't I putt over it!" said Booverman, brandishing his putter. "A thirty-foot putt that stops an inch short—did you ever see anything like it? By everything that's just and fair I should have had a three. You'd have had it, Picky. Lord! If I only could putt!"

"One under three," said Pickings to his fluttering inner self. "He can't realize it. If I can only keep his mind off the score!"

The seventh tee is reached by a carefully planned, fatiguing flight of steps to the top of a bluff, where three churches at the back beckon so many recording angels to swell the purgatory lists. As you advance to the abrupt edge, everything is spread before you; nothing is concealed. In the first plane, the entangling branches of a score of apple-trees are ready to trap a topped ball and bury it under impossible piles of dry leaves. Beyond, the wired tennis courts give forth a musical, tinny note when attacked. In the middle distance a glorious sycamore draws you to the left, and a file of elms beckon the sliced way to a marsh, a wilderness of grass and an overgrown gully whence no balls return. In front, one hundred and twenty yards away, is a formidable bunker, running up to which is a tract of long grass, which two or three times a year is barbered by charitable enterprise. The seventh hole itself lies two hundred and sixty yards away in a hollow guarded by a sunken ditch, a sure three or—a sure six.

Booverman was still too indignant at the trick fate had played him on the last green to yield to any other emotion. He forgot that a dozen good scores had ended abruptly in the swale to the right. He was only irritated. He plumped down his ball, dug his toes in the ground, and sent off another long, satisfactory drive, which added more fuel to his anger.

"Anyone else would have had a three on the sixth," he muttered as he left the tee. "It's too ridiculous."

He had a short approach and an easy putt, plucked his ball from the cup, and said in an injured tone:

"Picky, I feel bad about that sixth hole, and the fourth, too. I've lost a stroke on each of them. I'm playing two strokes more than I ought to be. Hang it all! That sixth wasn't right! You told me the green was fast."

"I'm sorry," said Pickings, feeling his fingers grow cold and clammy on the grip.

The eighth hole has many easy opportunities. It is five hundred and twenty yards long, and things may happen at every stroke. You may begin in front of the tee by burying your ball in the waving grass, which is always permitted a sort of poetical license. There are the traps to the seventh hole to be crossed, and to the right the paralleling river can be reached by a short stab or a long curling slice, which the prevailing wind obligingly assists to a splashing descent.

"And now we have come to the eighth hole," said Booverman, raising his hat in profound salutation. "Whenever I arrive here with a good score I take from eight to eighteen, I lose one to three balls. On the contrary, when I have an average of six, I always get a five and often a four. How this hole has changed my entire life!" He raised his ball and addressed it tenderly: "And now, little ball, we must part, you and I. It seems a shame; you're the nicest little ball I ever have known. You've stuck to me an awful long while. It's a shame."

He teed up, and drove his best drive, and followed it with a brassy that laid him twenty yards off the green, where a good approach brought the desired four.

"Even threes," said Pickings to himself, as though he had seen a ghost. Now he was only a golfer of one generation; there was nothing in his inheritance to steady him in such a crisis. He began slowly to disintegrate morally to revert to type. He contained himself until Booverman had driven free of the river, which flanks the entire green passage to the ninth hole, and then barely controlling the impulse to catch Booverman by the knees and implore him to discretion, he burst out:

"I say, dear boy, do you know what your score is?"

"Something well under four," said Booverman, scratching his head.

"Under four, nothing; even threes!"

"What?"

"Even threes."

They stopped, and tabulated the holes.

"So it is," said Booverman, amazed. "What an infernal pity!"

"Pity?"

"Yes, pity. If only someone else could play it out!"

He studied the hundred and fifty yards that were needed to reach the green that was set in the crescent of surrounding trees, changed his brassy for his cleek, and his cleek for his midiron.

"I wish you hadn't told me," he said nervously.

Pickings on the instant comprehended his blunder. For the first time Booverman's shot went wide of the mark, straight into the trees that bordered the river to the left.

"I'm sorry," said Pickings with a feeble groan.

"My dear Picky, it had to come," said Booverman, with a shrug of his shoulders. "The ball is now lost, and all the score goes into the air, the most miraculous score anyone ever heard of is nothing but a crushed egg!"

"It may have bounded back on the course," said Pickings desperately.

"No no, Picky; not that. In all the sixty thousand times I have hit trees, barns, car tracks, caddies, fences—"

"There it is!" cried Pickings with a shout of joy.

Fair on the course at the edge of the green itself lay the ball, which soon was sunk for a four. Pickings felt a strange, unaccountable desire to leap upon Booverman like a fluffy, enthusiastic dog; but he fought it back with the new sense of responsibility that came to him. So he said artfully:

"By George! Old man, if you hadn't missed on the fourth or the sixth, you'd have done even threes!"

"You know what I ought to do now—I ought to stop," said Booverman in profound despair—"quit golf and never lift another club. It's a crime to go on; it's a crime to spoil such a record. Twenty-eight for nine holes, only forty-two needed for the next nine to break the record, and I have done it in thirty-three—and in fifty-three! I ought not to try; it's wrong."

He teed his ball for the two-hundred-yard flight to the easy tenth, and took his cleek.

"I know just what'll happen now; I know it well."

But this time there was no varying in the flight; the drive went true to the green, straight on the flag, where a good but not difficult putt brought a two.

"Even threes again," said Pickings, but to himself. "It can't go on. It must turn."

"Now, Pickings, this is going to stop," said Booverman angrily. "I'm not going to make a fool of myself. I'm going right up to the tee, and I'm going to drive my ball right smack into the woods and end it. And I don't care."

"What!"

"No, I don't care. Here goes."

Again his drive continued true, the mashy pitch for the second was accurate, and his putt, after circling the rim of the cup, went down for a three.

The twelfth hole is another dip into the long grass that might serve as an elephant's bed, and then across the Housatonic River, a carry of one hundred and twenty yards to the green at the foot of an intruding tree.

"Oh, I suppose I'll make another three here, too," said Booverman moodily. "That'll only make it worse."

He drove with his midiron high in the air and full on the flag.

"I'll play my putt carefully for a three," he said, nodding his head. Instead, it ran straight and down for a two.

He walked silently to the dreaded thirteenth tee, which, with the returning fourteenth, forms the malignant Scylla and Charybdis of the course. There is nothing to describe the thirteenth hole. It is not really a golf hole; it is a long, narrow breathing spot, squeezed by the railroad tracks on one side and by the river on the other. Resolute and fearless golfers often cut them out entirely, nor are ashamed to acknowledge their terror. As you stand at the thirteenth tee, everything is blurred to the eye. Nearby are rushes and water, woods to the left and right; the river and the railroad and the dry land a hundred yards away look tiny and distant, like a rock amid floods.

A long drive that varies a degree is doomed to go out of bounds or to take the penalty of the river.

"Don't risk it. Take an iron—play it carefully," said Pickings in a voice that sounded to his own ears unrecognizable.

Booverman followed his advice and landed by the fence to the left, almost off the fair. A midiron for his second put him in position for another four, and again brought his score to even threes.

When the daring golfer has passed quaking up the narrow way and still survives, he immediately falls a victim to the fourteenth, which is a bend hole, with all the agonies of the preceding thirteenth, augmented by a second shot over a long, mushy pond. If you play a careful iron to keep from the railroad, now on the right, or to dodge the river on your left, you are forced to approach the edge of the swamp with a cautious fifty-yard-running-up stroke before facing the terrors of the carry. A drive with a wooden club is almost sure to carry into the swamp, and only a careful cleek shot is safe.

"I wish I were playing this for the first time," said Booverman, blackly. "I wish I could forget—rid myself of memories. I have seen class A amateurs take twelve, and professionals eight. This is the end of all things, Picky, the saddest spot on earth. I won't waste time. Here goes."

To Pickings's horror, the drive began slowly to slice out of bounds, toward the railroad tracks.

"I knew it," said Booverman calmly, "and the next will go there, too; then I'll put one in the river, two in the swamp, slice into—"

All at once he stopped, thunderstruck. The ball, hitting tie or rail, bounded high in the air, forward, back upon the course, lying in perfect position.

Pickings said something in a purely reverent spirit.

"Twice in sixty thousand times," said Booverman, unrelenting. "That only evens up the sixth hole. Twice in sixty thousand times!"

From where the ball lay an easy brassy brought it near enough to the green to negotiate another four. Pickings, trembling like a toy dog in zero weather, reached the green in ten strokes, and took three more putts.

The fifteenth, a short pitch over the river, eighty yards to a slanting green entirely surrounded by more long grass, which gave it the appearance of a chin spot on a full face of whiskers, was Booverman's favorite hole. While Pickings held his eyes to the ground and tried to breathe in regular breaths, Booverman placed his ball, drove with the requisite backspin, and landed dead to the hole. Another two resulted.

"Even threes—fifteen holes in even threes," said Pickings to himself, his head beginning to throb. He wanted to sit down and take his temples in his hands, but for the sake of history he struggled on.

"Damn it!" said Booverman all at once.

"What's the matter?" said Pickings, observing his face black with fury.

"Do you realize, Pickings, what it means to me to have lost those two strokes on the fourth and sixth greens, and through no fault of mine, either? Even threes for the whole course—that's what I could do if I had those two strokes—the greatest thing that's ever been seen on a golf course. It may be a hundred years before any human being on the face of this earth will get such a chance. And to think I might have done it with a little luck!"

Pickings felt his heart begin to pump, but he was able to say with some degree of calm:

"You may get a three here."

"Never. Four, three and four is what I'll end."

"Well, good heavens! What do you want?"

"There's no joy in it, though," said Booverman gloomily. "If I had those two strokes back, I'd go down in history, I'd be immortal. And you, too, Picky, because you went around with me. The fourth hole was bad enough, but the sixth was heartbreaking."

His drive cleared another swamp and rolled well down the farther plateau. A long cleek laid his ball off the green, a good approach stopped a little short of the hole, and the putt went down.

"Well, that ends it," said Booverman, gloomily. "I've got to make a two or three to do it. The two is quite possible; the three absurd."

The seventeenth hole returns to the swamp that enlivens the sixth. It is a full cleek, with about six mental hazards distributed in Indian ambush, and in five of them a ball may lie until the day of judgment before rising again.

Pickings turned his back, unable to endure the agony of watching. The click of the club was sharp and true. He turned to see the ball in full flight arrive unerringly hole high on the green.

"A chance for a two," he said under his breath. He sent two balls into the lost land to the left and one into the rough to the right.

"Never mind me," he said, slashing away in reckless fashion.

Booverman, with a little care, studied the ten-foot route to the hole and putted down.

"Even threes!" said Pickings, leaning against a tree.

"Blast that sixth hole!" said Booverman, exploding. "Think of what it might be, Picky—what it ought to be!"

Pickings retired hurriedly before the shaking approach of Booverman's frantic club. Incapable of speech, he waved him feebly to drive. He began incredulously to count up again, as though doubting his senses.

"One under three, even threes, one over, even, one under—"

"What the deuce are you doing?" said Booverman angrily. "Trying to throw me off?"

"I didn't say anything," said Pickings.

"You didn't—muttering to yourself."

"I must make him angry, keep his mind off the score," said Pickings feebly to himself. He added aloud, "Stop kicking about your old sixth hole! You've had the darndest luck I ever saw, and yet you grumble."

Booverman swore under his breath, hastily approached his ball, drove perfectly, and turned in a rage.

"Luck?" he cried furiously. "Pickings, I've a mind to wring your neck. Every shot I've played has been dead on the pin, now, hasn't it?"

"How about the ninth hole—hitting a tree?"

"Whose fault was that? You had no right to tell me my score, and, besides, I only got an ordinary four there, anyway."

"How about the railroad track?"

"One shot out of bounds. Yes, I'll admit that. That evens up for the fourth."

"How about your first hole in two?"

"Perfectly played; no fluke about it at all—once in sixty thousand times. Well, any more sneers? Anything else to criticize?"

"Let it go at that."

Booverman, in this heckled mood, turned irritably to his ball, played a long midiron, just cleared the crescent bank of the last swale, and ran up on the green.

"Damn that sixth hole!" said Booverman, flinging down his club and glaring at Pickings. "One stroke back, and I could have done it."

Pickings tried to address his ball, but the moment he swung his club his legs began to tremble. He shook his head, took a long breath, and picked up his ball.

They approached the green on a drunken run in the wild hope that a short putt was possible. Unfortunately the ball lay thirty feet away, and the path to the hole was bumpy and riddled with worm casts. Still, there was a chance, desperate as it was.

Pickings let his bag slip to the ground and sat down, covering his eyes while Booverman with his putter tried to brush away the ridges.

"Stand up!"

Pickings rose convulsively.

"For heaven's sake, Picky, stand up! Try to be a man!" said Booverman hoarsely. "Do you think I've any nerve when I see you with chills and fever? Brace up!"

"All right."

Booverman sighted the hole, and then took his stance; but the cleek in his hand shook like an aspen. He straightened up and walked away.

"Picky," he said, mopping his face, "I can't do it. I can't putt it."

"You must."

"I've got buck fever. I'll never be able to putt it—never."

At the last, no longer calmed by an invincible pessimism, Booverman had gone to pieces. He stood shaking from head to foot.

"Look at that," he said, extending a fluttering hand. "I can't do it; I can never do it."

"Old fellow, you must," said Pickings. "You've got to. Bring yourself together. Here!"

He slapped him on the back, pinched his arms, and chafed his fingers. Then he led him back to the ball, braced him into position, and put the putter in his hands.

"Buck fever," said Booverman in a whisper. "Can't see a thing."

Pickings, holding the flag in the cup, said savagely:

"Shoot!"

The ball advanced in a zigzag path, running from worm cast to worm cast, wobbling and rocking, and at the last, as though preordained, fell plump into the cup!

At the same moment, Pickings and Booverman, as though carried off by the same cannonball, flattened on the green.

III

Five minutes later, wild-eyed and hilarious, they descended on the clubhouse with the miraculous news. For an hour the assembled golfers roared with laughter as the two stormed, expostulated, and swore to the truth of the tale.

They journeyed from house to house in a vain attempt to find some convert to their claim. For a day they passed as consummate comedians, and the more they yielded to their rage, the more consummate was their art declared. Then a change took place. From laughing the educated town of Stockbridge turned to resentment, then to irritation, and finally to suspicion. Booverman and Pickings began to lose caste, to be regarded as unbalanced, if not positively dangerous. Unknown to them, a committee carefully examined the books of the club. At the next election another treasurer and another secretary were elected.

Since then, month in and month out, day after day in patient hope, the two discredited members of the educated community of Stockbridge may be seen, accompanied by caddies, toiling around the links in a desperate belief that the miracle that would restore them to standing may be repeated. Each time as they arrive nervously at the first tee and prepare to swing, something between a chuckle and a grin runs through the assemblage, while the left eyes contract waggishly, and a murmuring may be heard:

"Even threes."

The Stockbridge golf links is a course of ravishing beauty and the Housatonic River, as has been said, goes wriggling around it as though convulsed with merriment.

GOOD RESOLUTIONS

BERNARD DARWIN

The coming of each New Year's Day brings with it for golfers, as for other people, reflections on the past and resolutions for the future. As to the resolutions, we often have a greater opportunity of making them than of putting them into practice, for in the early days of January there is apt to be a wind so biting, even if the links be not carpeted with snow, that the wise man lays aside his clubs and the foolish one confines his attention to a captive ball. Reflections are always open to us, but, as we grow older, they are apt to become just a little sad. One of the more depressing that gradually forces itself upon us is that that which we are pleased to term "our game" is never going to get any better. There was a time when we hoped that a miracle would occur, and that the dash and strength and glory of hitting which are vouchsafed to the few might suddenly one fine morning descend upon us too, so that we should be as creatures transfigured and made splendid for evermore. Braid says that he went to bed a short driver and woke up a long one, and we, without knowing that curious piece of natural history, yet trusted that something of the kind was going to happen to us.

After a certain number of Januaries we know in our heart of hearts that beautiful New Year's day-dream is not coming true. We may possibly be going to play very well in the coming year: better and more steadily perhaps, than we have ever played before; but it will be our own old second-rate game, with just one or two mistakes the less, or perhaps a long-continued putting inspiration. We shall not really be hitting the ball any better, but just because we are not eating or drinking or smoking too much, or because we have got a new club that gives us confidence, we may be making fewer bad shots. Heaven knows that this is not a state of things to be despised, for it will lead to the acquisition of many half-crowns, but there is a pang in realising that we never shall tear the ball away with the brassy from a deep cup and send it hurtling on to a green two hundred yards away: never play those wonderful low, forcing shots with the iron that burrow their way through a solid wall of wind. We shall never do these heroic things, because we simply have not got it in us. And so we have just got to make the best of our own permanently pedestrian attainments.

Well, it is depressing, but the fact that we recognise our own limitations, or so at least we flatter ourselves, argues that there is in us a measure of sense and knowledge of the game which a good many people lack. I believe that there are golfers who think—nay, I have heard them say it— that the only difference between their game and that of Braid is that he does the holes in four more often than they do. They do not see any material distinction, between the hole as played by them and by a champion. They take two full shots, neither hit perfectly clean, a long putt from the outskirts of the green laid within five feet, and the fourth scrambled in: he has a drive, a crisp, firm half-shot with an iron, and a six-yard putt that goes in and out of the hole for three. Both holes were done in four, but that is the only point of resemblance. Yet there are some who, because they can sometimes successfully bring off these two half-hit drives and that scrambling putt throughout a whole round, imagine in their secret souls that they have for once attained to the level of really first-class golf. Let us pray to be delivered from similar blindness, even though it is wonderfully pleasant for a time.

If it is saddening to know that we have arrived, roughly speaking, at our fixed place in golfing society, increasing age can offer some compensating consolations. The small boy who is suddenly deprived of some eagerly expected pleasure cannot believe in the possibility of any further happiness in this world. He may not eat that bun or go to that children's party; therefore it is absurd—nay, it is actually insulting—to suggest that there can ever be other buns and other parties or any pleasure to be derived from them. In the same way, the young golfer who is in the throes of a hideous golfing malady cannot believe that the ball which now flies in a malignant curve to the right will one day go straight down the course again. It must surely be, he thinks, that he is condemned to slice for ever; he utterly refuses to admit the possibility of any improvement, even though he is trying a new swing every minute in order to effect one. After a certain number of years he learns by experience that no golfing disease—not even slicing—does go on for ever, and that the day will come when he will hit the ball again. Of course, he learns also that he will miss it again, that there is nothing before him but a series of hits and misses to the end of the chapter, whereas the callow youth, having once got rid of his slice, cannot believe that it will ever recur, and strikes the stars with his uplifted head accordingly. Which is better? Alternating despair and rapture, or an equable cynicism?

I said that New Year's Day reflections were gloomy, but I had no idea how gloomy they would be till I came to write them down. Now that I see them in black and white, I grow ashamed of a spirit so whimpering and unmanly. After all, I force myself to say, things are not really so very bad, and Mr. Charles Hutchings won the championship when he was fifty-three, and I am going to the course I love best in the world, and the weather looks promising. I shall play with some who are quite old and fat, and I can give them strokes—quite a lot of strokes. I must go and pack up my clubs—I am sure I shall improve this year, after all.

That, beyond doubt, is the braver spirit, and so, with all the old buoyant hopefulness, let us leave reflection and fall to upon our good resolutions for yet another year. What are they to be? They must be of a noble and lofty character, dealing with the general principles of golfing wisdom, and not stooping to some small trick or mannerism that we have discovered, and which, we fondly believe, has cured us permanently of some fell disease. These things are but evanescent: though at the moment we believe them to be among the eternal verities. We know that we make twenty or thirty such discoveries every year. Our New Year's resolutions must be on broader lines.

The first one that would rise to most golfers' minds is probably the best and most far-reaching—"Be up." Be up in our putts, be up in our short approaches, be up with any shot whereby we try to reach the green. How many strokes and half-crowns we should save, how very few holes we should lose, by being past the hole! The hole will not come to us, and yet to reach it is the hardest thing in the whole world of golf. There must surely be some scientific explanation of this almost universal failing. If our long approach, a little too firmly played, run over the green into a bunker, we are commiserated on all sides; nobody says "Bad luck!" if the shot drop feebly into trouble short of the green. Therefore the former disaster should clearly be less annoying than the latter. Why, then, do we not court it more strenuously? It is more common to be short, because it is so much more common to underclub rather than to overclub ourselves. Most people are more at ease with a spoon than a brassy, a driving iron than a spoon, and so on down to the mashie. They feel happier with the shorter club, and take it for safety if they have any excuse for doing so. Consequently they are often short from taking a club with which under no circumstances could they be up to the flag; if they do not hit the ball quite clean, they are, of course, shorter still.

One reason for this underclubbing is that for the average golfer it is less disastrous to press at a shot than to spare one. This is a bold statement, and is opposed to the views of those eminent persons who declare that it is easier to play a half-shot with a powerful club than a full shot with a less powerful one. I do not believe that for the average golfer this last doctrine is true. He finds himself, let us say 150 or 160 yards from the hole. Should he take his cleek he will be worried with the feeling that he is going too far; result, he will spare it, tuck his arms into his body instead of following through properly, and hook or slice the ball a thousand miles away. If he take his iron he may hit rather too hard, and make an indifferent shot, but the disaster will not be of the same magnitude. He will thus gradually get into a habit of taking the shorter club, and, as a result, his approaches will very generally be short of the hole.

A very good golfer once told me that he attributed a great part of his success to the fact that when in doubt between two clubs he always took the stronger one. On the other hand, another fine player, especially good with his cleek, informed me that he often took his cleek, even though he knew he could not quite get up with it, in preference to a brassy. Of these two teachers the second was the greater player, but his precepts appear the less sound: his tenets should be regarded as part of the eccentricity of his genius, and not to be imitated.

Another good resolution to make, at least from a match-winning point of view, would be that during a match one should concentrate one's entire attention on hitting the ball, and reserve all heart-searchings as to the causes of wrongdoing till the time of practice after the round. If we once begin to wonder in the middle of a game what we are doing wrong in executing some particular stroke, we lose interest in all other strokes, so that our whole game becomes disjointed, and any temporary improvement in respect of the diseased stroke is outweighed by a general feebleness and uncertainty in other departments. Probably every golfer has some word of wisdom, appropriate to himself, that he can add to this little New Year's sermon. We can always fall back on those precepts which are part of general as well as golfing morality, such as not to call one's opponent's best shot a beastly fluke or to pursue an irritating caddy with a niblick. These, however, are matters rather for the spiritual than the golfing pastor.

Of a different kind to these wise resolves made before a roaring fire, or haply as we lie snugly in bed listening to the wintry wind, are those that we make at the beginning of a summer holiday. There can surely be few more agreeable sensations in life than that of settling comfortably down for some considerable time in the neighbourhood of a first-class seaside golf course. We have ecstatic visions of all we are going to do: the final polish to be put upon the cruder of our armoury of shots, the deadly solidity of steadiness to which we shall attain. There need be none of that feverish anxiety to be up and at it which attends a brief visit of a few days. No, we will go about the business temperately and soberly. We will attend to our other avocations in the morning, loaf down after lunch, and practise some of those shots, and perhaps play one round in the cool of the evening. Whatever we do we will not play ourselves into a state of dotage by means of three rounds a day; practice is the way to improve and to practice we will devote a great part of our energies.

It is said that the great Mr. Travis, when he was educating himself to win our championship and that of his own country, would go out with a dozen balls and work away at just one shot for an hour and a half at a stretch. A gentleman who has been staying at our seaside course is working away on the same lines, and has brought his handicap down from 18 to 3 in less than no time. What a bright example! We will map out an elaborate educational schedule, and stick to it through thick and thin. First of all, of course, there is the art of driving, which is said to be the easiest thing in the world, when one is in constant practice, and which, beyond all doubt, is abominably difficult when one is not. We have often driven well for short spells, and have been hazily conscious of a series of sensations which have accompanied our success. Now we will run those sensations to earth, if such a metaphor be permissible, discover exactly what is the cause of them, and what exactly we are doing, and then, of course, it will be quite easy to drive well and steadily ever afterwards.

Now here in the very beginning the system will probably break down, and what will really happen will be something entirely different. After a few days, if it be not presumptuous to hope so much, we shall very likely begin to drive quite respectably just because we have had those few consecutive days' golf, and the club feels a familiar and comfortable thing. We shall, as we imagine, solve the mystery and attribute our success to some particular action which may have temporarily something to do with it. In all our preliminary swings we shall be careful to introduce and indeed exaggerate that action; and yet, in spite of our folly, we may not improbably continue to drive well, just because we are in good practice, and can therefore afford to do some foolish things and yet hit the ball. So at the end of our summer-time we set out for home under the blissful delusion that we have mastered driving once and for all. Alas! we shall soon find, when, we return to week-end habits again, that the virtue lay not in that particular kink or switch; that, had we only known it, had long since become a piece of useless lumber, and the secret was merely that of frequent play. Hope, of course, springs more or less eternal in every golfer's breast, or the suicide statistics would long since have been such as to arouse the attention of all thoughtful citizens. It was not very long since that I saw a gentleman but moderately old and extremely eminent in other walks of life, putting in an attitude of unconscionable discomfort, his right foot tucked far away behind his left, so that he leered at the ball over his left shoulder. This position, he declared, enabled him to keep his eye on the ball. I wonder how long it was before that ever-youthful spirit returned, chastened and humble, to his natural attitude, in which, by the way, he putts more than reasonably well.

I find, despite all my show of bravery for the New Year, that I grow cynical and depressed again over the memories of many summer holidays, and, among the disappointments that I recall, there are scarce any more poignant than those connected with the new club that I bought before setting out.

Why is it that a man becomes temporarily demented as soon as he enters a shop with the intention of buying a club? I do not allude to the fact that he spends his money on Dreadnoughts, when he ought to be getting bread for his starving children. He may be perfectly justified in buying a club, but he goes perfectly mad in choosing the club that he does buy. The moment he crosses the threshold and sees the tempting array of clubs, with their nice shining heads and their handles sacrificially adorned with pink paper, he loses all idea of the kind of club he wants. Put him on a golf course, and he would instantly reject the proffered implement. "As flat as a skate," he would say; or would dismiss it with justifiable contempt as more suitable for a cricket bat. In the shop, however, he becomes incapable of judging of the lie of a club; and he will buy one absurdly flat, or upright, as the case may be, and bear it home in unsuspecting triumph, only to find out on his first visit to the links that he has irretrievably wasted seven and sixpence.

Nor is it only as regards the lie that we lose our wits; our "judgment goes out a-wisitin'" equally in the matter of weight. A little while ago, a most excellent golfer showed me with some pride a new brassy. It was an admirable club, but had only become so through having had very nearly all the lead taken out, so that there was a perfect chasm in the back of the head. Yet its owner, one of the sanest of mankind in the ordinary way, had bought it in a shop under the impression that it exactly suited him in its primitive state.

I may perhaps quote myself as another and more aggravated instance of this lunacy. Some time ago I bought a kind of medium iron or "jigger." I bought it because I thought that it was a little more upright in the lie than the one I already possessed, and also, I must confess, because it had a crooked neck, which exercised a weird fascination over me. The moment I took it out on to the grass the scales dropped from my eyes, and I saw the club as it really was. It is, in fact, considerably flatter than my old friend; its neck is in the last degree distasteful to me, and it has a shaft so abominably supple that it twists out of my hand like an eel. Some day, when I have had a new shaft put in, and have caused the head to be bent in a fiery furnace, it may possibly be a passable club, but it will have been a very expensive one.

The vendors of clubs do wisely when they pitch their tents not upon the edge of the links, but in the heart of a great city. The additional rent that they have to pay must be a drop in the ocean compared with the sums that we pay them for clubs we shall never be able to play with. Whether it is that we cannot judge of a club when we are arrayed in tall hats and tail coats, or whether there is something subtly deceitful about a hard level floor in place of yielding and uneven turf, I do not know; but, as a rule, the only possible verdict on our actions is one of temporary insanity.

When we are once more in our right mind we have to decide on what to do with the new purchase, since we cannot play with it. Obviously our first attempt should be to sell it to a friend at as slight a reduction as possible. It may really be that what is our poison will be his meat, in which case we can proceed in an honest and straightforward manner. If that is not possible, we must, of course, take care that he should not have any opportunity of trying the club on a golf course, since he will at once detect its faults. We must lure him into our own house. The surroundings of an ordinary house are not so seductive as those of a shop, but still there is a reasonable hope that he will be deceived.

If we cannot sell the club, we must either throw it away or put it away, and the latter is the preferable course. For one thing, clubs are very difficult things to throw away. I once tried to throw away some old clubs by putting them in the waste-paper basket together with socks that were all holes and collars frayed past redemption. The socks and collars disappeared, but a too-faithful servant carefully replaced the clubs in the corner whence they had been extracted. Then, too, clubs, like razors, sometimes become reformed characters through a period of enforced seclusion. Put them in a cupboard till they are coated with rust and dirt. Nine will remain useless, but the tenth will emerge, having been born again in some mysterious way, the club we have been dreaming of.

It should be added that it is only when we are buying clubs for ourselves that we act so insanely. If our intention is to purchase a *gage d'amour* for a golfing friend, we may have the utmost confidence in our judgment. We shall inevitably pick out a club the most perfectly balanced in the world. The shaft will be a miracle of "steeliness" having the "music," to use Tom Morris's word, exactly in the right place, and the lines of the head will be such as bring tears to the eye. I have at different times bought several clubs for a near relation. Two of them have now found their way back to my own bag, and it is only an innate chivalry that restrains me from stealing a third. As to the two she has really no solid ground of complaint, for they were obviously too heavy for her, and I handed over in exchange an admirable specimen of the Schenectady putter. As I have pointed out to her with excellent clear common sense, I could not be expected to know that the Rules of Golf Committee were going to bar it.

THE HUMOROUS SIDE OF GOLF

A. W. TILLINGHAST

Golf has been described as a serious game, and indeed there are players who regard it so seriously that the casual observer of some melancholy match well might wonder if these solemn visaged ones really find enjoyment in it. Some become so absorbed that anything other than their strokes and the match is exiled from their thoughts. Frequently there are happenings which are absurdly funny, but the actors are unable to see that side of it.

For example the man in the bunker, crashing vainly away until finally he fairly explodes with wrath cannot understand why others are forced to laugh at his torrid and original remarks. You see it depends entirely on the viewpoint. Possibly we may find a laugh here and there as we regard the game from the humorous side. Every man who golfs generally has a golf story to tell—the observation of a caddie, one of the oft-repeated Scotch anecdotes of old vintage, and the like. It is not any of these that shall be recorded here, but rather actual occurrences in serious golf wherein tragedy goes arm in arm with comedy.

There is an old story of two players who visited old St. Andrew's one day for a double round. At the finish of the first eighteen they were on even terms, and they were still level when the home green was reached in the evening. Consequently they decided to play on through the village streets to the railway station, and the first to hole out in the box by the stove was to be the winner. Unfortunately one of them sliced through the second story window of one of the little gray houses, and their discussion of the rules has been the topic of considerable embellishment and humorous narrative. Surely, the situation was one which would spread a smile over the most dour countenance, but to the two players it was serious business. As a matter of fact this is not fable for the men were humble clerks in an Edinburgh countinghouse. They had one holiday each year, and for months they had been preparing for this match which was to decide supremacy. Not a day passed without bantering each other, for the great match was serious business with them, and when at last they were forced to take the train on the run, haggling over the rules but with the question of supremacy still unsettled, they surely gave no thought to the ridiculously funny finale, which has served to amuse thousands of golfers since.

Determined men have scrambled to roof tops to play lodged balls, climbed trees, waded into water, and there is recorded the story of one whose ball went down a chimney, but, undismayed, he played out through the open door from the fireplace. Yet, probably, at the time not one of them cracked a smile.

One of the most amusing situations imaginable resulted from the misunderstood directions of a caddie. His employer started his round over an entirely strange course. He was a terrific slicer, and to keep on the course at all, it was necessary for him to face many degrees to the left of the true line.

"What is my line, lad?" he asked.

"Bear on your steeple, sir," the boy answered.

But there were two steeples in the distance, one far to the right of the other which was on line. Seeing but one (and the wrong one), the player took his stance. Thinking that his man was standing for a pull the boy

held his tongue, but was startled by the weirdest slice he had ever seen. The ball came to rest far in the rough, almost at right angles to the line to the hole and from which point it required a number of strokes to regain the fairway, not far from the original starting place. It would have been suicide to have laughed at the unfortunate at the time, although the occurrence has given him much amusement since.

A number of years ago a delegation waited on a certain English nobleman, who was the owner of vast estates. They represented a newly-organized golf club and they craved permission to lay out a small course on his lordship's land. His consent was obtained and in due time the links were completed.

Again the delegation came, hats in hands to ask another favor, a very great one. Would his lordship graciously consent to be present for the opening ceremonies—and drive the first ball.

"But, my friends, I have never struck a ball in my life, and I am much too old to attempt it now," he expostulated.

However, when it was explained that he would not be expected to knock it very far—"Just a tap, sir! It is an honor which will be greatly appreciated, for you see, sir, we want to keep that ball as a constant reminder of your lordship's generosity."

Finally, pleased with the thought, the venerable gentleman gave his consent, and when the eventful day arrived the whole village in their Sunday clothes and smartest frocks assembled around the first teeing ground.

A murmur waved through the gathering as the great man drew near, and amid cheers and applause he stepped with dignity to the tee on which rested a glistening white ball. A great silence fell over them as a new driver was put into his hands and with uncovered heads they watched him waggle it. But after all he was only a man, and suddenly there was born in his breast the overwhelming desire to hit that ball. No gentle tap could satisfy his intense longing to—(only a vulgar term can express it) "to soak it."

Walking deliberately to the ball he poised the club high in the air and looked out over the fairway. Every eye hung on each moment and the crowd held its breath for history was in the making. Suddenly he swung with might and main, but sad to relate he missed the ball completely, whirled around like a top and loosing his feet, suddenly sat down on the ball. Thus was the course opened, for the great man had broken his collarbone. The story is a sad one, but it has its funny side, too.

At Newport there used to be a blind drive to a green which could be reached with an iron. During one of their tournaments the field found great congestion here because nearly every one had lost his ball. They were sure that the drives had been straight on the pin, but not a ball was in sight. While the search was on, a loud snore attracted one of the players to a tree close by the green. There in the shade reposed one who had passed quietly out of the tournament after a very hard night with the cups that cheer. Someone happened to turn him over, and there under him were the missing balls. For a while he had amused himself by craftily gathering each ball as it rolled onto the green, and after arranging his nest to his entire satisfaction, he had gone to sleep.

One of the most laughable sights of any tournament was that of a well-known player seated on a camp stool, calmly reading while his opponent was playing. It happened in this way. In the tournament was one whose dilatory tactics worried his rivals to defeat. He had won several matches against admittedly better players because his obviously studied slowness had angered them. However, he of the camp-stool outwitted him.

"Let him take all the time he wants," camp stool observed, "I am in no hurry." So he took three caddies: one for his bag; another to bear the seat, an umbrella and reading matter; while the third carried a bucket of iced drinks. The match was speedily ended.

A NOVEL GOLFING MATCH

A. NIBLICK

You say Beattie's horse *only* took two minutes to come home in the last four-mile heat from the bend into the straight. Why *only*? I'll bet Sir David Moncrieffe's horse, Negociator, that won the Royal Caledonian Gold Cup last year over the same course, would have come home from the bend in half the time.'

'Yes, I daresay, Melville; but Negociator is a thoroughbred, while this horse of Jack Beattie's is only a half-bred hunter that he has drilled during the whole time the Yeomanry were up, and had no pretensions to galloping.'

'What do you call the distance?' followed this explanation.

'Six furlongs,' was the reply.

'Bah! is that all!' said the other, lighting a fresh cigar. 'I have had a message carried further than that when out in India many a time without a horse.'

'Then you used a pigeon!' suggested the other.

'No, I did not; and I do not mind betting you ten guineas and a dinner for four at the 'Golfer's Arms' that I'll do it on Saturday morning next in ten seconds less time, the message to be brought from the six furlong post to the winning-post.'

'You are joking, man; there is not a man in Edinburgh, or even in old Scotland, who could do the distance in one minute fifty seconds.'

'Take the bet, my boy, and we'll see. You lawyers of the Court of Session do not know everything, and anything smart you do find out is generally from some poor, yet sharp-witted fellow in a witness-box, who could gammon you all if he had the education.'

'Well, then, a bet be it,' said the other, who felt a little annoyed at the sarcastic remarks regarding the bluntness of wit amongst the members of his profession. 'Mind you, whoever carries your message must keep within the regular posts, no crossing the course or that.'

'If the message is carried between the posts I suppose you cannot find any fault,' said the other.

'None whatever.'

'Then find a good check timekeeper if you wish to save your ten guineas, for I mean to win my wager very easily. I will be here at ten o'clock on Saturday morning. Good-night.'

The conversation took place in the club-house of the Ancient Golf Club at Edinburgh sixty years ago. The annual training of the Yeomanry had just taken place, and had been followed by the customary races. Jack Beattie had won the Officer's Cup with a horse which the Edinburgh hunting men declared to be a non-such and a flier, and some had gone so far as to say that it had come in from the bend of the course at the far end in less time than any recorded. Timing races in those days depended much upon the pace made in the four and two-mile heats, and it is possible that cracks like Negociator were never pushed into beating a record by local competitors. At any rate it occurred to Charlie Melville of the Scots Greys, which were then stationed at Piershill Barracks (Jock's Lodge), that the pace mentioned was nothing very extraordinary. Always on the outlook for a wager, it appeared clear that he might make a little towards his mess-bill out of one of these very fat and very fleecing Edinburgh lawyers. Indeed, there was nothing in which he so much delighted as getting on the wrong side of 'legal gentlemen,' because, as he used to explain, 'I have many a time had them on all sides of me.' He was noted in the service as one of the most astute men for laying a drag scent up to a sure and certain catch-bet, and the older officers generally gave the younger ones who had just joined, the tip to keep their weather eye on Melville. These were the great days of catch-bets and peculiar wagers, let it be remembered, and things which would be called sharp now were at that time thought to be quite excusable.

'I wonder how he'll do it,' said the lawyer, John Tailzie, who was one of the leading advocates of the Court of Session. 'He must have one or more fast runners in the regiment, which he means to bring into his use, but even then I cannot see how he will pull it off. One thing is very certain, he will have a good try. Ten pounds is a great deal to him just now, not to speak of the price of the dinner, which I suppose is meant for himself and his friend and fellow whist-partner, Fitzjames, the 'Scotch Grey wi' the red heid,' as the laddies of Portobello call him when they march out, and a genuine Irishman, though of Scottish parentage, the only one with a brogue in the regiment. Saturday morning, however, will soon come, and we'll see.'

That night, whilst John Tailzie, over the walnuts, was telling his friends of the Long Room (the favourite exercising ground of briefless barristers in Scotland) what a grand wager he had got on with Melville of the Greys, all over Jack Beattie's horse and the pace in which it did the last seven furlongs of the Musselburgh course, the astute Melville was busily engaged in the slums of that dirtiest of all golfing centres, Musselburgh, along with his friend Fitzjames. What they were after no one seemed able to conjecture, but it was pretty clear to all that they were up to some mischief. The little golfing howffs were visited in turn, and conversations held with the most noted caddies in hurried whispers at the door. These conversations were generally wound up with the injunctions, 'Keep your mouth shut,' and 'Do not fail me, but be certain to be there.'

Saturday morning came, a bright, breezy morning in May, with the wind blowing fresh from the southward, and so right up the Musselburgh

racecourse. A nice, clear, 'caller' morning as the Edinburgh folks say, and the belles of Portobello were to be seen in dozens in front of their bathing-boxes sporting with the white-crested waves, which came tumbling into the beach from the German Ocean. Lug-sail boats were scudding up from Musselburgh to the oyster-beds, there to get hold of the far-famed 'Caller Ou,' after which was named one of our greatest racehorses, and outward-bound ships were shaking out their sails as they flew, with foam at their bows, down past Bonnie Inchkeith.

'But, dear me, what's on at the links,' was the call of one Musselburgher to another as he saw numerous well-known Edinburgh golfers and members of the Yeomanry ride over the Esk Bridge and on to the racecourse.

'There's no a caddie in the place,' another would observe; 'there must be some grand match.'

'I'll wager it's against the officers o' the Greys,' said one, 'because every one o' them, no' missing the Cornel, has ridden over frae Jock's Lodge this morning, and that de'il o' a madman, Melville, at the heid o' them. There's something no very canny aboot that lad. I think we'll best gang doun and see.'

And so they did 'gang doun and see,' in such numbers that when the lawyer arrived with his friends there was quite a crowd of two hundred or more, including horsemen, gathered opposite the winning-post, the Grand Stand opposite then being used as the golf club-quarters.

'Where's your runner,' asked Tailzie, as he rode up on a hack, accompanied by Beattie on the very horse which was the cause of all the concern.

'I'll show you that directly,' was the reply; 'but in the meantime, will you have another ten guineas on the result?'

'I will have it,' said Beattie, whose eyes were still red with the wine of the previous evening, and who believed that no message could have been quicker carried than his horse had earned him in the race for the Cup. So the bet was booked.

'Now,' said Melville, 'a message is a message long or short. It may be a volume, or it may be a word, that you'll admit, so long as it is carried within the time and under the conditions of the match.'

'Agreed,' said the other, 'I have no objections to that.'

'Well, then, here is a peg of wood. Write on it the word "Victory," the regimental password last night, in your own handwriting, and put your own initials under it. You have done so. Well,' said Melville, with all the manners of a street conjuror, 'you will observe shortly that I shall place it within this little ball, and if you will come with me,' he said, with a sly twinkle, 'I will show you that it is properly fastened inside.'

He led the way over to the Club-house, where stood the green-keeper and professional, and said, 'Allan, I wish you to fasten this peg of wood into this golf ball so that it will remain fast for at least thirteen or fourteen good drives.' The professional, who had specially manufactured a ball for the purpose, lost no time in doing so, and it was handed to Beattie with the remark, 'You ride up to the bend with this, and place it on the tee opposite the six-furlong post. I will wait here at the winning-post, and Tailzie will pick it up and extract his message. Aitchison here, of Edinburgh, the clockmaker, will keep time from the fall of a red flag, which will announce the departure of the ball in this direction.'

Tailzie's complexion assumed the hue of well-watered milk, but he merely remarked to his friend, 'Ride down the line after the ball as hard as you can, Jack, and see that they drive it between the posts and keep to the course.'

'That's all right,' said the other; 'you can't object to the ball being returned if it does go aside, and our taking the course properly.'

There was little danger, however, of the ball being allowed to go wrong, as Beattie early observed. At intervals of fifty yards were stationed laddies, each carrying in their hands small lumps of clay with which to tee the ball when picked up. These were outside the course by the rails. Inside were all the best driving caddies and professionals of Edinburgh, at eighty yards intervals, each with his play club in his hand, and seeming eager and anxious for the novel match to commence. Allan, the green-keeper, had well coached them in their duties, which were not to try to swipe too far, but to send their ball straight up the course to their next neighbour. Behind these drivers were stationed attendant caddies, who were to tee the ball if it lay badly, but to lose not one single second if possible. Of all things to be careful about, they were to try and keep good line.

Beattie had not been longer than five minutes at the post when the flag was seen to fall, and he was observed to come galloping down the course as hard as his famous flier could carry him. But fast as he galloped the golf ball galloped faster. Once only did he catch it up, and that was when midway it rolled outside of one of the posts. Quickly was it thrown back, passed round the post, teed in the centre of the course, and sent flying onward again. Allan the green-keeper was the last man to take it up, and this he did as a chieftain would have seized the fiery cross in the days of old. Not waiting for it to be teed, he lifted it with a clean swing straight up to the inside of the winning-post, where the timekeeper picked it up.

'How much?' asked Tailzie of the latter, anxiously.

'One minute, forty-eight seconds,' was the reply.

'Then I have lost on the post,' was the reply. 'All I can say is that had the wind not favoured you I should have won easily; but here is Beattie. Did they keep the course?'

'Yes,' was the crestfallen reply of the latter. 'I must say that they did not pass outside of a single post.'

'Then we must pay and look pleasant,' said the other, as Allan the green-keeper extracted the little message with the ominous word 'Victory.' 'I did not really think it could have been done without the assistance of horses or pigeons, and certainly never dreamt of this method of sending a message. It certainly is a curious style of play in the links, golfing against time.'

A ONE-BALL MATCH

GERALD BATCHELOR

It was the first day of Spring and I arrived early on the links, eager to make the most of my holiday.

I found a solitary figure in the smoking-room, poring over the latest book on golf, and recognized him as a fellow member whom I knew to be a good golfer, a good sportsman and one of the pleasantest men in the Club.

Clerkson had retired early from Government service owing to ill-health, and it was understood that, in spite of being an unmarried man, he possessed hardly sufficient means to be able to afford the luxury of playing golf regularly.

"Hullo, Clerkson!" I said, "I haven't seen you here for ages. Have you been away?"

"No," he replied, "I—er—I've given up golf."

"Given up golf?" I repeated in amazement, "*you*, the keenest player in all—but you've been ill, perhaps?"

"Yes, I have," he said, "but that is not the real reason. The fact is, I found the game too expensive. I don't complain of my limited income—it is nobody's business but my own—but I don't mind telling you that many a time when I have played here and lost a ball I have been forced to economize by going without my lunch!

"Now you will understand why I have always been so anxious to avail myself of the full five minutes allowed for search, however hopeless the case might appear. It's my own fault for ever taking up golf. I wish I hadn't. No, I don't wish that, and I would willingly deny myself anything rather than be compelled to give it up.

"The limit came when they put up the price of balls. That extra sixpence meant everything to me, you see, so I had no choice but to depart from my earthly paradise.

"I thought I could do it, too, but I was wrong. The exercise of brain and muscle, so happily combined, had become as necessary to me as food and sleep.

"My health began to suffer. Doctors could do nothing. They failed to diagnose my case. I got worse and worse, until I was almost given up.

"This morning I took the matter out of their hands, for I have thought of a plan. I jumped out of bed, enjoyed a big breakfast, and hurried up to the links. I feel better already."

"Excellent!" I exclaimed, "will you have a match?"

"I should be ashamed to ask you to play with me," he replied, "for I'm afraid I might spoil your game."

"What do you mean?" I asked. "You are a better golfer than I am."

"Ah, but I fear you do not quite understand the conditions under which I am compelled to play," he said; "in future I shall always have to play *without a ball!*"

"Without a ball?" I repeated; "you are surely joking. How is it possible?"

"Well, if you really don't object to watching the experiment," said Clerkson, "I will show you."

"Perhaps you will remember," he continued as we made for the first tee, "that it is my custom to take a trial swing before every drive? It was this which suggested the idea. I was always able to judge fairly accurately by the feeling of the swing whether the stroke would have been successful. Will you take the honour?"

"Shall we have a ball on?" I asked as usual, forgetting for the moment the peculiar conditions of the coming match. Clerkson seemed to be engaged in a mental struggle. Then he answered, "Yes!"

I made a fair drive and stood aside to see what my opponent would do. He took some sand, pinched it into a tee, addressed it carefully, and played.

"Ah!" he exclaimed: "I was afraid I should slice. I must have been standing that way."

He made off towards the rough, where I saw him play two strokes, and we walked on together to my ball. I also played two more shots before reaching the green.

"Where are you?" I asked.

"Didn't you see it?" said Clerkson. "I was rather surprised that you did not compliment me on the stroke. It was a wicked lie."

"Are you—are you near the hole?" I inquired, as I settled down to a long putt.

"I don't see it at present," he replied, looking about, "I hope it hasn't run over. Good Heavens!" he went on, as he reached the pin. "It's *in the hole!*"

He stooped and seemed to pick it out.

"I really must apologize for that fluke," my opponent said, as we walked to the next tee, "but I knew it was a fine shot directly I had played it, and I thought it deserved to be pretty close."

"It looks as if this is going to be rather a one-sided match," I said to myself, as I watched him dispatch what he described as a "screamer", and I began to wonder whether Clerkson had planned this game in order to provide himself with the necessary ball. Knowing him to be a thoroughly good fellow however, I dismissed the suspicion from my mind.

These misgivings prevented me from concentrating my attention entirely on the game, with the result that I played very indifferently and reached the second green three strokes to the bad. After I had holed my putt, Clerkson kept walking up and down the green in his attempts to get into the hole.

"Your hole!" he cried at last; "putting was always my weak point."

The game continued to be very even. If I obtained a lead of one hole my opponent invariably seemed to hit a tremendous distance from the next tee. At the fourth he played a shot which must have easily beaten the record drive. On the other hand, if he happened to become one up he lost the next by taking three or four putts.

At the sixth hole his ball disappeared into a gorse bush. Formerly he would have been much disturbed by such an occurrence, but now he seemed to accept the situation with philosophic calm.

"Come along; never mind," he said, after a casual look round; "it's of no consequence; only an old gutta, you know. I'll drop another"—which he did. He must have lost quite half a dozen balls during the round.

At the ninth we were all square. I was beginning to find my game better now.

"Mark it!" cried Clerkson, directly after driving from the tenth tee; "I've lost it in the sun."

"I see it," I said; "you've pulled it rather badly, I'm afraid, and it has landed in 'Purgatory' bunker." I pointed out to him that it was lying in a hopeless position, and he gave up the hole.

At the twelfth hole Clerkson made a very serious error of judgement. I was diligently looking for his wild drive when I happened to stumble on a brand-new "Dunlop."

"What are you playing with?" I asked.

"Let me see," he said, watching my face very intently, "was it a 'Colonel', or a 'Zodiac', or a 'Silver King', or—oh, I know; it was a 'Challenger'."

I put the ball in my pocket.

At the fourteenth, where Clerkson had the honour, some workmen were walking across the fairway, quite three hundred yards away.

"Do you think I can reach them?" my opponent said. I thoughtlessly said, "No, of course not."

Directly he had driven he yelled "Fore!" at the top of his voice. The men looked round.

"That was a narrow escape," he gasped.

"But surely you were a long way short," I said.

"Short!" he exclaimed, "why, man, it was *right over their heads!*"

He gave me a rare fright at the next.

I had a splendid tee shot, for once, and Clerkson walked straight up to my ball.

"This is mine, I believe," he said.

"Certainly not," I cried, "I am playing with a 'Kite'."

"*So am I!*" said he.

Fortunately I was able to point out a private mark which I had made on my ball.

We were all square on the eighteenth. I drove out of bounds.

"Did you get a good one?" I asked anxiously, after he had played.

"A perfect peach," he replied.

I concluded that I had lost the match. I persevered, however, and was playing two more with my approach, while he (so I was informed) was less than a yard from the hole. My mashie shot looked like going in, but the ball came to rest on the edge of the tin.

Clerkson walked up, looked at the ball, went on one knee, then suddenly dashed his cap to the ground in disgust.

"Anything wrong?" I inquired.

"Wrong?" he repeated. "Can't you see that you have laid me *a dead stymie?*"

He studied the line with great care.

"I think there is just room to pull round," he muttered. He played, and watched, with an agonized expression, the course of his invisible ball. Suddenly there came a strong puff of wind, and my ball toppled into the hole.

"D—n it all," cried Clerkson, "I've *knocked you in!*" He picked up my ball, and with it, apparently, his own.

"A halved match," he said, "and I must thank you for an exceedingly interesting game."

I was due in London that evening, and on my return, some weeks later, I learnt that Clerkson had been laid up with a form of brain fever.

DORMIE ONE

HOLWORTHY HALL

It was five o'clock and rapidly shading into dusk. The September sun, which earlier had set the air to simmering in tremulous heatwaves, now moved reluctant to ambush behind the hills, and, as though sullen at the exigency of its time, gave warning by its bloodshot eye of pitiless heat to be renewed with tomorrow's dawn. From the curving line of trees—thin elms and maples, bordering upon the hard-packed road—long, soothing shadows edged out into the fresh green of the fairway, measuring with their deeper green the flight of hours and the peaceful ebbing of the afternoon.

From the distant Sound, a transient breeze, shy as a maiden in the manner of its coming, ventured out from the protection of the ridge, hesitated, wavered, and passed across the sward so fleetingly that almost before it seemed assured a fact, it was a memory.

Then, from the trees at the roadside, and from the trees beyond, and from the little brook dawdling along from east to west, and from the reeded lake far over to the right, a breath of evening crept out upon the lawns, and there was silence.

In a squared clearing at the southern end of the sinous line of maples there was a trim plateau, close-shorn of grass, and sharply defined by boundaries of sedge and stubble. From this spot forward an expansive belt of untrimmed land stretched northward for a hundred yards, to merge presently with the more aristocratic turf of the fairway. Thereafter, narrowing between the trees and a long alignment of arid pits, the trail of adventure ran through rolling country, skirted a grove of locusts, dipped down to ford the brook, climbed past a pair of shallow trenches which glistened with coarse sand, and finally found refuge on a terraced green protected by towering chestnuts and flanked by the arm of a colonial house which rested comfortably beneath the trees.

From clearing to terrace the crow, flying as crows are popularly supposed to fly, would have accomplished five hundred and twenty yards. It was the eighteenth hole at Kenilworth. The trim plateau, which was the eighteenth tee, now marked the apex of a human letter, a V of which a thousand men and women formed each stroke. Converging sharply toward that rectangle in the sedge, two thousand men and women—twin lines of white slashed here and there with vivid, burning color—restrained and held in check by twisted ropes, leaned out and gaped and wondered, breathless; now standing hushed by things already seen, now vibrant to the future, uneasy murmuring. And as in recompense for toiling through the humid afternoon, two thousand men and women held this privilege: to stand, and wait, and watch until a boy—a sturdy, laughing boy—and then a man—a grayed and quiet man—played, stroke by stroke, the eighteenth hole at Kenilworth.

And silhouetted in the background, nervous on the tee, stood man and boy, paired finalists for the Amateur Championship; two wizards of the links whose faces had gone rigid, whose palms were suddenly wet and cold, whose souls were newly strung upon the natural laws which govern flying objects. Each of them had reason for his agitation; their mutual loss of equilibrium was mutual in its cause; for of these two, the man—Hargrave, the present champion—was dormie one.

He was fifty–five, this Hargrave; in commercial life he had known bankruptcy at forty. Golf, which had been heretofore diversion, he made the solace of his penury; it had then constituted itself his religion. Within a decade he had snatched the national title for his keepsake; subsequently he had lost it, struggled for it desperately, regained, and twice defended it. The gold medal meant infinitely more to him than a mere visible token of success at golf; it was suggestive of success elsewhere; it was the embodiment of conquests he had never made, of victories he never might accomplish. In other years wealth had eluded him, power had been alien to him, social distinction was to be classed among the impossibilities; but when he stepped morosely out upon the course, he vaunted in his heart that he was highborn to the purple.

Granted that he was poor indeed in purse, he knew no multimillionaire in all the world who could undertake to meet him on equal terms; he could concede six strokes, and still administer a beating, to the finest gentleman and the finest golfer in the Social Register. And so, while golf was his theology, and the arbitrary standard of par his creed, he played the Scottish game as though it symbolized the life he had proved incapable of mastering—and he mastered the game instead. It was his single virtue; it was the hyphen which allied him to the rest of civilization.

To win was the wine of his existence; to surmount obstacles was the evidence of his regeneration; to come from behind, to turn impending downfall into disconcerting triumph, was his acrid compensation for the days and months and years when the man in him had cried out for recognition, and the weakling in him had earned his failure. And he was dormie one—and it was Stoddard's honor at the last hole.

The man stiffened perceptibly as Stoddard, nodding to the referee, took a pinch of sand from the box, and teed for the final drive. Then, in accordance with the grimmest of his grim theories of golf, he abruptly turned his back on his opponent, and stared fixedly at the ground. He had trained himself to this practice for two unrelated reasons: the moral effect upon his adversary, and the opportunity to detach himself from the mechanics of his surroundings and to visualize himself in the act of playing his next stroke.

Habitually he conjured up a vision of the ball, the club, himself in the address, the swing, the attack, the aftermath. He compelled his faculties to rivet upon a superb ideal. And it was largely by virtue of this preliminary concentration that he was enabled to bring off his shots with such startling absence of delay: the orders were transmitted to his muscles in advance; his swing was often started when, to the openmouthed observer, he had hardly reached the ball. And it was by virtue of his utter disregard of his opponent that he was never discouraged, never unnerved, never disheartened. He was neither cheered by the disaster of the enemy, nor cast down by the enemy's good fortune. He was contemptuous not only of the personality of the opponent, but also of his entity. He played his own game, and his best game, ironically ignoring the fact that it was competitive. To all intents and purposes, Hargrave in contest was the only man on the course; he even disregarded his caddy, and expected the proper club, as he demanded it, to be placed in his hand extended backward.

But as now he formally prepared to shut Stoddard out of his consciousness, and as he exerted his stern determination to picture himself in yet another perfect illustration of golfing form, he discovered that his will, though resolute, was curiously languid. It missed of its usual persistence. The ideal came and went, as though reflected on a motion film at lowered speed. There was no continuity; there was no welding of motor impulses. According to his theory, Hargrave should have been purely mechanical. On the contrary, he was thinking.

He entertained no sense of actual antagonism toward Stoddard. Indeed, from the inception of the finals, at ten o'clock this morning, the boy had shown himself considerate and generous, quick of applause and slow of alibi, a dashing, brilliant, dangerous golfer with the fire of an adventurer and the grace of a cavalier. He was confident yet modest, and he had performed a score of feats for which his modesty was none of that inverted conceit of mediocrity in luck, but literal modesty, sheer lack of self-aggrandizement. He was dogged while he smiled; he was still smiling with his lips when his eyes betrayed his chastened mood; and the smile faded and vanished only when he saw that Hargrave was in difficulty. The gallery, nine tenths of it, was with him boisterously. The gallery was frankly on the side of youth and spontaneity. The mass, unresponsive to the neutral tints of Hargrave's character, thrilled to the juvenile star ascendant.

The gray–haired champion, introspective on the tee, frowned and grimaced, and toyed with his dread-naught driver. Early in the morning he had confessed guiltily to himself that Stoddard was the sort of lad he should have liked to call his son. And yet he knew that if he had ever married, if he had ever glowed to the possession of an heir, the boy couldn't conceivably have been in the least like Stoddard. Too many generations forbade the miracle. The mold of ancestry would have stamped out another failure, another charge upon the good opinion of the world. The child would have been the father of the man. And Stoddard—witness his behavior and his generosity—was of no varnished metal. He was without alloy. He was a gentleman because his great–grandfathers had been gentlemen. He was rich because they had made him so. But Hargrave had allowed himself to experience an anomalous and paternal emotion toward Stoddard—Stoddard who at twenty was higher in rank, higher in quality, higher in the affection of the people than Hargrave at fifty-five. He had nourished this emotion by trying to imagine what he could have made of himself if, at his majority, he had been of the type of Stoddard.

And now, recalling this quondam sentiment, he shuddered in a spasm of self-pity; and simultaneously in one of those racking bursts of humanity which come to men unloving and unloved, he longed to whirl about, to stride toward Stoddard, to grip his hand and say—well, one of the common platitudes. "May the best man win"—something of that sort; anything to show that he, too, was living rapidly in the crisis.

In another moment he might have yielded; he might have bridged the fearful chasm of self-imposed restraint. But he was slothful to the impulse. Behind him there was the sharp, pistol-like crack of a clean and powerful drive; and before him, brought clear by reflex and by the will that had been lagging, the ghostly mirage of a ball, and of himself swinging steadily and hard, and of the joy of impact, and a tremendous carry and run, true to the flag. The champion had remembered that he was dormie one. A voice, low but distinct, came to him through a volume of incoherent sound: "Mr. Hargrave!"

The man turned slowly. He saw neither the referee, who had spoken to him, nor Stoddard, who had stepped aside; he saw no caddies; he saw no fairway. Both lines of the V were weaving, undulating; on the faces of the men and women nearest him he perceived beatific, partizan delight. The thousand-tongued shout which had gone up in praise of Stoddard was dwindling by degrees to a pleasant hum, which throbbed mercilessly in Hargrave's ears and challenged him. He knew, as he had known for hours, how earnestly the public hoped for his defeat. He knew that if he bettered Stoddard's drive his sole reward would be a trifling ripple of applause, smirched by a universal prayer that ineptly he might spoil his second shot.

He grinned sardonically at the throng. He rubbed his palms together, drying them. He teed a ball, and took his stance; glanced down the course, took back the club a dozen inches, carried it ahead, and rested for the fraction of a second; then, accurate, machinelike to the tiniest detail, swung up, hit down, and felt his body carried forward in the full, strong finish of a master drive.

"Good ball!" said Stoddard in a voice that trembled slightly. From the V—sporadic hand clapping. Hargrave, the national champion, had driven two hundred and sixty yards.

Ahead of him, as he walked defiantly through the rough, the fairway bobbed with men and women who, as they chattered busily, stumbled over the irregularities of the turf. Now and then a straggler threw a look of admiration over his shoulder, and, meeting the expressionless mask of the amateur champion, insouciantly shrugged that shoulder and resumed his march.

Hargrave's caddy, dour and uncommunicative as the champion himself, stalked abreast, the clubs rattling synchronously to his stride. Hargrave was studying the contour of the land in front; he glowered at the marshals who had suffered the gallery to break formation and overflow the course; and he was tempted to ask his caddy how, when the entire middle distance was blocked by gabbling spectators, the Golf Association thought a finalist could judge the hole. But he denied himself the question; it was seven years since he had condescended to complain of, or to criticize, the conditions of any tournament. Nevertheless he was annoyed; he was certain that the ground sloped off just where his second shot should properly be placed; his memory was positive. Blindfold, he could have aimed correctly to a surveyor's minute.

Still, he was impatient, irritated. He wanted to verify his scheme of play. He wanted to do it instantly. The muscles of his neck twitched spasmodically; and without warning, even to himself, his canker flared into red hate. His eyes flashed venomously; and when it seemed that unless that crowd dispersed, and gave him room, his nerves would shatter in a burst of rage, he saw the marshals tautening their lines, the gallery billowing out into a wide and spacious funnel, and felt the caddy's timid touch upon his sleeve.

"Look out, Mr. Hargrave! Stoddard's away!"

The champion halted, and without a glance toward Stoddard, stared at his own ball. It was an excellent lie; he nodded imperceptibly and took a brassey which the caddy, without instructions, placed in his outstretched hand. His fingers closed around the smooth-worn grip; he tested the spring of the shaft, and focused his whole attention upon the ball. He strove to summon that mental cinema of Hargrave, cool, collected, playing a full brassey to the green. But Stoddard again intruded.

In the morning round, Hargrave had won the first three holes in a row, and he had held the advantage, and brought in his man three down. He had made a seventy-four, one over par, and Stoddard had scored a creditable seventy-eight—doubly creditable in view of his ragged getaway. And in the afternoon Hargrave had won the first two holes, and stood five up with sixteen more to play, when Stoddard had begun an unexpected spurt. Hargrave scowled at the toe of his brassey as he recounted errors which, if they could have been eliminated from his total, would have erased five needless strokes, and ended the match long since. Cruelly three of those errors were on successive holes. On the fifteenth he had missed a simple putt for the win; on the sixteenth he had overapproached and thrown away a half; on the seventeenth he had topped an iron and still accomplished a par four—but Stoddard had made a three.

The champion felt his heart flutter and his knees yield a trifle as he reflected what havoc one more ineffectual shot would work upon his nerves. He was surely, steadily slipping, and he knew it. The bulk of his vitality was gone; and he was drawing heavily upon his light reserve. He realized, not in cowardice but in truth and in fact, that if the match should go to an extra hole, he, and not Stoddard, would be the loser. His customary command of his muscles was satisfactory, but his control of his nerves was waning. He was overgolfed; overstrained; stale. He could bear the strain of this hole, but that was all. His stamina had touched its limit; his fortitude could stand no more. He could gage it to a nicety; he had a debilitating intuition which told him that if he had to drive again from the first tee, he should founder wretchedly; and he believed this message from his soul, because he had never before received it.

If Stoddard won the eighteenth, it would be the fourth consecutive godsend for Stoddard, and Stoddard's game was improving, not deteriorating; he had moral courage behind him, he had the savage exhilaration of metamorphosing a forlorn chance into a delirious certainty, he had the stimulus and the impetus of his grand onrush, he had the responsive gallery to cheer him on. It was inevitable that Stoddard, if he won the eighteenth, would win the next; so that the champion, who was dormie one, must have a half—he must divide this hole with Stoddard. He *must!*

The champion grew restive. It needed the supreme effort of his career to force himself to inertia, to refrain from wheeling swiftly, and shrieking aloud to Stoddard, to demand why he didn't *play!* Was the boy asleep? Dead? Dreaming? Had he succumbed to paralysis? Was he gloating over his triumph? Hargrave wet his lips, and swallowed dustily.

A tremor ran through his limbs, and his wrists tightened in palsied fear. His eyes pained him; they reminded him of a doll's eyes, turning inward; he was aware that his face was drawn. He wondered stupidly whether the spoon would be safer than the brassey. He liked the spoon—but was the cleek surer yet? He caught his breath in a gasp, and at the same moment his spine was chilled in a paroxysm of futile terror. He essayed once more to swallow and thought he was strangling. His soul cried heartbreakingly out to Stoddard: "Shoot! For God's sake, *shoot!*"

The tension snapped. A roar of jubilance went up from twice a thousand throats, a roar which, dying momentarily, swelled up in glory, and hung, and splintered into a thousand reverberations against the hills. Hargrave shivered and cleared his throat. For the life of him he couldn't maintain his principles; his nature revolted; and jerking his head towards the north, he was gazing at a tiny fleck of white ten feet to the side of the terrace, which was the eighteenth green. Stoddard was hole high in two! A lucky ricochet from the stones of the brook! Five hundred and twenty yards in two! Hargrave went sickly white, and looked despairingly at his caddy.

He needed a half, and Stoddard was hole high. There was an outside possibility, then, that Stoddard could make a four—one under par. And Hargrave was nearly three hundred yards away. Could he, too, make a four—for the half?

The champion, with two alternatives looming bold before him, shuddered in exquisite incertitude. He could attempt a heroic stroke with the brassey, sacrificing accuracy for distance, or he could play his normal shot, which was practically sure to clear the brook, but still would leave him at a critical disadvantage. In the latter instance he could guarantee himself a five, but already Stoddard was assured of four. And that four, if he achieved it, meant a squared match for Stoddard, and a resultant victory. Hargrave would halve the hole only if Stoddard blundered; and for an hour and more Stoddard's golf had been flawless. There was no blunder in him.

But if Hargrave should risk his own crown on a mighty endeavor to equal Stoddard's titanic brassey shot, he would have the odds of war alarmingly against him. The trajectory must be perfect to a ruled, undeviating line. The ball must either fall short of the brook by ten yards, or clear it by ten, and bounding neither to the left, among the trees, nor to the right, among the sand pits, surmount the grade. An unfortunate angle of consequence, a mere rub of the green, would be doubly fatal. The ball might even be unplayable. There would yet be a hazardous last chance for a five; but again, there was no reason to expect that Stoddard would need so many. Stoddard had been deadly, uncannily deadly, on those short running approaches. Stoddard would make his four, and Hargrave knew it. He closed and unclosed his fingers around the grip of his brassey. A rim of ice, pressing inward, surrounded his heart. His brain was delicately clouded, as though he had just awakened out of the slumber of exhaustion, and looked upon the world without comprehending it, sensed it without perceiving its physiology. He passed a hand over his forehead, and found it damp with perspiration.

A year ago he had promised himself that, as champion, he would withdraw from competition. It was his dream to retire at the height of his prowess, to go down in the history of games as one of that rare company who have known when to file their resignations. Indeed, as late as February he had vowed not to defend his title this year. But when he had once sniffed the intoxicant atmosphere of a club grill, and after he had proved his strength in a practice round or two, he had diffidently entered for the Atlantic City tournament, and won it. Infectiously the old ardor had throbbed in his veins. He was keenly alive to his dominant tenure; his nostrils dilated, his jaws set.

He would add one consummating honor to those that had gone before; he would take his third successive championship with him into exile. And so at Deal, at Apawamis, at Sleepy Hollow and at Garden City, at Montclair and Wykagyl and Piping Rock, he had groomed himself, thoroughly and deliberately, for the fitting climax. The metropolitan supremacy was his for the fifth occasion; he had finished fourth in the Metropolitan Open, third in the National Open. In the handicap list of the great central association he stood proudly aloof at scratch. He was invincible.

And now, with six days of irreproachable golf behind him; with the greatest prize of a lifetime shining in his very eyes, he looked at a distant red flag, drooping on its staff, and looked at a ball lying in tempting prominence on the fairway, and felt his chin quiver in the excess of his passionate longing, and felt a white-hot band searing his forehead, and penetrating deep.

He kept the brassey. And as he took his stance, and struggled to centralize his wishes upon the problem of combining vast length with absolute precision, his mind became so acutely receptive to impression, so marvelously subjective, that he found himself repeating over and over to himself the series of simple maxims he had learned painfully by heart when he was a novice, striving to break through the dread barrier which divides those who play over and those who play under a hundred strokes for the single round.

He experienced, for the first time in years, a subtle premonition of ineptitude. He was again a tyro, whose margin of error was 95 percent. Where was the ball going? It was incredibly small, that sphere in the fairway; it was incredible that he should smite it so truly and so forcibly that it would fly even so far as a welcome furlong. Suppose he, a champion, with a champion's record, should slice, or pull, or top—or miss the ball completely?

Hargrave's teeth came grindingly together. His eyes dulled and contracted. He took the club back for a scant foot, raised it, took it forward, past the ball in the line of the hole, brought it to its original position, pressed it gently into the velvet turf with infinitesimal exertion of the left wrist, and swung. Wrists, forearms, shoulders and hips—his whole anatomy coordinated in that terrible assault. The click of the wood against the ball hadn't yet reached his ears when he knew, with exultation so stupendous that it nauseated him, that the shot had come off. His eager eyes picked up the ball in flight; and as he paused momentarily at the finish of his terrific drive, he was filled with a soft and yet an incongruously fierce content. Again he had foiled the gallery, and Stoddard! He saw the ball drop, across the brook; saw it leap prodigiously high in air, and fall again, and bound, and roll, slower and slower, and cease to roll—a good club's length from the lower pit, twenty yards from the green.

The champion and the challenger were on even terms.

Unlike the average man of gregarious instincts, Hargrave never sought proximity to his opponent during a match. His procedure was exactly as though, instead of playing against a flesh-and-blood antagonist, he were going around alone. He went his independent way, kept his peace, and entertained no thought of conversation or courtesy. If fortuitously he had to walk a course parallel to that of his opponent, and even if the interval between them were a matter of a scant rod or so, the champion was invariably thin-lipped, reflective, incommunicative.

He observed with a little flicker of amusement that Stoddard was eyeing him sidewise, and he felt that Stoddard was not a little affected by that enormous brassey as well as by Hargrave's outward indifference toward it. Hargrave, however, appraised his own flinty exterior as one of his championship assets. He never praised the other man; and if the other man chose to burst into fervid eulogy, the champion's manner was so arctic, so repelling, that not infrequently he gained a point on the very next shot through the adversary's dazed inefficiency and even one stroke in match play is worth saving.

He knew that he was unpopular, he knew that he was affirmatively disliked; he knew that the public, the good-natured and friendly public, yearned for Stoddard's triumph rather as a vindication of gentility than as a proof of might. But as he observed that Stoddard showed premonitory symptoms of increased nervousness, and that Stoddard was impelled to speak, and yet held his tongue to save himself from sure rebuff, the champion's breast expanded with golden hope.

Stoddard, after all, was a mere boy: a veteran golfer—yes, but immature in the mentality of golf. And Hargrave sometimes won his matches, especially from younger men, in the locker room before he put on his shoes. If Stoddard congratulated him now, he could send Stoddard into catastrophe with one glowing sentence. But Stoddard didn't speak.

In addition to his other reasons, he was anxious to beat Stoddard because of his very youth. It had galled Hargrave to be called, by the luck of the draw, to meet five of the youngest experts of the country in this tournament; it had galled him, not because he was loath to win from younger men, but because the public naturally discounted his victories over them.

On Tuesday he had overwhelmed a Western prodigy, a freckled schoolboy who had blushingly donned full-length trousers for this great event. On Wednesday he had won, three up and two to go, from a Harvard freshman, a clubable youngster who had capitulated to Hargrave primarily because his optimism had slowly been destroyed by Hargrave's rude acerbity. On Thursday he had met, and easily defeated, the junior champion of Westchester—defeated him by the psychology of the locker room, by knocking him off-balance at the outset, much as the gladiator Corbett once shook the poise of the gladiator Sullivan. In the semifinals yesterday he had beaten his man—browbeaten him—by diligently creating an atmosphere of such electric stress that a too-little-hardened Southron, sensitive as a girl, had gone to pieces at the ninth, surrendered at the twenty-seventh hole.

And Hargrave, whose bitterness toward the golfing world had progressed arithmetically through these earlier rounds, had come up to the finals in a mood of acid which, in the true analysis, was a form of specious envy and regret. He realized that in comparison with any of the men he had removed from brackets, he was unattractive, aged, cynical, repugnant. He envied youth—but how could he regain his own? How could he crystallize at fifty-five the secret ambitions of a boy too young to vote? He couldn't stand before this fashionable gallery and, indicating Stoddard, cry out to them: "But I *want* to be like him! I *want* to be! And it's too late! It's too late!"

A great wave of self-glorification swept over him, and left him calmer, more pragmatical. After all, he was Hargrave, phenomenon of the links, the man who, beginning serious golf at the age of forty, unaided by professional tutoring, unschooled by previous experience in the realm of sports, had wrenched three amateur championships and unnumbered lesser prizes from keen fields. He was the unconquerable Hargrave; the man who had victoriously invaded France, England, Austria, Canada, Scotland. He had averaged below seventy-five for the previous three years on all courses and at all seasons. He had been six down with nine to play in the finals of the English Amateur, and come romping home to triumph, four under par. It was said of him that he was never beaten until the last putt on the last hole. Better than that, it was true.

By this time the gallery was massed rows deep around the eighteenth green. Hargrave crossed the little footbridge over the brook and permitted the vestige of a smile to temper the severity of his face. They hoped to see him lose, did they? Well, he had often disappointed them in the past; he could disappoint them now! All he required was a half, and he was barely off the green in two.

But even in the vanity which somewhat relieved the strain upon him, he was conscious of a burdening weariness which wasn't solely physical. He was impatient, not only to end the hole, and the match, but also to end his tournament golf forever. He was sure now that, winner or loser, he should never enter an important contest again. His nerves were disintegrating. He was losing that essential balance without which no man, however skillful in the academics of the game, may be renowned for his examples.

Next year he should unquestionably play with less surety, less vigor. Some unknown duffer would catch him unawares and vanquish him; and after that the descent from scratch would be rapid—headlong. It had been so with the greatest golfers of old; it would be so with Hargrave. Great as he was, he wasn't immune to the calendar. But to retire as merely a runner-up—that was unthinkable! To retire in favor of a slim boy whose Bachelorhood of Arts was yet a fond delusion—that was impossible! He must win—and on the eighteenth green, after he had holed out, he would break his putter over his knee, and he would say to the gallery—and it ought to be dramatic . . .

He brought himself to a standstill. His heart pounded suffocatingly. A lump rose in his throat, and choked him, and his whole intellect seemed to melt into confusion and feeble horror; there was a crushing weight on his chest. A slow, insistent cacophony poured through his brain, and for an instant his universe went black. The ball, which had appeared to carry so magnificently, and roll so well, had found a bowl-shaped depression in the turf, a wicked concavity an inch and a half in depth, two in diameter; and there it lay, part in the sunlight, part nestling under the shelter of a dry leaf, a ball accursed and sinister.

Blindly, and apprehensive, the champion turned to look at Stoddard. The boy was struggling to conceal the manifestation of his hopes; the muscles of his lower face were flexed and unrelenting. Between him and the flag was level turf, untroubled by the slightest taint of trickery or unevenness. He knew, and Hargrave knew, that nothing short of superhuman skill could bring the like to Hargrave. He knew, and Hargrave knew, that at the playoff of a tie the champion was doomed. The champion had faltered on the last few holes; his game was destined to collapse as surely as Stoddard's game was destined to rise supreme. As Hargrave paused, aghast, there came a rustle and a murmur from the gallery. A clear voice— a woman's voice—said ecstatically, "Then Bobby'll *win*—won't he?"

Hargrave glared in the direction of that voice. The veil of horror had gradually dissolved, but Hargrave, as he weighed the enigma of the shot, was visited by a cold apathy which staggered him. It wasn't a phlegmatic calm which sat upon him; it was inappetency—as though he had just been roused to a sense of proportionate values.

The matter of coaxing a golf ball out of a casual depression—what significance had it? Tomorrow would yet be tomorrow; with breakfast, and the newspapers, and all the immaterial details of living and breathing. Why all this bother and heartache about it? What was golf, that it should stir a man to the otherwise unprobed depths of his soul? Why should he care, why should he squander so much mental torture as could be computed by one tick of a clock, why should he tremble at this ridiculous experiment with a little white ball and a bit of iron on the end of a shaft of hickory?

For one elemental moment he was almost irresistibly impelled to pick that ball out of its lie, and dash it in the face of the gallery, hurl his clubs after it, and empty himself of the accumulated passion of fifty-five years. Sulfurous phrases crowded to his lips . . .

And then he realized that all this time he had been glaring in the direction of a woman's voice. He exhaled fully and held his hand out backward to the caddy.

"Niblick!" said Hargrave thickly.

The distance to the hole was greater than he had fancied. The lie of the ball was worse than he had feared. His calculation intimated that he must strike hard, and stiffly, with a pronounced up-and-down swing to get at the back of the ball. The force of the extricating stroke must be considerable; the green, however, was too fast, too fine, to permit liberty in the manner of approaching it. The ball, if it were to carry the full thirty yards to the pin, couldn't possibly receive sufficient reverse power to fall dead. It must, therefore, be played to reach the nearer rim of the green, and to drift gently on to the hole.

Hargrave caught his breath. The knowledge that he distrusted himself was infinitely more demoralizing than any other factor in the personal equation; he was shocked and baffled by his own uncertainty. Through his brain ran unceasingly the first tenets of the kindergarten of golf. He didn't imagine himself playing this shot: he speculated as to how Braid, or Vardon, or Ray or Duncan would play it. He was strangely convinced that for anyone else on earth it would be the simplest of recoveries, the easiest of pitches to the green.

He glanced at his caddy, and in that glance there was hidden an appeal which bespoke genuine pathos. Hargrave wasn't merely disturbed and distressed: he was palpitatingly afraid. He was afraid to strike, and he was afraid not to strike. His mind had lost its jurisdictive functions; he felt that his thews and sinews were in process of revolt against his will. He was excruciatingly perceptive of people watching him; of Stoddard regarding him humorously.

The collective enmity of the gallery oppressed and befuddled him. He was crazily in dread that when he swung the niblick upright, someone would snatch at it and divert its orbit. His ears strained for a crashing sound from the void; his overloaded nerves expected thunder. He knew that the fall of an oak leaf would reverberate through his aching head like an explosion of maximite and make him strike awry. His vitals seemed suddenly to slip away from his body, leaving merely a febrile husk of clammy skin to hold his heartbeats. The throbbing of the veins in his wrists was agony.

The niblick turned in his perspiring hands. He gripped more firmly, and as his wrists reacted to the weight of the club head, he was automatic. The niblick rose, and descended, smashing down the hinder edge of the bowl-like cavity and tearing the ball free. A spray of dust sprang up, and bits of sod and dirt. The ball shot forward, overrunning the hole by a dozen feet. Almost before it came to rest, Stoddard played carefully with a jigger, and landed ten inches from the hole.

Hargrave's sensation was that he was encompassed with walls which were closing in to stifle and crush him. That they were living walls was evident by the continuous whisper of respiration, and by the cross-motion of the sides. He was buried under the tremendous weight of thousands of personalities in conflict with his own. He tottered on the verge of hysteria. He was nervously exhausted, and yet he was upheld, and compelled to go on, to play, to putt, by nervous energy which by its very goad was unendurable. Hargrave looked at the green under his feet, and fought back a mad impulse to throw himself prone upon it, to scream at the top of his lungs, and writhe, to curse and blaspheme, and claw the grass with his nails. Each breath he drew was cousin to a sob.

He stood behind the ball to trace the line, and recognized that he was seeing neither the ball nor the hole. He couldn't see clearly the grass itself. He was stricken, as far as his environment was concerned, with utter ophthalmia. And although the boy Stoddard was outside the scope of Hargrave's vision, the champion saw Stoddard's face, as he had seen it just now, before Stoddard turned away. He despised Stoddard; unreasonably but implacably he despised him, because of the light he had seen in Stoddard's eyes. The boy wasn't a philosopher, like Hargrave: he was a baby, a whining infant grasping for the moon. *He* had no sense of proportion. That expression in his eyes had convicted him. This tournament was to him the horizon of his life. It *was* his life!

Hargrave's mouth was parched and bitter. He tried to moisten his lips. Details of the green began to develop in his consciousness as in a photographic negative. He saw the zinc-lined hole twelve feet away. His eye traced an imaginary line, starting from his ball and leading, not straight to the cup, but perceptibly to the left, then curving in along the briefest of undulations, swerving past a tiny spot where the grass was sun-scorched, and so to the haven of the hole.

If he could sink that curling putt, nothing could deprive him of his victory. He would be down in four, and Stoddard now lay three. He would have a half—and the match by one up in thirty-six holes. He would be the Amateur Champion of the United States—and he could quit! He could quit as the only man who ever won in three successive years. And if he missed, and Stoddard took the hole in four to five, Hargrave knew that even if his legs would support him to the first tee, his arms would fall at the next trial. He doubted if sanity itself would stay with him for another hole.

The murmur of the gallery appalled him with its vehemence. The noise was as the rushing of the falls of Niagara. Hargrave stood wearily erect, and eyed that section of the crowd which was before him. He was puzzled by the excitement, the anxiety of that crowd. He was violently angered that no smile of encouragement, of good-fellowship, met his inquiring gaze. The misanthrope in him surged to the surface, and he was supercilious—just for a second!—and then that sense of impotence, of futility, of shaken poise fell upon him once more, and his throat filled.

He needed the half. He must hole this putt. He was thinking now not so much of the result of holing it as of the result of missing it. He could fancy the wretched spectacle he would make of himself on the playoff; he could fancy the explosive, tumultuous joy of the gallery; he could picture the dumb, stunned radiance of Stoddard. And Stoddard was so young. Hargrave wouldn't have minded defeat at the hands of an older man, he told himself fiercely—but at the hands of a boy! Hargrave, the man who had made more whirlwind finishes than any other two players of the game, beaten by a stripling who had come from behind!

On the sixteenth and seventeenth holes the champion had reviled himself, scourged himself, between shots. He had clenched his teeth and sworn to achieve perfection. He had persuaded himself that each of his mishaps had been due to carelessness; and he had known in his heart that each of them was due to a fault, a palpable fault of execution. On the eighteenth hole he had reverted to sincerity with himself. He was harrowed and upset, and in confessing his culpability he had removed at least the crime of over-confidence. But this was far worse! He was doubting his own judgment now: he had determined upon the line of his putt, and he was reconsidering it.

He peered again and, blinking, discovered that there were tears in his eyes. The hole seemed farther away than ever, the green less true, the bare spot more prominent, the cup smaller. He wondered dully if he hadn't better putt straight for the hole. He braced himself, and tremblingly addressed the ball with his putter. This was the shot that would take stomach! This was the end!

He had a vision of tomorrow, and the day after, and the day after that. If he missed this putt, and lost the match, how could he exonerate himself? He had no other pleasure in life, he had no other recreation, no other balm for his wasted years. If he tried again next season, he would lose in the first round. He knew it. And he might live to be seventy—or eighty—always with this gloomy pall of failure hanging over him. Another failure—another Waterloo! And this time he would be to himself the apotheosis of failure! Why—Hargrave's heart stopped beating—*he wouldn't be champion!*

With a final hum, which was somehow different from those that had preceded it, the gallery faded from his consciousness. Stoddard was as though he had never existed. Hargrave bent over the putter, and a curious echo rang not unpleasantly in his ears. He saw a white ball in the sunlight, a stretch of lawn, a zinc-lined hole in shadow. There was no longer an objective world in which he lived; there were no longer men and women. He himself was not corporeal. His brain, his rationality, were lost in the abysmal gulf of nothingness. He was merely a part of geometric space; he was an atom of that hypothetical line between two points. His whole being was, for the moment, the essence of the linear standard.

In a blank detachment—for he had no recollection of having putted— he saw the ball spinning on a course to the left of the hole. A terrible agony seized him, and for the second time a black curtain shut him off from actuality. It lifted, leaving him on the brink of apoplexy and he saw that the ball had curved correctly to the fraction of an inch, and was just dropping solidly and unerringly into the cup.

And from the morning paper:

Hargrave was dormie one. Both men drove two hundred and fifty yards straight down the course. Stoddard banged away with his brassey, and nearly got home when the ball caromed off a stone in the brook. Hargrave, playing with that marvelous rapidity which characterizes his game, wouldn't be downed, and promptly sent off a screaming brassey which found a bad lie just off the green, but after studying it fully ten seconds—twice his usual allowance—he chipped out prettily with a niblick. Stoddard ran up, dead. Hardly glancing at the line of his fifteen-footer, Hargrave confidently ran down the putt for a birdie four, and the match. Probably no man living would have played the hole under similar conditions, with such absence of nerves and such abnormal assurance. From tee to green Hargrave barely addressed the ball at all. And certainly in the United States, if not in the world, there is no player who can compete with Hargrave when the champion happens to be in a fighting mood.

To our reporter Hargrave stated positively after the match that he will defend his title next year.

MATHEMATICS FOR GOLFERS

STEPHEN LEACOCK

It is only quite recently that I have taken up golf. In fact, I have played for only three or four years, and seldom more than ten games in a week, or at most four in a day. I have had a proper golf vest for only two years. I bought a "spoon" only this year, and I am not going to get Scotch socks till next year.

In short, I am still a beginner. I have once, it is true, had the distinction "of making a hole in one," in other words, of hitting the ball into the pot, or can, or receptacle, in one shot. That is to say, after I had hit, a ball was found in the can, and my ball was not found. It is what we call circumstantial evidence—the same thing that people are hanged for.

Under such circumstances I should have little to teach to any body about golf. But it has occurred to me that from a certain angle my opinions may be of value. I at least bring to bear on the game all the resources of a trained mind and all the equipment of a complete education.

In particular I may be able to help the ordinary golfer, or "goofer"— others prefer "gopher"—by showing him something of the application of mathematics to golf.

Many a player is perhaps needlessly discouraged by not being able to calculate properly the chances and probabilities of progress in the game. Take for example the simple problem of "going round in bogey." The ordinary average player, such as I am now becoming—something between a beginner and an expert—necessarily wonders to himself, "Shall I ever be able to go around in bogey; will the time ever come when I shall make not one hole in bogey but all the holes?"

To this, according to my calculations, the answer is overwhelmingly "yes." The thing is a mere matter of time and patience.

Let me explain for the few people who never play golf (such as night watchmen, night clerks in hotels, night operators, and astronomers) that "bogey" is an imaginary player who does each hole at golf in the fewest strokes that a first-class player with ordinary luck ought to need for that hole.

Now an ordinary player finds it quite usual to do one hole out of nine "in bogey"—as we golfers, or rather, "us goofers," call it; but he wonders whether it will ever be his fate to do all the nine holes of the course in bogey. To which we answer again with absolute assurance, he will.

The thing is a simple instance of what is called the mathematical theory of probability. If a player usually and generally makes one hole in bogey, or comes close to it, his chance of making any one particular hole in bogey is one in nine. Let us say, for easier calculation, that it is one in ten. When he makes it, his chance of doing the same with the next hole is also one in ten; therefore, taken from the start, his chance of making the two holes successively in bogey is one tenth of a tenth chance. In other words, it is one in a hundred.

The reader sees already how encouraging the calculation is. Here at last something definite about his progress. Let us carry it farther. His chance of making three holes in bogey one after the other will be one in 1,000, his chance of four, one in 10,000, and his chance of making the whole round in bogey will be exactly one in 1,000,000,000—that is, one in a billion games.

In other words, all he has to do is to keep right on. But for how long? he asks. How long will it take, playing the ordinary number of games in a month, to play a billion? Will it take several years? Yes, it will.

An ordinary player plays about a hundred games in a year and will, therefore, play a billion games in exactly 10,000,000 years. That gives us precisely the time it will need for persons like the reader and myself to go around in bogey.

Even this calculation needs a little revision. We have to allow for the fact that in 10,000,000 years the shrinking of the earth's crust, the diminishing heat of the sun, and the general slackening down of the whole solar system, together with the passing of eclipses, comets, and showers of meteors, may put us off our game.

In fact, I doubt if we shall ever get around in bogey. Let us try something else. Here is a very interesting calculation in regard to "allowing for the wind."

I have noticed that a great many golf players of my own particular class are always preoccupied with the question of "allowing for the wind." My friend Amphibius Jones, for example, just before driving always murmurs something, as if in prayer, about "allowing for the wind." After driving he says with a sigh, "I didn't allow for the wind." In fact, all through my class there is a general feeling that our game is practically ruined by the wind. We ought really to play in the middle of the Desert of Sahara where there isn't any.

It occurred to me that it might be interesting to reduce to a formula the effect exercised by the resistance of the wind on a moving golf ball. For example, in our game of last Wednesday, Jones in his drive struck the ball with what, he assures me, was his full force, hitting it with absolute accuracy, as he himself admits, fair in the center, and he himself feeling, on his own assertion, absolutely fit, his eye being (a very necessary thing with Jones) absolutely "in," and he also having on his proper sweater—a further necessary condition of first-class play. Under all the favorable circumstances the ball advanced only fifty yards! It was evident at once that

it was a simple matter of the wind: The wind, which was of that treacherous character that blows over the links unnoticed, had impinged full upon the ball, pressed it backward, and forced it to the earth.

Here, then, is a neat subject of calculation. Granted that Jones—as measured on a hitting machine the week the circus was here—can hit two tons and that this whole force was pressed against a golf ball only one inch and a quarter in diameter. What happens? My reader will remember that the superficial area of a golf ball is Pi ★ r^3, that is 3.141567 × (5/8 inches)^3. [Editor's note: 3.14567 is Leacock's value for Pi] And all of this driven forward with the power of 4,000 pounds to the inch!

In short, taking Jones's statements at their face value, the ball would have traveled, had it not been for the wind, no less than six and a half miles.

I give next a calculation of even more acute current interest. It is in regard to "moving the head." How often is an admirable stroke at golf spoiled by moving the head! I have seen members of our golf club sit silent and glum all evening, murmuring from time to time, "I moved my head." When Jones and I play together I often hit the ball sideways into the vegetable garden from which no ball returns (they have one of these on every links; it is a Scottish invention). And whenever I do so Jones always says, "You moved your head." In return when he drives his ball away up into the air and down again ten yards in front of him, I always retaliate by saying, "You moved your head, old man."

In short, if absolute immobility of the head could be achieved, the major problem of golf would be solved.

Let us put the theory mathematically. The head, poised on the neck, has a circumferential sweep or orbit of about two inches, not counting the rolling of the eyes. The circumferential sweep of a golf ball is based on a radius of 250 yards, or a circumference of about 1,600 yards, which is very nearly equal to a mile. Inside this circumference is an area of 27,878,400 square feet, the whole of which is controlled by a tiny movement of the human neck. In other words, if a player were to wiggle his neck even 1/190 of an inch the amount of ground on which the ball might falsely alight would be half a million square feet. If at the same time he multiplies the effect by rolling his eyes, the ball might alight anywhere.

I feel certain that after reading this any sensible player will keep his head still.

A further calculation remains—and one perhaps of even greater practical interest than the ones above.

Everybody who plays golf is well aware that on some days he plays better than on others. Question—How often does a man really play his game?

I take the case of Amphibius Jones. There are certain days when he is, as he admits himself, "put off his game" by not having on his proper golf vest. On other days the light puts him off his game; at other times the dark; so, too, the heat, or again the cold. He is often put off his game because he has been up late the night before; or similarly because he has been to bed too early the night before; the barking of a dog always puts him off his game; so do children, or adults, or women. Bad news disturbs his game; so does good; so also does the absence of news.

All of this may be expressed mathematically by a very simple application of the theory of permutations and probability; let us say that there are altogether fifty forms of disturbance, any one of which puts Jones off his game. Each one of these disturbances happens, say, once in ten days. What chance is there that a day will come when not a single one of them occurs? The formula is a little complicated, but mathematicians will recognize the answer at once as

$$\frac{x^2}{1} + \frac{x}{1} + \frac{x^n}{1}$$

In fact, that is exactly how often Jones plays at his best;

$$\frac{x}{1} + \frac{x^2}{1} + \frac{x^n}{1}$$

worked out in time and reckoning four games to the week, and allowing for leap years and solar eclipses, come to about once in 2,930,000 years. And from watching Jones play I think that this is about right.

THE SCIENCE OF GOLF

ANONYMOUS

A certain make of field-glasses is advertised just now as "suitable for golf players, enabling them before striking to select a favourable spot for the descent of their ball." There can be little doubt that this brilliant hint will be further developed, with some such results as those outlined in the following anticipation.]

As I told Jones when he met me at the clubhouse, it was a year or more since I had last played, so the chances were that I should be a bit below form. Besides, I was told that the standard of play had been so raised—

"Raised? I should just think it has!" said Jones. "Why, a year ago they played mere skittles—not what you could properly call golf. Got your clubs? Come along then. Queer old-fashioned things they are, too! And you're never going out without your theodolite?"

"Well," I said with considerable surprise, "the fact is, I haven't got one. What do you use it for?"

"Taking levels, of course. And—bless me, you've no inflater, or glasses—not even a wind-gauge! Shall I borrow some for you?—Oh, just as you like, but you won't be able to put up much of a game without them."

"Does your caddie take all those things?" I asked, pointing to the curious assortment of machinery which Jones had put together.

"My caddies do," he corrected. "No one takes less than three nowadays. Good; there's only one couple on the first tee, so we shall get away in half an hour or so."

"I should hope so!" I remarked. "Do you mean that it will be half an hour before those men have played two shots?"

"There or thereabouts. Simkins is a fast player—wonderful head for algebra that man has—so it may be a shade less. Come and watch him; then you'll see what golf is!"

And indeed I watched him with much interest. First he surveyed the country with great care through a field-glass. Then he squinted along a theodolite at a distant pole. Next he used a strange instrument which was, Jones told me, a wind-gauge, and tapped thoughtfully at a pocket-barometer. After that he produced paper and pencil, and was immersed apparently in difficult sums. Finally, he summoned one of his caddies, who carried a metal cylinder. A golf ball was connected to this by a piece of india-rubber tubing, and a slight hissing noise was heard.

"Putting in the hydrogen," explained Jones. "Everything depends upon getting the right amount. New idea? Not very; even a year ago you must have seen pneumatic golf balls—filled with compressed air? Well, this is only an obvious improvement. There, he's going to drive now."

And this he did, using a club unlike anything I had seen before. Then he surveyed the putting-green—about half a mile away—through his glasses, and remarked that it was a fairish shot, the ball being within three inches of the hole. His companion, who went through the same lengthy preliminaries, was less fortunate. In a tone of considerable disgust he announced that he had over-driven the hole by four hundred yards.

"Too much hydrogen," murmured Jones, "or else he got his formulae muddled. Well, we can start now. Shall I lead the way?"

I begged him to do so. He in turn surveyed the country, consulted instruments, did elaborate sums, inflated his ball.

"Now," he said, at length settling into his stance, "now I'll show you." And then he missed the ball clean.

. . . Of course he ought not to have used such language, and yet it was a sort of relief to find something about the game which was entirely unchanged.

HIT THE BALL: A VALUABLE LESSON OF WHAT CONCENTRATION REALLY MEANS

EDDIE LOOS

A good many years ago I had a pupil who worried me. He could swing perfectly without a ball. In practice, he would hit fifty per cent of his shots with a surety that made your heart rejoice. But in actual play, he was the most erratic performer that ever topped his approach, missed his putt, sliced his drive, or dubbed an iron shot.

The more lessons I gave him, the worse his performance got. And the worst of it was, I liked him personally, so my feelings as well as my pride as an instructor were at stake.

He laughed—I guess he liked me too—I was an earnest if not a fully competent boy—and he told me something like this: "It isn't your fault, Eddie. I've been to some of the best instructors in the country before I came to you and while you haven't helped me, my game isn't any worse than it was before you took hold."

This was scant consolation for a young fellow who really wanted to help his pupils and who laid awake nights trying to figure out how—if you can imagine such a thing in golf.

I talked to some of the older pros. Outside of the fact that they were not much interested—in my problems, at least—the best I got was: "It's mental—"

I studied and I pondered and I questioned, but the more I questioned them on this "mental" thing, the closer I came to the conclusion that they had read it somewhere—didn't know what it meant.

My pupil himself gave me the clue—unwittingly. He came out one day, to take another lesson, and with the courage born of desperation, I told him the truth. "It isn't any use taking any more lessons. I just simply can't teach you anything and I don't want to take pay without giving something in return." And I needed the money, too.

He laughed and told me not to worry about that side of it, then he asked me a question.

"Eddie, what do you think of when you hit a golf ball?"

I had never considered the question before, so I stopped and thought carefully and when I answered, I told him truthfully, "I just think of hitting the ball."

My answer, incidentally, with a slight addition would be the same today. And then, on the spur of the moment, I impulsively asked him the same question. "What do you think of when *you* hit a golf ball?"

He looked at me, and then he replied, "Well, I think of my grip and my stance and keeping my head still and swinging back slowly and maintaining the correct arc and rolling my forearms as I come into the ball and not swaying—and following through—"

I stopped him—I was astounded. "Do you mean to say you think of all those things when you hit at a ball?"

"I try to"—he said slowly

And then it dawned on me that I couldn't hit a ball myself, if I tried to keep my mind on anything besides actually hitting it, let alone a dozen things—the swing is too fast to permit of consecutive thinking, although I didn't argue it out that way then.

He took a practice swing as I stood thinking. It looked fine—the arc was true—his wrists worked properly—everything co-ordinated perfectly.

I had an idea, and made a beginning. "I'm going to give you a lesson after all," I said, and teed up a ball, "but—" I added—"I'm going to learn more than you do and you've got to do just what I say."

He laughed and agreed.

"Now," I said slowly, trying to get my idea clear, "I want you to step up to that ball and look at it. Then I want you to make a swing without an idea in your head except to hit the ball—hit through it."

He did—and since this isn't a fairy story, I'll have to admit that he tightened—and the ball was badly topped.

I scratched my head. "What did you think of?" I asked.

"Hitting the ball," he answered.

"Anything else?" I asked.

"Well"—he grinned a little—"I guess I thought of hitting it—*hard*."

"Let's try it again," I said, and teed up another ball.

"I want you to hit this ball a hundred yards—only a hundred yards—do it by swinging easily not by trying to shorten your swing," I told him.

"Hit it a hundred yards," he repeated and then stepped up to the ball.

Out it sailed—two hundred and ten yards—the longest ball he had ever hit in his life. He reached for another ball without a word, started his club back and stopped.

"Getting ready to slug it," he explained. "Guess I'd better try again."

He did and the next ball went around two hundred.

I pulled the driver from his hands and gave him a mashie. We were both learning something.

At the end of that lesson, he had hit more perfect balls than ever before in his life at one sitting—or standing.

And from that time on I gave that man lessons by simply reminding him to hit the ball. His swing was all right except when he spoiled it by thinking about it or by tightening up to try and slug the ball.

When he realized that clean hitting brought distance, the tightening disappeared—and when he got the knack of thinking about hitting the ball, his handicap inside of one season went from 25 to 14—no miracle, but a splendid improvement.

And that was the beginning of my realization of something which has been of immense value to me in my teaching ever since. In my own mind, I make a distinct differential between teaching the swing and hitting the ball. In spite of the fact that practice swings mean nothing, a man with patience can better learn to play golf without a ball than he can with one—simply because every time he dubs or slices, or hooks or tops, he

begins to make a change in his swing and thereby defeats any possibility of really developing skill in the swing.

There are two sides to golf—the mechanical and the mental. And it's mighty simple and a sure recipe for improvement if you'll let it sink into your system.

The mechanical side is the swing—when you have learned the correct swing that part of your game should be behind you. It is a tool you have acquired and its use is in hitting the ball.

And the mental side of golf is not intense, wrinkle-browed concentration—it's simply stepping up to the ball with the determination to hit it where you want to go, or "hit through it," whichever expression you prefer—with no other thought in your mind—none whatever.

When I step up to the ball, no matter where it lies, I look at it—I determine the path it is going to take and suddenly I find my club has snapped it into space right in the direction pre-determined. When I try to think of anything else, my shot is spoiled.

No thought of turning wrists or top of swing or anything else—just hit the ball where you want it to go. Even people with ugly swings who have this knack can secure surprising results.

We all know men whose swings look like nothing this side of the nether regions, yet they shoot good golf. Their minds are on hitting the ball where they want it to go.

It's far better fun to play golf with a good swing than with a bad one, but the man with his mind on hitting the ball, no matter what his form is, is going to play better golf than the fellow with splendid form who is trying in a fraction of a second the golf swing takes to think of sixteen different parts of his anatomy.

I have talked with hundreds of professionals. They all tell me the same thing—when they're frank—their thoughts are on hitting the ball.

Their analysis of the swing for teaching purposes is the result of observation. Their swings are not consciously executed. Their instructions to you are the things they have noticed in their own swings when they studied them for tuition purposes. This plus the mouth to mouth methods of transmitting golf lore that have always been prevalent in professional ranks.

Golf is no more difficult than driving a nail or swinging an axe. True, the planes in golf are a little confusing to the beginner, but the most difficult part of golf is the part that we inject into it by making a mental thing of something that should be mechanical.

Try this experiment.

Go out and make a few practice swings without a ball—make sure your clubhead grazes the ground and comes through on a straight line for a few inches before and after the spot where the ball ought to be.

When this comes easily and naturally, lay down a ball. Fix the direction you want to go and step up to the ball in the same mental state that you would start to swing an axe. Think of the objective, not the physical motions necessary to attain it. Step up to hit that ball straight and true—never mind distance—just as you would drive a nail or chop a tree.

You may surprise yourself.

Now, of course, a good many people will feel that by taking this attitude, I am discounting the value of professional instruction, but this could hardly be true, considering the fact that I earn my living in that particular manner.

Professional instruction develops the ideal swing—the "good form" with which every ambitious man wants to play golf. And for that reason alone, professional coaching will always be in demand.

But the man who is going to play a good game of golf, with or without professional coaching, must make up his mind to divorce the mechanical and the mental sides of golf.

He will learn to swing so that his control over his club is exercised without any more thought than he uses a hammer or an axe or reaches for a glass of water.

And then, when he plays, he will forget his swing—put the mechanical part of it behind him. His mind will be on hitting the ball the distance he wants to go. His attention will be concentrated on that little flight path that starts a few inches before the ball and ends several inches past it pointing in the desired direction.

And with his mind and his attention concentrated right at the bottom of the swing where it belongs, he will find that handicaps go down and balls fly straight and true.

I firmly believe that a clear understanding of this principle will do wonders for any golfer.

And just as a last word—a confession. I have observed that when a shot fails to come off to my satisfaction, that my mind was elsewhere than on hitting the ball.

The danger of the amateur lies in filling his mind with so many things that he can't center on hitting the ball.

The danger of the professional is that his certainty is so great and his swing so true that he may let his mind wander entirely off the golf course.

And the fact that even when he does this, he brings off a good shot most times, shows that a good swing—a formed habit—is well worth cultivating.

A LESSON IN GOLF

ANONYMOUS

You won't dare!" said I.

"There is nothing else for it," said Amanda sternly. "You know perfectly well that we must practise every minute of the time, if we expect to have the least chance of winning. If she will come just now— well!" Amanda cocked her pretty chin in the air, and looked defiant.

"But—*Aunt Susannah!*" said I.

"It's quite time for you to go and meet her," said Amanda, cutting short my remonstrances; and she rose with an air of finality.

My wife, within her limitations, is a very clever woman. She is prompt: she is resolute: she has the utmost confidence in her own generalship. Yet, looking at Aunt Susannah, as she sat—gaunt, upright, and formidable— beside me in the dog-cart, I did not believe even Amanda capable of the stupendous task which she had undertaken. She would never dare—

I misjudged her. Aunt Susannah had barely sat down—was, in fact, only just embarking on her first scone—when Amanda rushed incontinently in where I, for one, should have feared to tread.

"Dear Aunt Susannah," she said, beaming hospitably, "I'm sure you will never guess how we mean to amuse you while you are here!"

"Nothing very formidable, I hope?" said Aunt Susannah grimly.

"You'll never, never guess!" said Amanda; and her manner was so unnaturally sprightly that I knew she was inwardly quaking. "We want to teach you—what do you think?"

"I think that I'm a trifle old to learn anything new, my dear," said Aunt Susannah.

I should have been stricken dumb by such a snub. Not so, however, my courageous wife.

"Well—golf!" she cried, with overdone cheerfulness.

Aunt Susannah started. Recovering herself, she eyed us with a stony glare which froze me where I sat.

"There is really nothing else to do in these wilds, you know," Amanda pursued gallantly, though even she was beginning to look frightened. "And it is such a lovely game. You'll like it immensely."

"*What* do you say it is called?" asked Aunt Susannah in awful tones.

"Golf," Amanda repeated meekly; and for the first time her voice shook.

"Spell it!" commanded Aunt Susannah.

Amanda obeyed, with increasing meekness.

"Why do you call it 'goff' if there's an 'l' in it?" asked Aunt Susannah.

"I—I'm afraid I don't know," said Amanda faintly.

Aunt Susannah sniffed disparagingly. She condescended, however, to inquire into the nature of the game, and Amanda gave an elaborate explanation in faltering accents. She glanced imploringly at me; but I would not meet her eye.

"Then you just try to get a little ball into a little hole?" inquired my relative.

"And in the fewest possible strokes," Amanda reminded her, gasping.

"And—is that all?" asked Aunt Susannah.

"Y—yes," said Amanda.

"Oh!" said Aunt Susannah.

A game described in cold blood sounds singularly insignificant. We both fell into sudden silence and depression.

"Well, it doesn't sound *difficult*," said Aunt Susannah. "Oh, yes, I'll come and play at ball with you if you like, my dears."

"*Dear* Auntie!" said Amanda affectionately. She did not seem so much overjoyed at her success, however, as might have been expected. As for me, I saw a whole sea of breakers ahead; but then I had seen them all the time.

We drove out to the Links next day. We were both very silent. Aunt Susannah, however, was in good spirits, and deeply interested in our clubs.

"What in the world do you want so many sticks for, child?" she inquired of Amanda.

"Oh, they are for—for different sorts of ground," Amanda explained feebly; and she cast an agonised glance at our driver, who had obviously overheard, and was chuckling in an offensive manner.

We both looked hastily and furtively round us when we arrived. We were early, however, and fortune was kind to us; there was no one else there.

"Perhaps you would like to watch us a little first, just to see how the game goes?" Amanda suggested sweetly.

"Not at all!" was Aunt Susannah's brisk rejoinder. "I've come here to play, not to look on. Which stick—?"

"*Club*—they are called clubs," said Amanda.

"Why?" inquired Aunt Susannah.

"I—I don't know," faltered Amanda. "Do you, Laurence?"

I did not know, and said so.

"Then I shall certainly call them sticks," said Aunt Susannah decisively. "They are not in the least like clubs."

"Shall I drive off?" I inquired desperately of Amanda.

"Drive off? Where to? Why are you going away?" asked Aunt Susannah. "Besides, you can't go—the carriage is out of sight."

"The way you begin is called driving off," I explained laboriously. "Like this." I drove nervously, because I felt her eye upon me. The ball went some dozen yards.

"That seems easy enough," said Aunt Susannah. "Give me a stick, child."

"Not that end—the *other* end!" cried Amanda, as our relative prepared to make her stroke with the butt-end.

"Dear me! Isn't that the handle?" she remarked cheerfully; and she reversed her club, swung it, and chopped a large piece out of the links. "Where is it gone? Where is it gone?" she exclaimed, looking wildly round.

"It—it isn't gone," said Amanda nervously and pointed to the ball still lying at her feet.

"What an extraordinary thing!" cried Aunt Susannah; and she made another attempt, with a precisely similar result. "Give me another stick!" she demanded. "Here, let me choose for myself—this one doesn't suit me. I'll have that flat thing."

"But that's a putter," Amanda explained agonisedly.

"What's a putter? You said just now that they were all clubs," said Aunt Susannah, pausing.

"They are all clubs," I explained patiently. "But each has a different name."

"You don't mean to say you give them names like a little girl with her dolls?" cried Aunt Susannah. "Why, what a babyish game it is!" She laughed very heartily. "At any rate," she continued, with that determination which some of her friends call by another name, "I am sure that this will be easier to play with!" She grasped the putter, and in some miraculous way drove the ball to a considerable distance.

"Oh, splendid!" cried Amanda. Her troubled brow cleared a little, and she followed suit, with mediocre success. Aunt Susannah pointed out that her ball had gone farther than either of ours, and grasped her putter tenaciously.

"It's a better game than I expected from your description," she conceded. "Oh, I daresay I shall get to like it. I must come and practise every day." We glanced at each other in a silent horror of despair, and Aunt Susannah after a few quite decent strokes, triumphantly holed out. "What next?" said she.

I hastily arranged her ball on the second tee: but the luck of golf is proverbially capricious. She swung her club, and hit nothing. She swung it again, and hit the ground.

"*Why* can't I do it?" she demanded, turning fiercely upon me.

"You keep losing your feet," I explained deferentially.

"Spare me your detestable slang terms, Laurence, at least!" she cried, turning on me again like a whirlwind. "If you think I have lost my temper—which is absurd!—you might have the courage to say so in plain English!"

"Oh, no, Aunt Susannah!" I said. "You don't understand—"

"Or want to," she snapped. "Of all silly games—"

"I mean you misunderstood me," I pursued, trembling. "Your foot slipped, and that spoilt your stroke. You should have nails in your boots, as we have."

"Oh!" said Aunt Susannah, only half pacified. But she succeeded in dislodging her ball at last, and driving it into a bunker. At the same moment, Amanda suddenly clutched me by the arm. "Oh, Laurence!" she said in a blood-curdling whisper. "What shall we do? Here is Colonel Bartlemy!"

The worst had happened. The hottest-tempered man in the club, the oldest member, the best player, the greatest stickler for etiquette, was hard upon our track; and Aunt Susannah, with a red and determined countenance, was urging her ball up the bunker, and watching it roll back again.

"Dear Auntie," said Amanda, in her sweetest voice, "you had much better take it out."

"Is that allowed?" inquired our relative suspiciously.

"Oh, you may always do that and lose a stroke!" I assured her eagerly.

"I shan't dream of losing a stroke!" said Aunt Susannah, with decision. "I'll get it out of this ditch by fair means, if I have to spend all day over it!"

"Then do you mind waiting one moment?" I said, with the calmness of despair. "There is a player behind us—"

"Let him stay behind us! I was here first," said Aunt Susannah; and she returned to her bunker.

The Links rose up in a hillock immediately behind us, so that our successor could not see us until he had reached the first hole. I stood with my eye glued to the spot where he might be expected to appear. I saw, as in a nightmare, the scathing remarks that would find their way into the Suggestion Book. I longed for a sudden and easy death.

At the moment when Colonel Bartlemy's rubicund face appeared over the horizon, Aunt Susannah, flushed but unconquered, drew herself up for a moment's rest from toil. He had seen her. Amanda shut her eyes. For myself, I would have run away shamelessly, if there had been any place to run to. The Colonel and Aunt Susannah looked hard at each other. Then he began to hurry down the slope, while she started briskly up it.

"Miss Cadwalader!" said the Colonel.

"Colonel Bartlemy!" cried Aunt Susannah; and they met with effusion.

I saw Amanda's eyes open, and grow round with amazed interest. I knew perfectly well that she had scented a bygone love affair, and was already planning the most suitable wedding-garb for Aunt Susannah. A frantic hope came to me that in that case the Colonel's affection might prove stronger than his zeal for golf. They were strolling down to us in a leisurely manner, and the subject of their conversation broke upon my astonished ears.

"I'm afraid you don't think much of these Links, after yours," Colonel Bartlemy was saying anxiously. "They are rather new—"

"Oh, I've played on many worse," said Aunt Susannah, looking round her with a critical eye. "Let me see—I haven't seen you since your victory at Craigmory. Congratulations!"

"Approbation from Sir Hubert Stanley!" purred the Colonel, evidently much gratified. "You will be here for the twenty-seventh, I hope?"

"Exactly what I came for," said Aunt Susannah calmly.

"Though I don't know what our ladies will say to playing against the Cranford Champion!" chuckled the Colonel; and then they condescended to become aware of our existence. We had never known before how exceedingly small it is possible to feel.

"Aunt Susannah, what am I to say? What fools you must think us!" I murmured miserably to her, when the Colonel was out of earshot looking for his ball. "We are such raw players ourselves—and of course we never dreamt—"

Aunt Susannah twinkled at me in a friendly manner. "There's an ancient proverb about eggs and grandmothers," she remarked cheerfully. "There should be a modern form for golf-balls and aunts—hey Laurence?"

Amanda did not win the prize brooch; but Aunt Susannah did, in spite of an overwhelming handicap, and gave it to her. She does not often wear it—possibly because rubies are not becoming to her: possibly because its associations are too painful.

A MIXED THREESOME

P. G. WODEHOUSE

It was the holiday season, and during the holidays the Greens Commit-
tees have decided that the payment of one hundred dollars shall entitle
fathers of families not only to infest the course themselves, but also to
decant their nearest and dearest upon it in whatever quantity they please.
All over the links, in consequence, happy, laughing groups of children had
broken out like a rash. A wan-faced adult, who had been held up for ten
minutes while a drove of issue quarrelled over whether little Claude had
taken two hundred or two hundred and twenty approach shots to reach
the ninth green sank into a seat beside the Oldest Member.

"What luck?" inquired the Sage.

"None to speak of," returned the other, moodily. "I thought I had
bagged a small boy in a Lord Fauntleroy suit on the sixth, but he ducked.
These children make me tired. They should be bowling their hoops in the
road. Golf is a game for grownups. How can a fellow play, with a platoon
of progeny blocking him at every hole?"

The Oldest Member shook his head. He could not subscribe to these
sentiments.

No doubt (said the Oldest Member) the summer golf-child is, from the point of view of the player who likes to get round the course in a single afternoon, something of a trial; but, personally, I confess, it pleases me to see my fellow human beings—and into this category golf-children, though at the moment you may not be broad-minded enough to admit it, undoubtedly fall—taking to the noblest of games at an early age. Golf, like measles, should be caught young, for, if postponed to riper years, the results may be serious. Let me tell you the story of Mortimer Sturgis, which illustrates what I mean rather aptly.

Mortimer Sturgis, when I first knew him, was a carefree man of thirty-eight, of amiable character and independent means, which he increased from time to time by judicious ventures on the Stock Exchange. Although he had never played golf, his had not been altogether an ill-spent life. He swung a creditable racket at tennis, was always ready to contribute a baritone solo to charity concerts, and gave freely to the poor. He was what you might call a golden-mean man, good-hearted rather than magnetic, with no serious vices and no heroic virtues. For a hobby, he had taken up the collecting of porcelain vases, and he was engaged to Betty Weston, a charming girl of twenty-five, a lifelong friend of mine.

I liked Mortimer. Everybody liked him. But, at the same time, I was a little surprised that a girl like Betty should have become engaged to him. As I said before, he was not magnetic; and magnetism, I thought, was the chief quality she would have demanded in a man. Betty was one of those ardent, vivid girls, with an intense capacity for hero-worship, and I would have supposed that something more in the nature of a plumed knight or a corsair of the deep would have been her ideal. But, of course, if there is a branch of modern industry where the demand is greater than the supply, it is the manufacture of knights and corsairs; and nowadays a girl, however flaming her aspirations, has to take the best she can get. I must admit that Betty seemed perfectly content with Mortimer.

Such, then, was the state of affairs when Eddie Denton arrived, and the trouble began.

I was escorting Betty home one evening after a tea-party at which we had been fellow-guests, when, walking down the road, we happened to espy Mortimer. He broke into a run when he saw us, and galloped up, waving a piece of paper in his hand. He was plainly excited, a thing which was unusual in this well-balanced man. His broad, good-humoured face was working violently.

"Good news!" he cried. "Good news! Dear old Eddie's back!"

"Oh, how nice for you, dear!" said Betty. "Eddie Denton is Mortimer's best friend," she explained to me. "He has told me so much about him. I have been looking forward to his coming home. Mortie thinks the world of him."

"So will you, when you know him," cried Mortimer. "Dear old Eddie! He's a wonder! The best fellow on earth! There's nobody like Eddie! He landed yesterday. Just home from Central Africa. He's an explorer, you know," he said to me. "Spends all his time in places where it's death for a white man to go."

"An explorer!" I heard Betty breathe, as if to herself. I was not so impressed, I fear, as she was. Explorers, as a matter of fact, leave me a trifle cold. It has always seemed to me that the difficulties of their life are greatly exaggerated—generally by themselves. In a large country like Africa, for instance, I should imagine that it was almost impossible for a man not to get somewhere if he goes on long enough. Give me the fellow who can plunge into the bowels of the earth at Times Square and find the right subway train with nothing but a lot of misleading signs to guide him. However, we are not all constituted alike in this world, and it was apparent from the flush on her cheek and the light in her eyes that Betty admired explorers.

"I wired to him at once," went on Mortimer, "and insisted on his coming down here. It's two years since I saw him. You don't know how I have looked forward, dear, to you and Eddie meeting. He is just your sort. I know how romantic you are and keen on adventure and all that. Well, you should hear Eddie tell the story of how he brought down the bull *bongo* with his last cartridge after all the *pongos*, or native bearers, had fled into the *dongo*, or undergrowth."

"I should love to!" whispered Betty, her eyes glowing. I suppose to an impressionable girl these things really are of absorbing interest. For myself, *bongos* intrigue me even less than *pongos*, while *dongos* frankly bore me. "When do you expect him?"

"He will get my wire to-night. I'm hoping we shall see the dear old fellow tomorrow afternoon some time. How surprised old Eddie will be to hear that I'm engaged. He's such a confirmed bachelor himself. He told me once that he considered the wisest thing ever said by human tongue was the Swahili proverb—'Whoso taketh a woman into his kraal depositeth himself straightway in the *wongo*,' *Wongo*, he tells me, is a sort of broth composed of herbs and meat-bones, corresponding to our soup. You must get Eddie to give it you in the original Swahili. It sounds even better."

I saw the girl's eyes flash, and there came into her face that peculiar set expression which married men know. It passed in an instant, but not before it had given me material for thought which lasted me all the way to my house and into the silent watches of the night. I was fond of Mortimer Sturgis, and I could see trouble ahead for him as plainly as though I had been a palmist reading his hand at two guineas a visit. There are other proverbs fully as wise as the one which Mortimer had translated from the Swahili, and one of the wisest is that quaint old East London saying, handed down from one generation of costermongers to another, and whispered at midnight in the wigwams of the whelk-sellers: "Never introduce your donah to a pal." In those seven words is contained the wisdom of the ages.

I could read the future so plainly. What but one thing could happen after Mortimer had influenced Betty's imagination with his stories of his friend's romantic career, and added the finishing touch by advertising him as a woman-hater? He might just as well have asked for his ring back at once. My heart bled for Mortimer.

I happened to call at his house on the second evening of the explorer's visit, and already the mischief had been done.

Denton was one of those lean, hard-bitten men with smouldering eyes and a brick-red complexion. He looked what he was, the man of action and enterprise. He had the wiry frame and strong jaw without which no explorer is complete, and Mortimer, beside him, seemed but a poor, soft product of our hot-house civilisation. Mortimer, I forgot to say, wore glasses; and, if there is one time more than another when a man should not wear glasses, it is while a strong-faced, keen-eyed wanderer in the wilds is telling a beautiful girl the story of his adventures.

For this was what Denton was doing. My arrival seemed to have interrupted him in the middle of a narrative. He shook my hand in a strong, silent sort of way, and resumed:

"Well, the natives seemed fairly friendly, so I decided to stay the night."

I made a mental note never to seem fairly friendly to an explorer. If you do, he always decides to stay the night.

"In the morning they took me down to the river. At this point it widens into a *kongo*, or pool, and it was here, they told me, that the crocodile mostly lived, subsisting on the native oxen—the short-horned *jongos*—which, swept away by the current while crossing the ford above, were carried down on the *longos*, or rapids. It was not, however, till the second evening that I managed to catch sight of his ugly snout above the surface. I waited around, and on the third day I saw him suddenly come out of the water and heave his whole length on to a sandbank in mid-stream and go to sleep in the sun. He was certainly a monster—fully thirty—you have never been in Central Africa, have you, Miss Weston? No? You ought to go there!—fully fifty feet from tip to tail. There he lay, glistening. I shall never forget the sight."

He broke off to light a cigarette. I heard Betty draw in her breath sharply. Mortimer was beaming through his glasses with the air of the owner of a dog which is astonishing a drawing-room with its clever tricks.

"And what did you do then, Mr. Denton?" asked Betty, breathlessly.

"Yes, what did you do then, old chap?" said Mortimer.

Denton blew out the match and dropped it on the ash-tray.

"Eh? Oh," he said, carelessly, "I swam across and shot him."

"Swam across and shot him!"

"Yes. It seemed to me that the chance was too good to be missed. Of course, I might have had a pot at him from the bank, but the chances were I wouldn't have hit him in a vital place. So I swam across to the sandbank, put the muzzle of my gun in his mouth, and pulled the trigger. I have rarely seen a crocodile so taken aback."

"But how dreadfully dangerous!"

"Oh, danger!" Eddie Denton laughed lightly. "One drops into the habit of taking a few risks out there, you know. Talking of danger, the time when things really did look a little nasty was when the wounded *gongo* cornered me in a narrow *tongo* and I only had a pocket-knife with everything in it broken except the corkscrew and the thing for taking stones out of horses' hoofs. It was like this—"

I could bear no more. I am a tender-hearted man, and I made some excuse and got away. From the expression on the girl's face I could see that it was only a question of days before she gave her heart to this romantic newcomer.

As a matter of fact, it was on the following afternoon that she called on me and told me that the worst had happened. I had known her from a child, you understand, and she always confided her troubles to me.

"I want your advice," she began. "I'm so wretched!"

She burst into tears. I could see the poor girl was in a highly nervous condition, so I did my best to calm her by describing how I had once done the long hole in four. My friends tell me that there is no finer soporific, and it seemed as though they may be right, for presently just as I had reached the point where I laid my approach-putt dead from a distance of thirty feet, she became quieter. She dried her eyes, yawned once or twice, and looked at me bravely.

"I love Eddie Denton!" she said.

"I feared as much. When did you feel this coming on?"

"It crashed on me like a thunderbolt last night after dinner. We were walking in the garden, and he was just telling me how he had been bitten by a poisonous *zongo*, when I seemed to go all giddy. When I came to myself I was in Eddie's arms. His face was pressed against mine, and he was gargling."

"Gargling?"

"I thought so at first. But he reassured me. He was merely speaking in one of the lesser-known dialects of the Walla-Walla natives of eastern Uganda, into which he always drops in moments of great emotion. He soon recovered sufficiently to give me a rough translation, and then I knew that he loved me. He kissed me. I kissed him. We kissed each other."

"And where was Mortimer all this while?"

"Indoors, cataloguing his collection of vases."

For a moment, I confess, I was inclined to abandon Mortimer's cause. A man, I felt, who could stay indoors cataloguing vases while his *fiancée* wandered in the moonlight with explorers deserved all that was coming to him. I overcame the feeling.

"Have you told him?"

"Of course not."

"You don't think it might be of interest to him?"

"How can I tell him? It would break his heart. I am awfully fond of Mortimer. So is Eddie. We would both die rather than do anything to hurt him. Eddie is the soul of honour. He agrees with me that Mortimer must never know."

"Then you aren't going to break off your engagement?"

"I couldn't. Eddie feels the same. He says that, unless something can be done, he will say good-bye to me and creep far, far away to some distant desert, and there, in the great stillness, broken only by the cry of the prowling *yongo*, try to forget."

"When you say 'unless something can be done,' what do you mean? What can be done?"

"I thought you might have something to suggest. Don't you think it possible that somehow Mortimer might take it into his head to break the engagement himself?"

"Absurd! He loves you devotedly."

"I'm afraid so. Only the other day I dropped one of his best vases, and he just smiled and said it didn't matter."

"I can give you even better proof than that. This morning Mortimer came to me and asked me to give him secret lessons in golf."

"Golf! But he despises golf."

"Exactly. But he is going to learn it for your sake."

"But why secret lessons?"

"Because he wants to keep it a surprise for your birthday. Now can you doubt his love?"

"I am not worthy of him!" she whispered.

The words gave me an idea.

"Suppose," I said, "we could convince Mortimer of that!"

"I don't understand."

"Suppose, for instance, he could be made to believe that you were, let us say, a dipsomaniac."

She shook her head. "He knows that already."

"What!"

"Yes; I told him I sometimes walked in my sleep."

"I mean a secret drinker."

"Nothing will induce me to pretend to be a secret drinker."

"Then a drug-fiend?" I suggested, hopefully.

"I hate medicine."

"I have it!" I said. "A kleptomaniac."

"What is that?"

"A person who steals things."

"Oh, that's horrid."

"Not at all. It's a perfectly ladylike thing to do. You don't know you do it."

"But, if I don't know I do it, how do I know I do it?"

"I beg your pardon?"

"I mean, how can I tell Mortimer I do it if I don't know?"

"You don't tell him. I will tell him. I will inform him to-morrow that you called on me this afternoon and stole my watch and"—I glanced about the room—"my silver matchbox."

"I'd rather have that little vinaigrette."

"You don't get either. I merely say you stole it. What will happen?"

"Mortimer will hit you with a cleek."

"Not at all. I am an old man. My white hairs protect me. What he will do is to insist on confronting me with you and asking you to deny the foul charge."

"And then?"

"Then you admit it and release him from his engagement."

She sat for a while in silence. I could see that my words had made an impression.

"I think it's a splendid idea. Thank you very much." She rose and moved to the door. "I knew you would suggest something wonderful." She hesitated. "You don't think it would make it sound more plausible if I really took the vinaigrette?" she added, a little wistfully.

"It would spoil everything," I replied, firmly, as I reached for the vinaigrette and locked it carefully in my desk.

She was silent for a moment, and her glance fell on the carpet. That, however, did not worry me. It was nailed down.

"Well, good-bye," she said.

"Au revoir," I replied. "I am meeting Mortimer at six-thirty to-morrow. You may expect us round at your house at about eight."

Mortimer was punctual at the tryst next morning. When I reached the tenth tee he was already there. We exchanged a brief greeting and I handed him a driver, outlined the essentials of grip and swing, and bade him go to it.

"It seems a simple game," he said, as he took his stance. "You're sure it's fair to have the ball sitting up on top of a young sand-hill like this?"

"Perfectly fair."

"I mean, I don't want to be coddled because I'm a beginner."

"The ball is always teed up for the drive," I assured him.

"Oh, well, if you say so. But it seems to me to take all the element of sport out of the game. Where do I hit it?"

"Oh, straight ahead."

"But isn't it dangerous? I mean, suppose I smash a window in that house over there?"

He indicated a charming bijou residence some five hundred yards down the fairway.

"In that case," I replied, "the owner comes out in his pajamas and offers you the choice between some nuts and a cigar."

He seemed reassured, and began to address the ball.

I watched him curiously. I never put a club into the hand of a beginner without something of the feeling of the sculptor who surveys a mass of shapeless clay. I experience the emotions of a creator. Here, I say to myself, is a semi-sentient being into whose soulless carcass I am breathing life. A moment before, he was, though technically living, a mere clod. A moment hence he will be a golfer.

While I was still occupied with these meditations Mortimer swung at the ball. The club, whizzing down, brushed the surface of the rubber sphere, toppling it off the tee and propelling it six inches with a slight slice on it.

"Damnation!" said Mortimer, unravelling himself.

I nodded approvingly. His drive had not been anything to write to the golfing journals about, but he was picking up the technique of the game.

"What happened then?"

I told him in a word.

"Your stance was wrong, and your grip was wrong, and you moved your head, and swayed your body, and took your eye off the ball, and pressed, and forgot to use your wrists, and swung back too fast, and let the hands get ahead of the club, and lost your balance, and omitted to pivot on the ball of the left foot, and bent your right knee."

He was silent for a moment.

"There is more in this pastime," he said, "than the casual observer would suspect."

I have noticed, and I suppose other people have noticed, that in the golf education of every man there is a definite point at which he may be said to have crossed the dividing line—the Rubicon, as it were—that separates the golfer from the non-golfer. This moment comes immediately after his first good drive. In the ninety minutes in which I instructed Mortimer Sturgis that morning in the rudiments of the game, he made every variety of drive known to science; but it was not till we were about to leave that he made a good one.

A moment before he had surveyed his blistered hands with sombre disgust.

"It's no good," he said. "I shall never learn this beast of a game. And I don't want to either. It's only fit for lunatics. Where's the sense in it? Hitting a rotten little ball with a stick! If I want exercise, I'll take a stick and go and rattle it along the railings. There's something *in* that! Well, let's be getting along. No good wasting the whole morning out here."

"Try one more drive, and then we'll go."

"All right. If you like. No sense in it, though."

He teed up the ball, took a careless stance, and flicked moodily. There was a sharp crack, the ball shot off the tee, flew a hundred yards in a dead straight line never ten feet above the ground, soared another seventy yards in a graceful arc, struck the turf, rolled, and came to rest within easy mashie distance of the green.

"Splendid!" I cried.

The man seemed stunned.

"How did that happen?"

I told him very simply.

"Your stance was right, and your grip was right, and you kept your head still, and didn't sway your body and never took your eye off the ball, and slowed back, and let the arms come well through, and rolled the wrists, and let the club-head lead, and kept your balance, and pivoted on the ball of the left foot, and didn't duck the right knee."

"I see," he said. "Yes, I thought that must be it."

"Now, let's go home."

"Wait a minute. I just want to remember what I did while it's fresh in my mind. Let me see, this was the way I stood. Or was it more like this? No, like this." He turned to me, beaming. "What a great idea it was, my taking up golf. It's all nonsense what you read in the comic papers about people foozling all over the place and breaking clubs and all that. You've only to exercise a little reasonable care. And what a corking game it is! Nothing like it in the world! I wonder if Betty is up yet. I must go round and show her how I did that drive. A perfect swing, with every ounce of weight, wrist, and muscle behind it. I meant to keep it a secret from the dear girl till I had really learned, but of course I *have* learned now. Let's go round and rout her out."

He had given me my cue. I put my hand on his shoulder and spoke sorrowfully.

"Mortimer, my boy, I fear I have bad news for you."

"Slow back—keep the head—What's that? Bad news?"

"About Betty."

"About Betty? What about her? Don't sway the body—keep the eye on the—"

"Prepare yourself for a shock, my boy. Yesterday afternoon Betty called to see me. When she had gone I found that she had stolen my silver matchbox."

"Stolen your matchbox?"

"Stolen my matchbox."

"Oh, well, I dare say there were faults on both sides," said Mortimer. "Tell me if I sway my body this time."

"You don't grasp what I have said! Do you realise that Betty, the girl you are going to marry, is a kleptomaniac?"

"A kleptomaniac!"

"That is the only possible explanation. Think what this means, my boy. Think how you will feel every time your wife says she is going out to do a little shopping! Think of yourself, left alone at home, watching the clock, saying to yourself, 'Now she is lifting a pair of silk stockings!' 'Now she is hiding gloves in her umbrella!' 'Just about this moment she is getting away with a pearl necklace!' "

"Would she do that?"

"She would! She could not help herself. Or, rather, she could not refrain from helping herself. How about it, my boy?"

"It only draws us closer together," he said.

I was touched, I own. My scheme had failed, but it had proved Mortimer Sturgis to be of pure gold. He stood gazing down the fairway, wrapped in thought.

"By the way," he said, meditatively, "I wonder if the dear girl ever goes to any of those sales—those auction-sales, you know, where you're allowed to inspect the things the day before? They often have some pretty decent vases."

He broke off and fell into a reverie.

From this point onward Mortimer Sturgis proved the truth of what I said to you about the perils of taking up golf at an advanced age. A lifetime of observing my fellow-creatures has convinced me that Nature intended us all to be golfers. In every human being the germ of golf is implanted at birth, and suppression causes it to grow and grow till—it may be at forty, fifty, sixty—it suddenly bursts its bonds and sweeps over the victim like a tidal wave. The wise man, who begins to play in childhood, is enabled to let the poison exude gradually from his system, with no harmful results. But a man like Mortimer Sturgis, with thirty-eight golfless years behind him, is swept off his feet. He is carried away. He loses all sense of proportion. He is like the fly that happens to be sitting on the wall of the dam just when the crack comes.

Mortimer Sturgis gave himself up without a struggle to an orgy of golf such as I have never witnessed in any man. Within two days of that first lesson he had accumulated a collection of clubs large enough to have enabled him to open a shop; and he went on buying them at the rate of two and three a day. On Sundays, when religious scruples would not permit him to buy clubs, he was like a lost spirit. True, he would do his regular four rounds on the day of rest, but he never felt happy. The thought, as he sliced into the rough, that the patent wooden-faced cleek which he intended to purchase next morning might have made all the difference, completely spoiled his enjoyment.

I remember him calling me up on the telephone at three o'clock one morning to tell me that he had solved the problem of putting. He intended in future, he said, to use a croquet mallet, and he wondered that no one had ever thought of it before. The sound of his broken groan when I informed him that croquet mallets were against the rules haunted me for days.

His golf library kept pace with his collection of clubs. He bought all the standard works, subscribed to all the golfing papers, and, when he came across a paragraph in a magazine to the effect that Mr. Hutchings, a British ex-amateur champion, did not begin to play till he was past forty and that his opponent in the final, Mr. S. H. Fry, had never held a club till his thirty-fifth year, he had it engraved on vellum and framed and hung up beside his shaving-mirror.

And Betty, meanwhile? She, poor child, stared down the years into a bleak future, in which she saw herself parted for ever from the man she loved, and the golf-widow of another for whom—even when he won a medal for lowest net at a weekly handicap with a score of a hundred and three minus twenty-four—she could feel nothing warmer than respect. Those were dreary days for Betty. We three—she and I and Eddie Denton—often talked over Mortimer's strange obsession. Denton said that, except that Mortimer had not come out in pink spots, his symptoms were almost identical with those of the dreaded *mongo-mongo*, the scourge of the West African hinterland. Poor Denton! He had already booked his passage for Africa, and spent hours looking in the atlas for good deserts.

In every fever of human affairs there comes at last the crisis. We may emerge from it healed or we may plunge into still deeper depths of soul-sickness; but always the crisis comes. I was privileged to be present when it came in the affairs of Mortimer Sturgis and Betty Weston.

I had gone into the club-house one afternoon at an hour when it is usually empty, and the first thing I saw, as I entered the main room, which looks out on the ninth green, was Mortimer. He was grovelling on the floor, and I confess that, when I caught sight of him, my heart stood still. I feared that his reason, sapped by dissipation, had given way. I knew that for weeks, day in and day out, the niblick had hardly ever been out of his hand, and no constitution can stand that.

He looked up as he heard my footstep.

"Hallo," he said. "Can you see a ball anywhere?"

"A ball?" I backed away, reaching for the door-handle. "My dear boy," I said, soothingly, "you have made a mistake. Quite a natural mistake. One anybody would have made. But, as a matter of fact, this is the club-house. The links are outside there. Why not come away with me very quietly and let us see if we can't find some balls on the links? If you will wait here a moment, I will call up Doctor Smithson. He was telling me only this morning that he wanted a good spell of ball-hunting to put him in shape. You don't mind if he joins us?"

"It was a Silver King with my initials on it," Mortimer went on, not heeding me. "I got on the ninth green in eleven with a nice mashie-niblick, but my approach-putt was a little too strong. It came in through that window."

I perceived for the first time that one of the windows facing the course was broken, and my relief was great. I went down on my knees and helped him in his search. We ran the ball to earth finally inside the piano.

"What's the local rule?" inquired Mortimer. "Must I play it where it lies, or may I tee up and lose a stroke? If I have to play it where it lies, I suppose a niblick would be the club?"

It was at this moment that Betty came in. One glance at her pale, set face told me that there was to be a scene, and I would have retired, but that she was between me and the door.

"Hallo, dear," said Mortimer, greeting her with a friendly waggle of his niblick. "I'm bunkered in the piano. My approach-putt was a little strong, and I over-ran the green."

"Mortimer," said the girl, tensely, "I want to ask you one question."

"Yes, dear? I wish, darling, you could have seen my drive at the eighth just now. It was a pip!"

Betty looked at him steadily.

"Are we engaged," she said, "or are we not?"

"Engaged? Oh, to be married? Why, of course. I tried the open stance for a change, and—"

"This morning you promised to take me for a ride. You never appeared. Where were you?"

"Just playing golf."

"Golf! I'm sick of the very name!"

A spasm shook Mortimer.

"You mustn't let people hear you saying things like that!" he said. "I somehow felt, the moment I began my up-swing, that everything was going to be all right. I—"

"I'll give you one more chance. Will you take me for a drive in your car this evening?"

"I can't."

"Why not? What are you doing?"

"Just playing golf!"

"I'm tired of being neglected like this!" cried Betty, stamping her foot. Poor girl, I saw her point of view. It was bad enough for her being engaged to the wrong man, without having him treat her as a mere acquaintance. Her conscience fighting with her love for Eddie Denton had kept her true to Mortimer, and Mortimer accepted the sacrifice with an absent-minded carelessness which would have been galling to any girl. "We might just as well not be engaged at all. You never take me anywhere."

"I asked you to come with me to watch the Open Championship."

"Why don't you ever take me to dances?"

"I can't dance."

"You could learn."

"But I'm not sure if dancing is a good thing for a fellow's game. You never hear of any first-class pro. dancing. James Barnes doesn't dance."

"Well, my mind's made up, Mortimer, you must choose between golf and me."

"But, darling, I went round in a hundred and one yesterday. You can't expect a fellow to give up golf when he's at the top of his game."

"Very well. I have nothing more to say. Our engagement is at an end."

"Don't throw me over, Betty," pleaded Mortimer, and there was that in his voice which cut me to the heart. "You'll make me so miserable. And, when I'm miserable, I always slice my approach shots."

Betty Weston drew herself up. Her face was hard.

"Here is your ring!" she said, and swept from the room.

For a moment after she had gone Mortimer remained very still, looking at the glistening circle in his hand. I stole across the room and patted his shoulder.

"Bear up, my boy, bear up!" I said.

He looked at me piteously.

"Stymied!" he muttered.

"Be brave!"

He went on, speaking as if to himself.

"I had pictured—ah, how often I had pictured!—our little home! Hers and mine. She sewing in her arm-chair, I practising putts on the hearth-rug—" He choked. "While in the corner, little Harry Vardon Sturgis played with little J. H. Taylor Sturgis. And round the room—reading, busy with their childish tasks—little George Duncan Sturgis, Abe Mitchell Sturgis, Harold Hilton Sturgis, Edward Ray Sturgis, Horace Hutchinson Sturgis, and little James Braid Sturgis."

"My boy! My boy!" I cried.

"What's the matter?"

"Weren't you giving yourself rather a large family?"

He shook his head moodily.

"Was I?" he said, dully. "I don't know. What's par?"

There was a silence.

"And yet—" he said, at last, in a low voice. He paused. An odd, bright look had come into his eyes. He seemed suddenly to be himself again, the old, happy Mortimer Sturgis I had known so well. "And yet," he said, "who knows? Perhaps it is all for the best. They might all have turned out tennis-players!" He raised his niblick again, his face aglow. "Playing thirteen!" he said. "I think the game here would be to chip out through the door and work round the club-house to the green, don't you?"

Little remains to be told. Betty and Eddie have been happily married for years. Mortimer's handicap is now down to eighteen, and he is improving all the time. He was not present at the wedding, being unavoidably detained by a medal tournament; but, if you turn up the files and look at the list of presents, which were both numerous and costly, you will see— somewhere in the middle of the column, the words:

STURGIS, J. MORTIMER.
Two dozen Silver King Golf-balls and one patent Sturgis Aluminum Self-Adjusting, Self-Compensating Putting-Cleek.

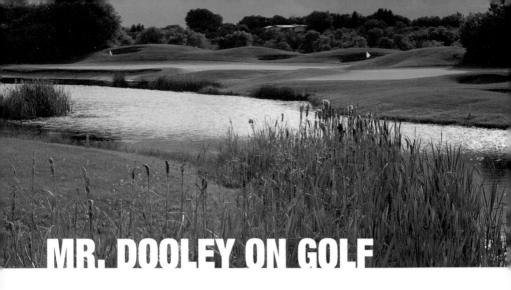

MR. DOOLEY ON GOLF

FINLEY PETER DUNNE

B
ut 'tis a gr-reat game, a gr-rand, jolly, hail-fellow-well-met spoort.
With the exciption maybe iv th' theery iv infant damnation, Scotland has given nawthin' more cheerful to th' wurruld thin th' game
iv goluf."

"An' what's this game iv goluf like, I dinnaw?" said Mr. Hennessy,
lighting his pipe with much unnecessary noise. "Ye're a good deal iv a
spoort, Jawnny: did ye iver thry it?"

"No," said Mr. McKenna. "I used to roll a hoop onct upon a time, but
I'm out of condition now."

"It ain't like base-ball," said Mr. Hennessy, "an' it ain't like shinny, an'
it ain't like lawn-teems, an' it ain't like forty-fives an' it ain't"—

"Like canvas-back duck or anny other game ye know," said Mr.
Dooley.

"Thin what is it like?" said Mr. Hennessy. "I see be th' pa-aper that
Hobart What-d'ye-call-him is wan iv th' best at it. Th' other day he made
a scoor iv wan hundherd an' sixty-eight, but whether 'twas miles or stitch-
es I cudden't make out fr'm th' raypoorts."

"'Tis little ye know," said Mr. Dooley. "Th' game iv goluf is as old as th' hills. Me father had goluf links all over his place, an', whin I was a kid, 'twas wan iv th' principal spoorts iv me life, afther I'd dug the turf f'r th' avenin', to go out and putt"—

"Poot, ye mean," said Mr. Hennessy. "They'se no such wurrud in th' English language as putt. Belinda called me down ha-ard on it no more thin las' night."

"There ye go!" said Mr. Dooley, angrily. "There ye go! D'ye think this here game iv goluf is a spellin' match? 'Tis like ye, Hinnissy, to be refer-eein' a twinty-round glove contest be th' rule iv three. I tell ye I used to go out in th' avenin' an' putt me mashie like hell-an'-all, till I was knowed fr'm wan end iv th' county to th' other as th' champeen putter. I putted two men fr'm Roscommon in wan day, an' they had to be took home on a dure.

"In America th' ga-ame is played more ginteel, an' is more like ciga-reet-smokin', though less onhealthy f'r th' lungs. 'Tis a good game to play in a hammick whin ye're all tired out fr'm social duties or shovel-lin' coke. Out-iv-dure golf is played be th' followin' rules. If ye bring ye'er wife f'r to see th' game, an' she has her name in th' paper, that counts ye wan. So th' first thing ye do is to find th' raypoorter, an' tell him ye're there. Thin ye ordher a bottle iv brown pop, an' have ye'er second fan ye with a towel. Afther this ye'd dhress, an' here ye've got to be dam particklar or ye'll be stuck f'r th' dhrinks. If ye're necktie is not on sthraight, that counts ye'er opponent wan. If both ye an' ye'er opponent have ye'er neckties on crook-ed, th' first man that sees it gets th' stakes. Thin ye ordher a carredge"—

"Order what?" demanded Mr. McKenna.

"A carredge."

"What for?"

"F'r to take ye 'round th' links. Ye have a little boy followin' ye, car-ryin' ye'er clubs. Th' man that has th' smallest little boy it counts him two. If th' little boy has th' rickets, it counts th' man in th' carredge three. The little boys is called caddies; but Clarence Heaney that tol' me all this—he

belongs to th' Foorth Wa-ard Goluf an' McKinley Club—said what th' little boys calls th' players'd not be fit f'r to repeat.

"Well, whin ye dhrive up to th' tea grounds"—

"Th' what?" demanded Mr. Hennessy.

"Th' tea grounds, that's like th' homeplate in baseball or ordherin' a piece iv chalk in a game iv spoil five. Its th' beginnin' iv ivrything. Whin ye get to th' tea grounds, ye step out, an' have ye're hat irned be th' cad-die. Thin ye'er man that ye'er goin' aginst comes up, an' he asks ye, 'Do you know Potther Pammer?' Well, if ye don't know Potther Pammer, it's all up with ye: ye lose two points. But ye come right back at him with an' upper cut: 'Do ye live on th' Lake Shore dhrive?' If he doesn't, ye have him in th' nine hole. Ye needn't play with him anny more. But, if ye do play with him, he has to spot three balls. If he's a good man an' shifty on his feet, he'll counter be askin' ye where ye spend th' summer. Now ye can't tell him that ye spent th' summer with wan hook on th' free lunch an' another on th' ticker tape, an' so ye go back three. That needn't discour-age ye at all, at all. Here's yer chance to mix up, an' ye ask him if he was iver in Scotland. If he wasn't, it counts ye five. Thin ye tell him that ye had an aunt wanst that heerd th' Jook iv Argyle talk in a phonograph; an', onless he comes back an' shoots it into ye that he was wanst run over be th' Prince iv Wales, ye have him groggy. I don't know whether th' Jook iv Argyle or th' Prince iv Wales counts f'r most. They're like th' right an' left bower iv thrumps. Th' best players is called scratch-men."

"What's that f'r?" Mr. Hennessy asked.

"It's a Scotch game," said Mr. Dooley, with a wave of his hand. "I won-der how it come out to-day. Here's th' pa-aper. Let me see, McKinley at Canton. Still there. He niver cared to wandher fr'm his own fireside. Col-lar-button men f'r th' goold standard. Statues iv Heidelback, Ickleheimer an' Company to be erected in Washington. Another Vanderbilt weddin' That sounds like goluf, but it ain't. Newport society livin' in Mrs. Pot-ther Pammer's cellar. Green-goods men declare f'r honest money. Anson in foorth place some more. Pianny tuners f'r McKinley. Li Hung Chang smells a rat. Abner McKinley supports th' goold standard. Wait a minyit.

Here it is: 'Goluf in gay attire.' Let me see. H'm. 'Foozled his aproach,'—nasty thing. 'Topped th' ball.' 'Three up an' two to play' Ah, here's the scoor. 'Among those prisint were Messrs. an' Mesdames"—

"Hol' on!" cried Mr. Hennessy, grabbing the paper out of his friend's hands. "That's thim that was there."

"Well," said Mr. Dooley, decisively "that's th' goluf scoor."

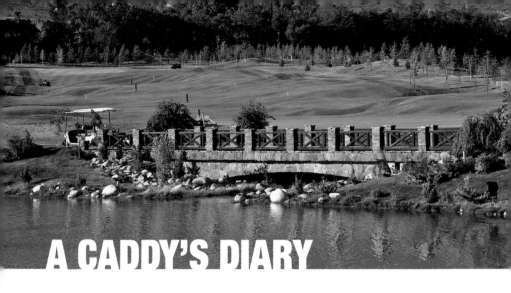

A CADDY'S DIARY

RING LARDNER

Wed. Apr. 12.

I am 16 of age and am a caddy at the Pleasant View Golf Club but only temporary as I expect to soon land a job some wheres as asst pro as my game is good enough now to be a pro but to young looking. My pal Joe Bean also says I have not got enough swell head to make a good pro but suppose that will come in time, Joe is a wise cracker.

But first will put down how I come to be writeing this diary, we have got a member name Mr Colby who writes articles in the newspapers and I hope for his sakes that he is a better writer then he plays golf but any way I cadded for him a good many times last yr and today he was out for the first time this yr and I cadded for him and we got talking about this in that and something was mentioned in regards to the golf articles by Alex Laird that comes out every Sun in the paper Mr Colby writes his articles for so I asked Mr Colby did he know how much Laird got paid for the articles and he said he did not know but supposed that Laird had to split 50-50 with who ever wrote the articles for him. So I said don't he write the articles himself and Mr Colby said why no he guessed not. Laird may be a master mind in regards to golf he said, but that is no sign he can write about it as very few men can write decent let alone a pro. Writeing is a nag.

How do you learn it I asked him.

Well he said read what other people writes and study them and write things yourself, and maybe you will get on to the nag and maybe you wont.

Well Mr Colby I said do you think I could get on to it?

Why he said smileing I did not know that was your ambition to be a writer.

Not exactly was my reply, but I am going to be a golf pro myself and maybe some day I will get good enough so as the papers will want I should write them articles and if I can learn to write them myself why I will not have to hire another writer and split with them.

Well said Mr Colby smileing you have certainly got the right temperament for a pro, they are all big hearted fellows.

But listen Mr Colby I said if I want to learn it would not do me no good to copy down what other writers have wrote, what I would have to do would be write things out of my own head.

That is true said Mr Colby.

Well I said what could I write about?

Well said Mr Colby why don't you keep a diary and every night after your supper set down and write what happened that day and write who you cadded for and what they done only leave me out of it. And you can write down what people say and what you think and etc., it will be the best kind of practice for you, and once in a wile you can bring me your writeings and I will tell you the truth if they are good or rotten.

So that is how I come to be writeing this diary is so as I can get some practice writeing and maybe if I keep at it long enough I can get on to the nag.

Friday, Apr. 14.

We been haveing Apr. showers for a couple days and nobody out on the course so they has been nothing happen that I could write down in my diary but dont want to leave it go to long or will never learn the trick so will try and write a few lines about a caddys life and some of our members and etc.

Well I and Joe Bean is the 2 oldest caddys in the club and I been cadding now for 5 yrs and quit school 3 yrs ago tho my mother did not like it for me to quit but my father said he can read and write and figure so what is the use in keeping him there any longer as greek and latin dont get you no credit at the grocer, so they lied about my age to the trunce officer and I been cadding every yr from March till Nov and the rest of the winter I work around Heismans store in the village.

Dureing the time I am cadding I genally always manage to play at least 9 holes a day myself on wk days and some times 18 and am never more than 2 or 3 over par figures on our course but it is a cinch.

I played the engineers course 1 day last summer in 75 which is some golf and some of our members who has been playing 20 yrs would give their right eye to play as good as myself.

I used to play around with our pro Jack Andrews till I got so as I could beat him pretty near every time we played and now he wont play with me no more, he is not a very good player for a pro but they claim he is a good teacher. Personly I think golf teachers is a joke tho I am glad people is suckers enough to fall for it as I expect to make my liveing that way. We have got a member Mr Dunham who must of took 500 lessons in the past 3 yrs and when he starts to shoot he trys to remember all the junk Andrews has learned him and he gets dizzy and they is no telling where the ball will go and about the safest place to stand when he is shooting is between he and the hole.

I dont beleive the club pays Andrews much salary but of course he makes pretty fair money giveing lessons but his best graft is a 3 some which he plays 2 and 3 times a wk with Mr Perdue and Mr Lewis and he gives Mr Lewis a stroke a hole and they genally break some wheres near even but Mr Perdue made a 83 one time so he thinks that is his game so he insists on playing Jack even, well they always play for $5.00 a hole and Andrews makes $20.00 to $30.00 per round and if he wanted to cut loose and play his best he could make $50.00 to $60.00 per round but a couple of wallops like that and Mr Perdue might get cured so Jack figures a small stedy income is safer.

I have got a pal name Joe Bean and we pal around together as he is about my age and he says some comical things and some times will wisper some thing comical to me while we are cadding and it is all I can do to help from laughing out loud, that is one of the first things a caddy has got to learn is never laugh out loud only when a member makes a joke. How ever on the days when theys ladies on the course I dont get a chance to caddy with Joe because for some reason another the woman folks dont like Joe to caddy for them wile on the other hand they are always after me tho I am no Othello for looks or do I seek their flavors, in fact it is just the opp and I try to keep in the back ground when the fair sex appears on the seen as cadding for ladies means you will get just so much money and no more as theys no chance of them loosning up. As Joe says the rule against tipping is the only rule the woman folks keeps.

Theys one lady how ever who I like to caddy for as she looks like Lillian Gish and it is a pleasure to just look at her and I would caddy for her for nothing tho it is hard to keep your eye on the ball when you are cadding for this lady, her name is Mrs Doane.

Sat. Apr. 15.

This was a long day and I am pretty well wore out but must not get behind in my writeing practice. I and Joe carried all day for Mr Thomas and Mr Blake. Mr Thomas is the vice president of one of the big banks down town and he always slips you a $1.00 extra per round but beleive me you earn it cadding for Mr Thomas, there is just 16 clubs in his bag includeing

5 wood clubs tho he has not used the wood in 3 yrs but says he has got to have them along in case his irons goes wrong on him. I dont know how bad his irons will have to get before he will think they have went wrong on him but persony if I made some of the tee shots he made today I would certainly consider some kind of change of weppons.

Mr Thomas is one of the kind of players that when it has took him more than 6 shots to get on the green he will turn to you and say how many have I had caddy and then you are suppose to pretend like you was thinking a minute and then say 4, then he will say to the man he is playing with well I did not know if I had shot 4 or 5 but the caddy says it is 4. You see in this way it is not him that is cheating but the caddy but he makes it up to the caddy afterwards with a $1.00 tip.

Mr Blake gives Mr Thomas a stroke a hole and they play a $10.00 nassua and neither one of them wins much money from the other one but even if they did why $10.00 is chickens food to men like they. But the way they crab and squak about different things you would think their last $1.00 was at stake. Mr Thomas started out this A. M. with a 8 and a 7 and of course that spoilt the day for him and me to. Theys lots of men that if they dont make a good score on the first 2 holes they will founder all the rest of the way around and raze H with their caddy and if I was laying out a golf course I would make the first 2 holes so darn easy that you could not help from getting a 4 or better on them and in that way everybody would start off good natured and it would be a few holes at least before they begun to turn sour.

Mr Thomas was beat both in the A. M. and P. M. in spite of my help as Mr Blake is a pretty fair counter himself and I heard him say he got a 88 in the P. M. which is about a 94 but any way it was good enough to win. Mr Blakes regular game is about a 90 takeing his own figures and he is one of these cocky guys that takes his own game serious and snears at men that cant break 100 and if you was to ask him if he had ever been over 100 himself he would say not since the first yr he begun to play. Well I have watched a lot of those guys like he and I will tell you how they keep from going over 100 namely by doing just what he done this A. M. when he come to the 13th hole. Well he missed his tee shot and dubbed along and finely he got in a trap on his 4th shot and I seen him take 6 wallops in the trap and when he had took the 6th one his ball was worse off then when he started so he picked it up and marked a X down on his score card. Well if he had of played out the hole why the best he could of got was a 11 by holeing his next niblick shot but he would of probly got about a 20 which would of made him around 108 as he admitted takeing a 88 for the other 17 holes. But I bet if you was to ask him what score he had made he would say O I was terrible and I picked up on one hole but if I had played them all out I guess I would of had about a 92.

These is the kind of men that laughs themselfs horse when they hear of some dub takeing 10 strokes for a hole but if they was made to play out every hole and mark down their real score their card would be decorated with many a big casino.

Well as I say I had a hard day and was pretty sore along towards the finish but still I had to laugh at Joe Bean on the 15th hole which is a par 3 and you can get there with a fair drive and personly I am genally hole high with a midiron, but Mr Thomas topped his tee shot and dubbed a couple with his mashie and was still quiet a ways off the green and he stood studying the situation a minute and said to Mr Blake well I wonder what I better take here. So Joe Bean was standing by me and he said under his breath take my advice and quit you old rascal.

Mon. Apr. 17.

Yesterday was Sun and I was to wore out last night to write as I cadded 45 holes. I cadded for Mr Colby in the A. M. and Mr Langley in the P. M. Mr Thomas thinks golf is wrong on the sabath tho as Joe Bean says it is wrong any day the way he plays it.

This A. M. they was nobody on the course and I played 18 holes by myself and had a 5 for a 76 on the 18th hole but the wind got a hold of my drive and it went out of bounds. This P. M. they was 3 of us had a game of rummy started but Miss Rennie and Mrs Thomas come out to play and asked for me to caddy for them, they are both terrible.

Mrs Thomas is Mr Thomas wife and she is big and fat and shakes like jell and she always says she plays golf just to make her skinny and she dont care how rotten she plays as long as she is getting the exercise, well maybe so but when we find her ball in a bad lie she aint never sure it is hers till she picks it up and smells it and when she puts it back beleive me she don't cram it down no gopher hole.

Miss Rennie is a good looker and young and they say she is engaged to Chas Crane, he is one of our members and is the best player in the club and dont cheat hardly at all and he has got a job in the bank where Mr Thomas is the vice president. Well I have cadded for Miss Rennie when she was playing with Mr Crane and I have cadded for her when she was playing alone or with another lady and I often think if Mr Crane could hear her talk when he was not around he would not be so stuck on her. You would be surprised at some of the words that falls from those fare lips.

Well the 2 ladies played for 2 bits a hole and Miss Rennie was haveing a terrible time wile Mrs Thomas was shot with luck on the greens and sunk 3 or 4 putts that was murder. Well Miss Rennie used some expressions which was best not repcated but towards the last the luck changed around and it was Miss Rennie that was sinking the long ones and when they got to the 18th tee Mrs Thomas was only 1 up.

Well we had started pretty late and when we left the 17th green Miss Rennie made the remark that we would have to hurry to get the last hole played, well it was her honor and she got the best drive she made all day about 120 yds down the fair way. Well Mrs Thomas got nervous and looked up and missed her ball a ft and then done the same thing right over and when she finely hit it she only knocked it about 20 yds and this made her lay 3. Well her 4th went wild and lit over in the rough in the apple trees. It was a cinch Miss Rennie would win the hole unless she dropped dead.

Well we all went over to hunt for Mrs Thomas ball but we would of been lucky to find it even in day light but now you could not hardly see under the trees, so Miss Rennie said drop another ball and we will not count no penalty. Well it is some job any time to make a woman give up hunting for a lost ball and all the more so when it is going to cost her 2 bits to play the hole out so there we stayed for at lease 10 minutes till it was so dark we could not see each other let alone a lost ball and finely Mrs Thomas said well it looks like we could not finish, how do we stand? Just like she did not know how they stood.

You had me one down up to this hole said Miss Rennie.

Well that is finishing pretty close said Mrs Thomas.

I will have to give Miss Rennie credit that what ever word she thought of for this occasion she did not say it out loud but when she was paying me she said I might of give you a quarter tip only I have to give Mrs Thomas a quarter she dont deserve so you dont get it.

Fat chance I would of had any way

Thurs. Apr. 20.

Well we have been haveing some more bad weather but today the weather was all right but that was the only thing that was all right. This P. M. I cadded double for Mr Thomas and Chas Crane the club champion who is stuck on Miss Rennie. It was a 4 some with he and Mr Thomas against Mr Blake and Jack Andrews the pro, they was only playing best ball so it was really just a match between Mr Crane and Jack Andrews and Mr Crane win by 1 up. Joe Bean cadded for Jack and Mr Blake. Mr Thomas was terrible and I put in a swell P. M. lugging that heavy bag of his besides Mr Cranes bag.

Mr Thomas did not go off the course as much as usual but he kept hitting behind the ball and he ran me ragged replaceing his divots but still I had to laugh when he was playing the 4th hole which you have to drive over a ravine and every time Mr Thomas misses his tee shot on this hole why he makes a squak about the ravine and says it ought not to be there and etc.

'Today he had a terrible time getting over it and afterwards he said to Jack Andrews this is a joke hole and ought to be changed. So Joe Bean wispered to me that if Mr Thomas kept on playing like he was the whole course would be changed.

Then a little wile later when we come to the long 9th hole Mr Thomas got a fair tee shot but then he whiffed twice missing the ball by a ft and the 3d time he hit it but it only went a little ways and Joe Bean said that is 3 trys and no gain, he will have to punt.

But I must write down about my tough luck, well we finely got through the 18 holes and Mr.Thomas reached down in his pocket for the money to pay me and he genally pays for Mr Crane to when they play together as Mr Crane is just a employ in the bank and dont have much money but this time all Mr Thomas had was a $20.00 bill so he said to Mr Crane I guess you will have to pay the boy Charley so Charley dug down and got the money to pay me and he paid just what it was and not a dime over, where if Mr Thomas had of had the change I would of got a $1.00 extra at lease and maybe I was not sore and Joe Bean to because of course Andrews never gives you nothing and Mr Blake dont tip his caddy unless he wins.

They are a fine bunch of tight wads said Joe and I said well Crane is all right only he just has not got no money.

He aint all right no more than the rest of them said Joe.

Well at lease he dont cheat on his score I said.

And you know why that is said Joe, neither does Jack Andrews cheat on his score but that is because they play to good. Players like Crane and Andrews that goes around in 80 or better cant cheat on their score because they make the most of the holes in around 4 strokes and the 4 strokes includes their tee shot and a couple of putts which everbody is right there to watch them when they make them and count them right along with them. So if they make a 4 and claim a 3 why people would just laugh in their face and say how did the ball get from the fair way on to the green, did it fly? But the boys that takes 7 and 8 strokes to a hole can shave their score and you know they are shaveing it but you have to let them get away with it because you cant prove nothing. But that is one of the penaltys for being a good player, you cant cheat.

To hear Joe tell it pretty near everybody are born crooks, well maybe he is right.

Wed. Apr. 26.

Today Mrs Doane was out for the first time this yr and asked for me to caddy for her and you bet I was on the job. Well how are you Dick she said, she always calls me by name. She asked me what had I been doing all winter and was I glad to see her and etc.

She said she had been down south all winter and played golf pretty near every day and would I watch her and notice how much she had improved.

Well to tell the truth she was no better than last yr and wont never be no better and I guess she is just to pretty to be a golf player but of course when she asked me did I think her game was improved I had to reply yes indeed as I would not hurt her feelings and she laughed like my reply pleased her. She played with Mr and Mrs Carter and I carried the 2 ladies bags wile Joe Bean cadded for Mr Carter. Mrs. Carter is a ugly dame with things on her face and it must make Mr Carter feel sore when he looks at Mrs Doane to think he married Mrs Carter but I suppose they could not all marry the same one and besides Mrs Doane would not be a sucker enough to marry a man like he who drinks all the time and is pretty near always stood, tho Mr Doane who she did marry aint such a H of a man himself tho dirty with money.

They all gave me the laugh on the 3d hole when Mrs Doane was makeing her 2d shot and the ball was in the fair way but laid kind of bad and she just ticked it and then she asked me if winter rules was in force and I said yes so we teed her ball up so as she could get a good shot at it and they gave me the laugh for saying winter rules was in force.

You have got the caddys bribed Mr Carter said to her.

But she just smiled and put her hand on my shoulder and said Dick is my pal. That is enough of a bribe to just have her touch you and I would caddy all day for her and never ask for a cent only to have her smile at me and call me her pal.

Sat. Apr. 29.

Today they had the first club tournament of the yr and they have a monthly tournament every month and today was the first one, it is a handicap tournament and everybody plays in it and they have prizes for low net score and low gross score and etc. I cadded for Mr Thomas today and will tell what happened.

They played a 4 some and besides Mr Thomas we had Mr Blake and Mr Carter and Mr Dunham. Mr Dunham is the worst man player in the club and the other men would not play with him a specialy on a Saturday only him and Mr Blake is partners together in business. Mr Dunham has got the highest handicap in the club which is 50 but it would have to be 150 for him to win a prize. Mr Blake and Mr Carter has got a handicap of about 15 a piece I think and Mr Thomas is 30, the first prize for the low net score for the day was a dozen golf balls and the second low score a ½ dozen golf balls and etc.

Well we had a great battle and Mr Colby ought to been along to write it up or some good writer. Mr Carter and Mr Dunham played partners against Mr Thomas and Mr Blake which ment that Mr Carter was playing Thomas and Blakes best ball, well Mr Dunham took the honor and the first ball he hit went strate off to the right and over the fence outside of the grounds, well he done the same thing 3 times. Well when he finely did hit one in the course why Mr Carter said why not let us not count them 3 first shots of Mr Dunham as they was just practice. Like H we wont count them said Mr Thomas we must count every shot and keep our scores correct for the tournament.

All right said Mr Carter.

Well we got down to the green and Mr Dunham had about 11 and Mr Carter sunk a long putt for a par 5, Mr Blake all ready had 5 strokes and so did Mr Thomas and when Mr Carter sunk his putt why Mr Thomas picked his ball up and said Carter wins the hole and I and Blake will take 6s. Like H you will said Mr Carter, this is a tournament and we must play every hole out and keep our scores correct. So Mr Dunham putted and went down in 13 and Mr Blake got a 6 and Mr Thomas missed 2 easy putts and took a 8 and maybe he was not boiling.

Well it was still their honor and Mr Dunham had one of his dizzy spells on the 2d tee and he missed the ball twice before he hit it and then Mr Carter drove the green which is only a mid-iron shot and then Mr Thomas stepped up and missed the ball just like Mr Dunham. He was wild and yelled at Mr Dunham no man could play golf playing with a man like you, you would spoil anybodys game.

Your game was all ready spoiled said Mr Dunham, it turned sour on the 1st green.

You would turn anybody sour said Mr Thomas.

Well Mr Thomas finely took a 8 for the hole which is a par 3 and it certainly looked bad for him winning a prize when he started out with 2 8s, and he and Mr Dunham had another terrible time on No 3 and wile they was messing things up a 2 some come up behind us and hollered fore and we left them go through tho it was Mr Clayton and Mr Joyce and as Joe Bean said they was probly dissapointed when we left them go through as they are the kind that feels like the day is lost if they cant write to some committee and preffer charges.

Well Mr Thomas got a 7 on the 3d and he said well it is no wonder I am off of my game today as I was up ½ the night with my teeth.

Well said Mr Carter if I had your money why on the night before a big tournament like this I would hire somebody else to set up with my teeth.

Well I wished I could remember all that was said and done but any way Mr.Thomas kept getting sore and sore and we got to the 7th tee and he had not made a decent tee shot all day so Mr Blake said to him why dont you try the wood as you cant do no worse?

By Geo I believe I will said Mr Thomas and took his driver out of the bag which he had not used it for 3 yrs.

Well he swang and zowie away went the ball pretty near 8 inchs distants wile the head of the club broke off clean and saled 50 yds down the course. Well I have got a hold on myself so as I dont never laugh out loud and I beleive the other men was scarred to laugh or he would of killed them so we all stood there in silents waiting for what would happen.

Well without saying a word he come to where I was standing and took his other 4 wood clubs out of the bag and took them to a tree which stands a little ways from the tee box and one by one he swang them with all his strength against the trunk of the tree and smashed them to H and gone, all right gentlemen that is over he said.

Well to cut it short Mr Thomas score for the first 9 was a even 60 and then we started out on the 2d 9 and you would not think it was the same man playing, on the first 3 holes he made 2 4s and a 5 and beat Mr Carter even and followed up with a 6 and a 5 and that is how he kept going up to the 17th hole.

What has got in to you Thomas said Mr Carter.

Nothing said Mr Thomas only I broke my hoodoo when I broke them 5 wood clubs.

Yes I said to myself and if you had broke them 5 wood clubs 3 yrs ago I would not of broke my back lugging them around.

Well we come to the 18th tee and Mr Thomas had a 39 which give him a 99 for 17 holes, well everybody drove off and as we was following along why Mr Klabor come walking down the course from the club house on his way to the 17th green to join some friends and Mr Thomas asked him what had he made and he said he had turned in a 93 but his handicap is only 12 so that give him a 81.

That wont get me no wheres he said as Charley Crane made a 75.

Well said Mr Thomas I can tie Crane for low net if I get a 6 on this hole.

Well it come his turn to make his 2d and zowie he hit the ball pretty good but they was a hook on it and away she went in to the woods on the left, the ball laid in behind a tree so as they was only one thing to do and that was waste a shot getting it back on the fair so that is what Mr Thomas done and it took him 2 more to reach the green.

How many have you had Thomas said Mr Carter when we was all on the green.

Let me see said Mr Thomas and then turned to me, how many have I had caddy?

I dont know I said.

Well it is either 4 or 5 said Mr Thomas.

I think it is 5 said Mr Carter.

I think it is 4 said Mr Thomas and turned to me again and said how many have I had caddy?

So I said 4.

Well said Mr Thomas personly I was not sure myself but my caddy says 4 and I guess he is right.

Well the other men looked at each other and I and Joe Bean looked at each other but Mr Thomas went ahead and putted and was down in 2 putts.

Well he said I certainly come to life on them last 9 holes.

So he turned in his score as 105 and with his handicap of 30 why that give him a net of 75 which was the same as Mr Crane so instead of Mr Crane getting 1 dozen golf balls and Mr Thomas getting ½ a dozen golf balls why they will split the 1st and 2d prize makeing 9 golf balls a piece.

Tues. May 2.

This was the first ladies day of the season and even Joe Bean had to carry for the fair sex. We cadded for a 4 some which was Miss Rennie and Mrs Thomas against Mrs Doane and Mrs Carter. I guess if they had of kept their score right the total for the 4 of them would of ran well over a 1000.

Our course has a great many trees and they seemed to have a traction for our 4 ladies today and we was in amongst the trees more then we was on the fair way.

Well said Joe Bean theys one thing about cadding for these dames, it keeps you out of the hot sun.

And another time he said he felt like a boy scout studing wood craft.

These dames is always up against a stump he said.

And another time he said that it was not fair to charge these dames regular ladies dues in the club as they hardly ever used the course.

Well it seems like they was a party in the village last night and of course the ladies was talking about it and Mrs Doane said what a lovely dress Miss Rennie wore to the party and Miss Rennie said she did not care for the dress herself.

Well said Mrs Doane if you want to get rid of it just hand it over to me.

I wont give it to you said Miss Rennie but I will sell it to you at ½ what it cost me and it was a bargain at that as it only cost me a $100.00 and I will sell it to you for $50.00.

I have not got $50.00 just now to spend said Mrs Doane and besides I dont know would it fit me.

Sure it would fit you said Miss Rennie, you and I are exactly the same size and figure, I tell you what I will do with you I will play you golf for it and if you beat me you can have the gown for nothing and if I beat you why you will give me $50.00 for it.

All right but if I loose you may have to wait for your money said Mrs Doane.

So this was on the 4th hole and they started from there to play for the dress and they was both terrible and worse then usual on acct of being nervous as this was the biggest stakes they had either of them ever played for tho the Doanes has got a bbl of money and $50.00 is chickens food.

Well we was on the 16th hole and Mrs Doane was 1 up and Miss Rennie sliced her tee shot off in the rough and Mrs Doane landed in some rough over on the left so they was clear across the course from each other. Well I and Mrs Doane went over to her ball and as luck would have it it had come to rest in a kind of a groove where a good player could not hardly make a good shot of it let alone Mrs Doane. Well Mrs Thomas was out in the middle of the course for once in her life and the other 2 ladies was over on the right side and Joe Bean with them so they was nobody near Mrs Doane and I.

Do I have to play it from there she said. I guess you do was my reply.

Why Dick have you went back on me she said and give me one of her looks.

Well I looked to see if the others was looking and then I kind of give the ball a shove with my toe and it come out of the groove and laid where she could get a swipe at it.

This was the 16th hole and Mrs Doane win it by 11 strokes to 10 and that made her 2 up and 2 to go. Miss Rennie win the 17th but they both took a 10 for the 18th and that give Mrs Doane the match.

Well I wont never have a chance to see her in Miss Rennies dress but if I did I aint sure that I would like it on her.

Fri. May 5.

Well I never thought we would have so much excitement in the club and so much to write down in my diary but I guess I better get busy writeing it down as here it is Friday and it was Wed. A. M. when the excitement broke loose and I was getting ready to play around when Harry Lear the caddy master come running out with the paper in his hand and showed it to me on the first page.

It told how Chas Crane our club champion had went south with $8000 which he had stole out of Mr Thomas bank and a swell looking dame that was a stenographer in the bank had eloped with him and they had her picture in the paper and I will say she is a pip but who would of thought a nice quiet young man like Mr Crane was going to prove himself a gay Romeo and a specialy as he was engaged to Miss Rennie tho she now says she broke their engagement a month ago but any way the whole affair has certainly give everybody something to talk about and one of the caddys Lou Crowell busted Fat Brunner in the nose because Fat claimed to of been the last one that cadded for Crane. Lou was really the last one and cadded for him last Sunday which was the last time Crane was at the club.

Well everybody was thinking how sore Mr Thomas would be and they would better not mention the affair around him and etc. but who should show up to play yesterday but Mr Thomas himself and he played with Mr Blake and all they talked about the whole P. M. was Crane and what he had pulled.

Well Thomas said Mr Blake I am curious to know if the thing come as a surprise to you or if you ever had a hunch that he was libel to do a thing like this.

Well Blake said Mr Thomas I will admit that the whole thing come as a complete surprise to me as Crane was all most like my son you might say and I was going to see that he got along all right and that is what makes me sore is not only that he has proved himself dishonest but that he could be such a sucker as to give up a bright future for a sum of money like $8000 and a doll face girl that cant be no good or she would not of let him do it. When you think how young he was and the carreer he might of had why it certainly seems like he sold his soul pretty cheap.

That is what Mr Thomas had to say or at least part of it as I cant remember a ½ of all he said but any way this P. M. I cadded for Mrs Thomas and Mrs Doane and that is all they talked about to, and Mrs Thomas talked along the same lines like her husband and said she had always thought Crane was to smart a young man to pull a thing like that and ruin his whole future.

He was getting $4000 a yr said Mrs Thomas and everybody liked him and said he was bound to get ahead so that is what makes it such a silly thing for him to of done, sell his soul for $8000 and a pretty face.

Yes indeed said Mrs Doane.

Well all the time I was listening to Mr Thomas and Mr Blake and Mrs Thomas and Mrs Doane why I was thinking about something which I wanted to say to them but it would of ment me looseing my job so I kept it to myself but I sprung it on my pal Joe Bean on the way home tonight.

Joe I said what do these people mean when they talk about Crane selling his soul?

Why you know what they mean said Joe, they mean that a person that does something dishonest for a bunch of money or a gal or any kind of a reward why the person that does it is selling his soul.

All right I said and it dont make no differents does it if the reward is big or little?

Why no said Joe only the bigger it is the less of a sucker the person is that goes after it.

Well I said here is Mr Thomas who is vice president of a big bank and worth a bbl of money and it is just a few days ago when he lied about his golf score in order so as he would win 9 golf balls instead of a ½ a dozen.

Sure said Joe.

And how about his wife Mrs Thomas I said, who plays for 2 bits a hole and when her ball dont lie good why she picks it up and pretends to look at it to see if it is hers and then puts it back in a good lie where she can sock it.

And how about my friend Mrs Doane that made me move her ball out of a rut to help her beat Miss Rennie out of a party dress.

Well said Joe what of it?

Well I said it seems to me like these people have got a lot of nerve to pan Mr. Crane and call him a sucker for doing what he done, it seems to me like $8000 and a swell dame is a pretty fair reward compared with what some of these other people sells their soul for, and I would like to tell them about it.

Well said Joe go ahead and tell them but maybe they will tell you something right back.

What will they tell me?

Well said Joe they might tell you this, that when Mr Thomas asks you how many shots he has had and you say 4 when you know he has had 5, why are you selling your soul for a $1.00 tip. And when you move Mrs Doanes ball out of a rut and give it a good lie, what are you selling your soul for? Just a smile.

O keep your mouth shut I said to him.

I am going to said Joe and would advice you to do the same.

HOW I BEGAN TO PLAY GOLF

FRANCIS OUIMET

B ig brothers" have a lot of responsibility in life, more than most of them realize. "Little brother" is reasonably certain to follow their example, to a greater or lesser degree, hence the better the example set, the better for all concerned. My own case is just one illustration. Whether I was destined to become a golfer anyway, I cannot say; but my first desire to hit a golf ball, as I recall, arose from the fact that my older brother, Wilfred, became the proud possessor of a couple of golf clubs when I was five years old, and at the same time I acquired the idea that the thing I wanted most in the world was to have the privilege of using those clubs.

Thus it was that, at the age of five, my acquaintance with the game of golf began. To say that the game has been a wonderful source of pleasure to me might lead the reader to think that the greatest pleasure of all has been derived from winning tournaments and prizes. I can truthfully say that nothing is further from the truth. Of course, I am pleased to have won my fair share of tournaments; I appreciate the honor of having won the national open championship; but the winning is absolutely secondary. It is the game itself that I love. Of all the games that I have played and like to see played, including baseball, football, hockey, and tennis, no other, to my mind, has quite so many charms as golf—a clean and wholesome pastime, requiring the highest order of skill to be played successfully and a game suitable alike for the young, the middle-aged, and the old.

The first "golf course" that I played over was laid out by my brother and Richard Kimball in the street in front of our home on Clyde Street, Brookline, Massachusetts, a street which forms the boundary of one side of the Country Club property. This golf course, as I call it, was provided by the town of Brookline, without the knowledge of the town's officials. In other words, my brother and Kimball simply played between two given points in the street. With the heels of their shoes they made holes in the dirt at the base of two lampposts about one hundred and twenty yards apart, and that was their "course."

Nearly every afternoon they played, and I looked on enviously. Once in a while they let me take a club and try my hand, and then was I not delighted! It made no difference that the clubs were nearly as long as I was and too heavy for me to swing, or that the ball would only go a few yards, if it went at all. After all, as I look back, the older boys were only dealing me scanty justice when they occasionally allowed me to take a club, for when they lost a ball, I used to go searching for it, and, if successful, they always demanded its return. In the case of such a demand from two older boys, it is not always wise to refuse.

"Big brother" was responsible for getting me interested in golf; "big brother" likewise was in great measure responsible for keeping me interested. On my seventh birthday, he made me a birthday present of a club—a short brassy. Here was joy indeed! Not only had I now a club all my own with which to practice, but I already had amassed a private stock of seven or eight golf balls. The way this came about was that the journey from my house to school (this school, by the way, had only eight pupils in it, and the schoolhouse was built in Revolutionary days) took me past the present sixth hole of the Country Club course, and I generally managed to get a little spare time to look for lost golf balls.

Some boys do not like to get up early in the morning. Any boy or girl who becomes as interested in golf as I was at the age of seven, will have no difficulty on that score. It was my custom to go to bed at eight o'clock, and then get up by six o'clock the next morning, and go out for some golf play before time to get ready for school. The one hole in the street where my brother and Richard Kimball first played had now been superseded by a more exacting golf layout in a bit of pasture land in back of our house.

Here the older boys had established a hole of about one hundred and thirty yards that was a real test for them, and, at first, a little too much for me. On the left, going one way, the ground was soft and marshy, an easy place to lose a ball. If the ball went on a straight line from the tree, it generally went into a gravel pit, which had an arm extending out to the right. There also was a brook about a hundred yards from the tee, when the play was in this same direction. Here, then, was a hole requiring accuracy; and I cannot but think that a measure of what accuracy my game now possesses had its foundation back in those days when I was so young and just taking up the game. I believe, moreover, that any boy or girl who becomes interested in golf should not pick out the easy places to play at the start, simply because they like the fun of seeing the ball go farther.

What bothered me most, in those days, was the fact that I could not drive over that brook going one way The best I could do was to play short of the brook, and then try to get the second on the improvised green. Every now and then, I became bold enough to have another try to carry the brook, though each time it was with the knowledge that failure possibly meant the loss of the ball in the brook, in a time when one ball represented a small fortune. At last came the memorable morning when I did manage to hit one over the brook.

If ever in my life a shot gave me satisfaction, it was that one. It did more—it created ambition. I can remember thinking that if I could get over the brook once, I could do it again. And I did do it again—got so I could do it a fair proportion of my tries. Then the shot over the brook, coming back, began to seem too easy, for the carry one way was considerably longer than the other. Consequently I decided that for the return I

would tee up on a small mound twenty-five to thirty yards in back of the spot from which we usually played, making a much harder shot. Success brought increased confidence, and confidence brought desired results, so that, in course of time, it did not seem so difficult to carry the brook playing either way.

This was done with the old hard ball then generally known as the "gutty," made from gutta-percha. About this time I picked up, one morning, a ball which bounced in a much more lively fashion than the kind I had found previously. Now, of course, I know that it was one of the early makes of rubber-cored balls, but at that time, I simply knew that it would go much farther than the others, and that, above all things, I must not lose it. That ball was my greatest treasure. Day after day I played with it, until all the paint was worn off, and it was only after long searching that I managed always to find it after a drive.

Realizing that something must be done to retain the ball, I decided to repaint it, and did so with white lead. Next, I did something that was almost a calamity in my young life. To dry the white lead, I put the ball into a hot oven and left it there for about an hour. I went back thinking to find a nice new ball, and found what do you suppose? Nothing but a soft mass of gutta-percha and elastic. The whole thing simply had melted. The loss of a brand-new sled or a new pair of skates could not have made me grieve more, and I vowed that in the future, no matter how dirty a ball became, I would never put another into a hot oven to dry after repainting.

All this time I had been playing with the brassy that Brother gave me, and all my energies were devoted to trying to see how far I could hit the ball. My next educational step in play came when Wilfred made me a present of a mashy, whereupon I realized that there are other points to the game than merely getting distance. Previous practice with the brassy had taught me how to hit the ball with fair accuracy, so that learning something about mashy play came naturally. Being now possessed of two clubs, my ambitions likewise grew proportionately. The cow pasture in back of our house was all right enough, as far as it went, but why be so limited in my surroundings? There was the beautiful course of the Country Club across the street, with lots of room and smoother ground; nothing would do but that I should play at the Country Club. I began going over there mornings to play, but soon discovered that the groundskeeper and I did not hold exactly the same views concerning my right to play there. Whatever argument there was in the matter was all in favor of the groundskeeper. Of course I know now that he only did his duty when he chased me off the course.

While my brother's interest in golf began to wane, because football and baseball became greater hobbies with him, other boys in our neighborhood began to evince an interest in it, until it became a regular thing for three or four of us to play in the cow pasture after school hours and most of the day Saturday. We even had our matches, six holes in length, by playing back and forth over the one-hundred-and-thirty-yard hole three times, each using the same clubs. We even got to the point where we thought it would add excitement by playing for balls, and one day I found myself the richer by ten balls. But let me add that it is a bad practice for boys. There is too much hard feeling engendered.

As we became more proficient in play, we began to look over the ground with an eye to greater distance and more variety until finally we lengthened out the original hole to what was a good drive and pitch for us, about two hundred and thirty yards; likewise we created a new hole of about ninety yards, to play with the mashy. From the new green, back to the starting point, under an old chestnut tree, was about two hundred yards, which gave us a triangle course of three holes. In this way we not only began gradually to increase the length of our game, but also to get in a great variety of shots.

As I look back now, I become more and more convinced that the manner in which I first took up the game was to my subsequent advantage. With the old brassy I learned the elementary lesson of swinging a club and hitting the ball squarely, so as to get all the distance possible for one of my age and physical make-up. Then, with the mashy I learned how to hit the ball into the air, and how to drop it at a given point. I really think I could not have taken up the clubs in more satisfactory order. Even to this day, I have a feeling of confidence that I shall be sure to hit the ball cleanly when using a brassy, which feeling probably is a legacy from those old days.

And a word of caution right here to the boy or girl, man or woman, taking up the game: do not attempt at the start to try to hit the ball as far as you have seen some experienced player send it. Distance does not come all at once, and accuracy is the first thing to be acquired.

The first time that I had the pleasure of walking over a golf course without the feeling that, at any moment, I should have to take to my heels to escape an irate greenskeeper was when I was about eleven years old. I was on the Country Club links, looking for lost golf balls, when a member who had no caddy came along and asked me if I would carry his clubs. Nothing could have suited me better. As this member was coming to the first tee, I happened to be swinging a club, and he was kind enough to hand me a ball, at the same time asking me to tee up and hit it.

That was one occasion in my golfing career when I really felt nervous, though by this time I had come to the point where I felt reasonably confident of hitting the ball. But to stand up there and do it with an elderly person looking on was a different matter. It is a feeling which almost any golfer will have the first time he tries to hit a ball before some person or persons with whom he had not been in contact previously. I can remember doubting that I should hit the ball at all, hence my agreeable surprise in getting away what, for me, was a good ball.

Evidently the gentleman, who was not an especially good player himself, was satisfied with the shot, for he was kind enough to invite me to play with him, instead of merely carrying his clubs. He let me play with his clubs, too. That was the beginning of my caddying career. Some of the other members, for whom I carried clubs occasionally made me a present of some clubs, so that it was not long before my equipment contained not only the original brassy and mashy but also a cleik, mid-iron, and putter.

Needless to say they were not all exactly suited to my size and style of play; yet to me each one of them was precious. I took great pride in polishing them up after every usage. The second time I played with the gentleman who first employed me as caddy, I had my own clubs. I had the pleasure of playing with him two years later, after he came home from abroad, in which round I made an eighty-four, despite a nine at one hole.

All this time, my enthusiasm for the game increased, rather than diminished, so that, during the summer of 1906, I was on the links every moment that I could be there until school opened in September; after which I caddied or played afternoons and Saturdays until the close of the playing season.

SHUSH!!! AN AUTHORITY ON ATHALETICS MAKES A SUGGESTION

RING LARDNER

To the Editor: I want to call your tension to something about golf that has been ranking in my bosom for a long wile and I would have said something about it yrs. ago only I thought a man of your brains and intelligents would take steps, but I suppose you are afraid of the Old Guard amist your readers and scared of offending them, but where they's a principal involved I never fail to speak out my mind and my friends say I have done it so often that it is what you might call spoken out.

Well, it looks to me like they was room for improvement in the game and when I say the game I don't mean my game but the game itself as gotten up by St. Andrew and Simon Peter his brother and the next time the rules committee gets together I wished they would make a change in the code witch looks to me to be a whole lot more important than takeing the endearing terms out of tennis or makeing a pitcher keep his finger nails pared so as he can't scratch baseball or self.

According to what I have read golf is suppose to be the most sociable game in the world and in my $1.50 dictionary one of the definitions of sociable is "suited for, or characterized by, much conversation." Well, then, why and the he-ll don't they mend the golf rules so as a man can talk wile they're playing? Instead of witch, if you say a word to a regular golfer wile he is makeing a shot, why the first thing he will do is suffer a nervous break down and then he will give you a dirty look and likely as not he will pick up his toys and walk off the links, as I have nicknamed them. And when you ask somebody what was the idear they will tell you that your ethics is rancid and you must be scum, because how can a man concentrate on their shot when somebody is makeing remarks at them. And if you was in the gallery at the national amateur and even wispered wile Bobby Ouimet was trying to run down a millimeter put, why the head linesman would reach in his hip pocket for a sawed off niblick and knock you for a safety.

Well, gents, I have seen a good many different kinds of athaletics and took a small part in a few of them and I ask you as man to man what other event is they where comments is barred?

"Yes," you will say, "but they's no other sport where a man has got to concentrate on what they are doing. If your mind is distracted wile you are playing golf you're gone."

How true.

And now leave us suppose that Ty Cobb is up in the ninth inning of a ball game with 2 out and the score 7 to 4 vs. Detroit like it usually is and Young and Bush on base. Well, the bench warmers on the other club is yelling "Pop up, Ty! You been a good old wagon but you done broke down." And the catcher is wispering "What shall I have him throw up here, Ty? Do you want a slow ball?" And the boys in the stands is hollering "Strike the big cheese out, Lefty. He's through."

But all this don't worry Ty because he is thinking to himself "I mustn't forget to send my laundry out when I get back to the hotel." His mind ain't on the game at all and when Lefty throws one up there, why it's just from force of habit that he swings and next thing you know Felsch is beating it back to the left center field fence and Jackson is getting set to make the relay. But suppose Ty had been thinking about that next pitch instead

of his shirts, why the uproar would of give him neurasthenia and they'd of had to send the trainer up to hit for him.

Or suppose for inst. they's a horse race and they are comeing down the stretch and Vagabond the favorite is out in front and the second horse is Willie the Wisp that's 20 to 1 and a lot of waiters has a bet down on him and they all begin screaming "Come on Willie" so loud that Vagabond can't help from hearing them, but he don't even look up as he is thinking about a couple of library books that he promised to bring home to his mare.

Or you take what happened down to Toledo last 4 of July. Dempsey lept up and crowned Jessica in the left eye and Jessica suddenly set down but he got up again and 60 thousand and no hundreds larnyxs was shreeking "Kill the big dog, Jack!" and as I recall it, instead of the remarks bothering Dempsey, why he hit Jessica again with the same Gen. results and I would of swore he was concentrateing, but I found out afterwards that he was trying to figure out weather he would have veal chops or a steak for supper. Otherwise he would of raised his hand unlocked and told the referee that he wouldn't go on unlest the fans shut up their d-m noise.

Or leave us consider that extra inning game that wound up in Europe a couple yrs. ago and they was a guy name Frank Foch or something that was suppose to be figureing out how to put on the finishing touchs to it and he was setting down with a map in front of him, but the Germans kept on shooting Big Bertha and Little Eva with the loud pedal on, so finely a orderly come in and asked Mr. Foch if the noise bothered him. And Mr. Foch says "Oh no. It might if I was rapped up in what I am doing. But I was just wondering if I would look better with my mustache off or on, so let them keep on shooting." So it looks like if Mr. Foch had of been really forced to think about the job they had wished on him the Germans would probably be in Harrisburg by this time, changeing engines.

And then they's examples in the more intimate sports like shooting craps or driveing a car. For inst. you have made four passes and you've left it all ride and you come out with a deuce and a four and all the boys that's fadeing you begins yelping "Billy Hicks can't six" and "How many wonders in the world?" and etc. and you might get rattled and seven only that you ain't concentrated on the crap game a-tall, but you're thinking what a good time you might of had in Yellowstone Park last summer if you hadn't went to the 1000 Islands. Or let's say you're driveing up Fifth Ave. at 4 PM and your wife keeps pinching one of your arms and the gals in the back seat screek every little wile and say "Look out be careful!" why you might bump somebody if your mind was on the traffic instead of Dr. C. Roach Straton's latest sermon.

Now in regards to golf itself leave me give you a couple of incidence that happened to me personly witch will show that the boys who crabs against a little sociability is makeing a mountain climber out of a mole trap. Well, once I was playing out to Riverside near Chi with Albert Seckel and he was giveing me seven and no hundreds strokes per hole and when we came to the last tee we was even up. Well, the last hole was about 260 yds. but you had to drive over the Blue Ridge Mts. of Virginia and you couldn't see the green from the tee and if you didn't get your drive over the Mts. you was utterly lost. Well, for some reason another Seck had the honor and just as he was going to drive, I says "I hope you don't miss the ball entirely" so he drove onto the green and went down in two.

And down to Toledo last July, a few days before Willard became an acrobat, I and Rube Goldberg met in a match game out to Inverness and we was playing for a buck a hole and my caddy was Harry Witwer and he had broughten along a alarm clock and when we would get on the green, witch was seldom, why just as Rube was going to put, Harry would set off the alarm, and Rube got so nervous that on the 15th. hole Harry throwed my towel into the ring and I was seven down.

So all and all, Mr. Editor, I say pass a rule makeing it legal to open your clam when you feel like it and leave us forget this old obsleet law of silent golf witch was gotten up in Scotland where they wouldn't no more talk for nothing than Harry Lauder would sing for the same price. But weather the rule is past or no, when I am playing at golf I am going to say what I want to when I want to and if my oppts. don't like my ethics, why they's showers in the locker room.

Yours Truely,

ETIQUETTE AND BEHAVIOUR

HORACE HUTCHINSON

In connection with the game of golf there are certain points of etiquette which, though not of such a nature as to fall within the jurisdiction of written law, are pretty accurately defined by the sanction of custom. Breach of these observances is not punished by the loss of the hole or of a stroke, but rather by the loss of social status in the golfing world. You do not exact an immediate penalty from him who thus outrages *les convenances*; but in your heart of hearts you propose to yourself the severest of all forms of punishment, viz. never to play with him again.

Of all delinquents against the unwritten code, the grossest offender is perhaps he who stands over you, with triumph spiced with derision, as you labour in a bunker, and aggressively counts your score aloud. The act of ostentatiously coming out of his own path to look at you is, of itself, almost on the boundary line between good and bad form. Apart from the indecent gloating over your misfortunes which such conduct on his part would seem to imply, it also contains the infinitely more offensive suggestion of a suspicion of your possible unfair dealing when shielded by the bunker's cliff from his espionage. But when he goes the length of audibly counting up your unhappy efforts, with undisguised satisfaction as the sum increases, you can scarcely look upon it otherwise than as an impugnment either of your arithmetic or of your honesty.

There are, indeed, certain circumstances which may almost, in a medal competition, justify such a proceeding; for in a medal competition, in the absence of markers, each player is responsible for the correctness of the score, as returned, of the other, and, setting the question of honesty—as it is to be hoped we may—on one side, there are medal-players whose arithmetic, as a matter of fact, is not above suspicion. It is, moreover, far more difficult than is generally recognised to keep exact account of the strokes at those unfortunate holes where the total approaches the two figures. It is scarcely possible for a man to be in honest doubt as to whether he has played four strokes or five; but it is a very different thing where a question arises as to whether he has played eight or nine. One among so many is a small item easily forgotten. Nevertheless, unless the player for whom one is scoring is known to be what is called a 'bad counter'—which not a few perfectly honourable gentlemen and golfers unquestionably are—there is no justification for the *audible* enumeration, one by one, of his strokes. One's duty to one's neighbour—in this case, to all the others engaged in the competition—can be adequately performed, without offence to the sufferer, by silently marking off on the card each stroke as it is played. Should the player think fit to contest the accuracy of this marking, each stroke may for the future be audibly impressed upon him, as it is played, without any regard to the sufferings which he will then have deservedly brought upon himself.

But all such espionage can only be justified by a sense of your responsibility to the other competitors. In a match there is no conceivable excuse for it. If it be a friendly match, to start with, it cannot long continue such if either subject the other to such indignities; and if it be a big match, there will be a sufficient number of onlookers to check any possible inaccuracy of scoring. If you have not faith in a man's scoring, do not play with him; and if you play with a man, do not act in such a way as to suggest that you are suspicious.

But there is a subtler crime than that of miscounting his score, of which a man may be, and of which many often are, guilty in a bunker; and it is a crime which again raises another delicate point of etiquette. He may be touching the sand with his iron. Every golfer knows the rule that you must not touch sand in a bunker, with the club, as you address yourself to the ball—that you must not rest the club-head behind the ball. Almost every golfer does so, however, accidentally now and again, and some do it habitually. Etiquette has its word to say not about the touching of the sand, which is a distinct breach of a hard-and-fast rule of the game, but about the tempering justice with mercy in bringing the criminal to account. Let us first see what the custom is, in regard to breach of this rule, and let us then see what the custom ought to be.

With the first class, of those who touch sand accidentally occasionally, the custom certainly is to continue playing on, lightheartedly as if they were all unconscious of the rule and of their breach of it. And no one thinks of claiming the stroke as a foul one. Why?—because it is the custom not to claim it, and in the presence of this custom the man who claimed his rights, under the rule, would be regarded as a sharp practitioner. There are, doubtless, also many cases in which the player is himself quite unconscious of having touched the sand; he will indignantly deny having done so, and in the absence of a referee the just claim results in nothing but mutual irritation.

Next, what is the custom with regard to the habitual touchers of the sand? The first two offences probably go unnoticed. At the third they are possibly cautioned. At the fourth a threat is made to claim the hole. Probably this is about as often as their opponent will have seen their bunker performances, and when the round is over they will tell all their friends what an ungentlemanly fellow their late opponent is, and will probably meet with a great amount of sympathy!

Even in a match with money depending on the result, it would be deemed a quite unheard-of thing to claim a hole for a first offence of this nature; and yet it is an offence which may just give the culprit the match. Do not be deceived upon this point: it is not that by resting the club on the sand the lie of the ball is materially improved, but it is that by the faint impress a guide is given to the eye, if the sand be soft; or if it be hard and caked, a guide is given to the hand, by the sense of touch, of the distance from hand to ball. And on the one stroke thus feloniously aided who shall say how many matches may have turned? But if the difficulty were confined to match-playing alone, we might perhaps allow the custom, absurd as it is, to rest without reproach. A man has, there, but his own moral weakness to blame for allowing another to get the advantage of him by a breach of the rules. But where it becomes a question of medal play, where one of two partners is responsible to all the other competitors for the score of the other, how can it then consist with his duty to allow to go unnoticed direct breaches, each of which should be counted a stroke, of a rule written down in black and white?

What the custom ought to be it seems almost absurd to need to state. The custom ought, of course, to be that the rule should be enforced, just as much as any other rule of the game of golf. A conscientious man, with a proper regard for the rules of the game, should as little think of not counting a stroke when he has inadvertently touched the sand in addressing his ball as he should when he has missed a short putt. By the rules of the game one is as much a stroke as the other, and either is as much a stroke as the longest shot ever driven from the tee. And if we do not play golf by the rules of golf, by what are we to be guided? Shall we not call anything a stroke with which the player of it is dissatisfied? That would make a pleasant game, possibly, but it would not be very much like golf.

Why all this immorality has crept into the game, especially with reference to the touching of sand, it is hard enough to say. If a man makes a foul shot by hitting the ball twice, and is conscious of it, he will ordinarily tell you so, and give up the hole without further parley. Or if he were himself unaware of it, and if you draw his attention to it, on the evidence of a disinterested spectator or of that little tell-tale mark of white paint which chips off the ball when struck in the air, he will generally yield the point without demur. Some of us are indeed rather sensitive about drawing attention to an error of this nature also, but we have fewer scruples than in pointing out that the sand has been touched—yet most inconsistently, for the double shot can be but an accident, and, moreover, an accident that is not in the interests of the player, while the sand touching is, with many, an habitual sin, and gives a distinct advantage.

Altogether there is no so-called petty infringement of the rules about which there is so much custom-sanctioned laxity as in the matter of touching sand, and we greatly need that some of our leading golfers should inaugurate a change in that particular. But there are certain other little points wherein a laxity of custom sometimes appears, wherein a rigid application of the rules of golf would make the game far pleasanter, and far less liable to those little roughnesses of temper which at times crop up in the course of matches.

For instance, it will sometimes happen that, in spite of a player's utmost carefulness in the removal of loose sticks and straws from the neighbourhood of his ball, the latter will roll ever so little from its place. This, by clearly expressed rules of the game, counts against him; but there are those who, with full knowledge of the rule, instead of manfully paying the penalty, will appeal to you with a question as to 'whether you want them to count that?'

This in itself is a distinct breach of etiquette, for it throws you who are innocent into a position in which a question of etiquette upon your side arises. Of course the proper and honest answer is 'Yes,' because that is the answer given by the rules of golf, and because, at the moment, you are supposed to be playing golf. But it is just this latter fact that your opponent does not seem to realise; and if you are too authoritative in pointing it out to him it is not impossible, in consequence of the laxity on these points introduced by custom, that he may however absurdly, regard himself as rather hardly treated by your assertion of your rights. The very fact of his asking the question indeed is a suggestion that he will so regard it. What are you to say? Is the point at issue, and your respect for your own strength of mind, of sufficient value to compensate for the chance of losing your opponent's good opinion?

These are questions which each will answer according to his temperament; but our great point is that such questions ought never to arise. Nor would they ever arise but for the reprehensible laxity in the application of the rules of the game, which thus gives openings for those very unpleasantnesses which their lax interpretation was presumably intended to avert. Let the rules be applied in their proper strictness; let us play golf according to the rules of golf, and in the strict game we shall find freedom from all such annoyance.

An ingenious method has been suggested whereby, under stress of the question proposed above—as to whether the penalty imposed by the rules shall be exacted—a hypersensitive person may escape from the immediate difficulty and yet administer a rebuke to his opponent. Let him allow the breach of the rule to his opponent, without penalty; let him then, in his opponent's presence, himself commit a similar error, but on his opponent's requesting him not to count it (as he can scarcely fail to have the grace to do), let him reply with such emphasis as he is capable of that he always plays the game. This is true etiquette and courtesy; but it is poor golf, indeed; nor shall we ever get golf in its integrity and to our satisfaction until we play it according to the rules formulated for its guidance.

Now on many links, as at St. Andrews, it oftentimes happens that after a shower of rain there will be left what is termed 'casual water' on the links—puddles of rain-water not contemplated in the rules. It is very customary on such occasions for parties to make, before starting, a mutual arrangement, whereby it is agreed to take out of these pools of 'casual water' without penalty. This is, however, distinctly a matter of special arrangement. In the absence of any such arrangement, it is scarcely fair to ask your opponent, 'What are we to do about casual water?' as soon as you find your ball in one of these puddles. The strict rule is that you lose a stroke for taking it out, and no arrangement made on a previous occasion has any jurisdiction over this one. Any suggestion that such an arrangement was tacitly understood should be left to emanate from you—not from him, to whose advantage it will be; and it is your part, in all etiquette, if there is reasonable cause for supposing any such tacit understanding, to suggest and insist upon it. And so it is in all cases of a possible doubt of this nature; it is from the party to whose disadvantage it will be that the question and its answer should arise. The opponent should never be left in the position of plaintiff for his rights. If you make a double shot, if you touch sand, if you move your ball, give up the hole, or pay the penalty whatever it may be, without question, and if a question of genuine etiquette arise, always endeavour to answer it in your opponent's favour; for all you will lose in golf matches by thus dealing you will more than compensate in self-respect, which is nearly as important.

So far, then, the license introduced by custom has been somewhat of an offence. There is a point, which is chiefly seen in playing on the St. Andrews links, in which it makes matters smooth and easy. A ball lost in the burn is always treated, not as a lost ball, but as a ball in the burn, which involves, of course, more or less of an assumption. You are allowed to take another ball and drop it, with one stroke as penalty, just behind the burn. This concession has extended itself to other pieces of water upon other links. According to the strict rules, it is probably open to a vexatious objector to say that he does not believe the ball went into the burn, that it is lying in some hole on the green, and that, unless recovered, it must be treated as a lost ball. A purely vexatious appeal of this nature would assuredly be given against him by the committee of the club, who would certainly support the immemorial usage in preference to the letter of the law.

An amusing controversy of this kind occurred at Hoylake. A player's ball went down a rabbit-hole. It could be seen at the bottom of the hole, but all efforts to scoop it up with the iron were fruitless. The player was about to drop another ball behind the rabbit-hole, with the loss of one stroke, according to the rule for a ball found in a rabbit-hole. His opponent objected. 'You cannot do that,' he said. 'That is a lost ball.'

'Lost ball!' said the other. 'What do you mean by lost? Why, there it is!'

'Yes,' said the first, 'there it is, and you cannot get it from there. I say that a ball is lost, unless you can *gather* it.'

And the case was referred to the committee, who gave it against the player, who expressed his intention of never returning to play golf at Hoylake till he had trained a ferret to draw golf balls.

This was pressing the strictness of the law somewhat far; but there is another class of instances in which laxity of enforcement has led to considerable immorality—viz. with regard to the limits within which it is permissible to clear the putting-green of loose impediments. Twenty yards is the distance allowed by law; but we often see, in unimportant matches, players clearing the ground for a much larger radius. For the most part they do so thoughtlessly; though there are probably a certain number who sin with deliberation, salving their apologies for consciences by the thought that they are no worse than their neighbours. Now no one likes to be too severely critical about a yard or so, because it is the general custom not to be thus critical, and because he whom it especially behoves to be so—the player himself—is not careful. If it were but fully realised how great is the effect on the match of one long putt laid dead, which might not have been laid dead had the player taken his iron in hand to loft over the obstacle at twenty-one yards from the hole which he feloniously removed, there would not be this laxity of practice, and this sensitiveness about claiming the penalty for the rule transgressed. This rule, however, is not treated with the universal contempt, as if it were quite beneath the notice of a gentleman, which is evinced for the rule which refers to the touching of sand.

Broadly speaking, there is no breach of true etiquette in enforcing rules; the breaches of etiquette consist, for the most part, in the breaches of the rules.

There are certainly a good many golfers who consider themselves grossly ill-treated if they are asked to hole out a short putt; and, singularly enough, it is just those very golfers who most often justify the request, by missing the short putt, who are most indignant at it. You have a perfect right to ask a golfer to hole out every single putt; and no golfer ought to take offence at your so asking him. There are, of course, putts which it is positively vexatious to ask the veriest duffer to hole. Common sense ought, and does, draw a fair line in the matter. Perhaps one of the most offensive of all breaches of etiquette is committed by him who, after missing one of these little putts, says to his opponent, airily, 'Oh, I thought you'd have given me that!' It is a remark one is very apt to make in the irritation of the moment, and it is a remark which it well becomes the opponent, in the magnanimity of his triumph, to forgive; but we can only excuse it to ourselves in proportion as we feel a shameful repentance for it afterwards.

Sometimes the remark will take the yet more offensive, and usually mendacious, form of 'I thought you *had* given it to me.'

There is often a genuine misunderstanding about these short putts. Players are in the habit of giving them to each other, and are apt to assume them given before such is really the case; but in all these instances he who has missed should as cheerfully as possible, hold himself bound by the results of his own unwarranted assumption, and not try to shame his opponent into weak-minded liberality, or an uncomfortable feeling that his action may be held open to the charge of sharp practice. Neither is it altogether the best of form to ask your opponent (if the putt be one that can, conceivably at all, be missed) whether or no he expects you to hole it out. It is hardly a fair question, as it may put him in a dilemma between conceding you a stroke which he does not consider an absolute certainty or feeling that you may, perhaps, consider him a little severe upon you if he request you to play it. All these delicate questions would be avoided if it were established as a constant and universal custom that all putts should be holed in match play, as in medal play.

It is impossible to frame rules which shall cover every possible contingency, and there should be, between gentlemen, a certain amount of give and take, such as will smooth off the rough edges of injustice or absurdity which in exceptional circumstances appear under the strict letter of the law. In a match played a few years back, a dog seized the ball of one of the players, as it rolled over the putting-green, and bore it off into a carriage which was standing near. According to the written law it was incumbent on the player to play the ball out of the carriage, where the dog had deposited it. This, surely, was one of those exceptional cases wherein the courtesy of the opponent might have suggested a fairer alternative to the, in this case, unjust requirement of the generally fair rule.

In the amateur championship meeting of 1888, held at Prestwick, one of the competitors played his ball into a spectator's pocket. This was a 'lie' of which the rules took no special cognisance, and the only general rule applicable to the case, viz. that every ball shall be played where it lies, except as otherwise provided for, would have been strenuously contested by the spectator who owned the pocket. It was a case in which the mutual courtesy of the players had to step in to suggest some reasonable solution, which, in point of fact, was speedily forthcoming.

How such questions could have been determined had they arisen with respect to a scoring round, it is happily not for us to determine; but the safest rule is to play the stroke according to each of any reasonable suggestions, and to leave to the committee of the club under whose auspices the competition is being held the task of deciding as to which solution is the right and fair one. These are points which, as they arise from time to time in match play will probably, as we have said, be determined by the mutual courtesy of the players; but in any case it should be remembered that in these points of etiquette it is more graceful to concede than to claim, and should mutual courtesy fail to suggest a satisfactory solution, it is better to play under protest—that is to say, subject to a subsequent appeal to the committee—than to persist in a protracted wrangle.

Discussion of these points opens another subject which is ruled rather by custom than by written law, viz. the respect to be paid to the feelings and wagers of 'outside bettors'—that is, of parties who have no active part in the match, but have made bets upon it. The outside bettor is rather in the habit of assuming very high ground, speaking as if the fact of his having wagered a sum varying from a shilling upwards upon the result had bought over into his service for the time being the player whom he has honoured with his confidence. He is apt to feel himself somewhat injured if the man he is backing yields a point of merest courtesy to the opponent, and he seems to consider that by the mere fact of having wagered an

insignificant sum he has formed some subtle contract with the player so favoured, that he will play in accordance with his backer's fancy.

This way of looking at the case is so very absurd, that it is scarcely possible to state it in reasonable terms; but it is a view which largely prevails in the golfing world, that a player engaged in a big match has to consider, besides his own interests, the interests of any number of people who, without taking him into their confidence, have seen fit to put their money on him. It is practically equivalent to saying that the player becomes, for the time being, the property of the public. The public, at all events, deems itself entitled to grumble very audibly if the favourite of its choice does not struggle, in the public interest, to the bitter end. The golfer is, in fact, treated as if he were a race-horse.

The sooner the outside bettor can dispel from his mind this idea of proprietorship, the better for all concerned—for the game generally, and therefore, so far, for the bettor himself, and infinitely better, certainly, for the player in big matches. It is not, of course, as if the bettor had come to the player before the match, and had said to him, 'I am going to back you, and I hope you will play up.' This may, indeed, savour of impertinence, if backer and player are not well acquainted; but if the player acquiesce in the backer's proposition, thus stated, it undoubtedly places the matter upon a somewhat different footing. But, apart from some such previous colloquy, the bettor has no conceivable claim upon him whom he is so apt to regard as his *protégé*. Should the *protégé* be four up and five to play, and should it then for inscrutable reasons please him to give up the match, his backer may indeed, and undoubtedly will, level curses upon his fortune; but he has no standpoint whatever from which to find fault with the player. He is nothing to the player, he has made no contract with him, tacit or express; he has chosen to back him, with all his caprices and foibles, not as a machine, not even as a race-horse, but as a free-volitioned man.

There is a further injury that this false 'respect for outside bettors' inflicts upon the golfing world; it is not unfrequently made the cloak of little meannesses which would not be attempted were not the player thus given the opportunity of shifting his responsibility upon an absent or fictitious scapegoat. Thus: A questionable point is at issue, and the cunning and mean golfer thus clothes himself in the garb of magnanimity—'Well, if it was only myself to be considered, I would give it to you; but there is outside money on this match, and so I feel that I ought to claim my full rights;' and his full rights, in the mouth of this man, are very apt to encroach a little beyond their province, and to become the opponent's wrongs. No, no! let us put back the outside bettor into his proper place—that is to say, let us show him that he has no *locus standi* at all whence to dictate to the player he favours, but that he must consider his money to be laid out at his own peril—and thus will this one at least of the many occasions for petty meannesses be abolished.

Possibly next upon the little list of these delinquents against the un-written code of golf etiquette comes he who complains outrageously of the good luck which falls to his opponent's share. We all know that there is a great deal of luck in the game; but we also know, in moments of sober reflection, that on the whole the balance of luck, good or bad, for us or against us, hangs very nearly even. Complaints of one's own bad luck are in infinitely bad taste. But this class of offence is nothing compared with aggressive outcries against the good fortune of an opponent. If circum-stances can aggravate a sin so intrinsically evil, it is even more criminal to complain of the good luck that befalls him with whom you are partnered in a scoring competition than your antagonist in a hand-to-hand match. Generally recognised etiquette goes so far as a kind sympathy and inter-est in the efforts of your partner for the medal round. A community of trials makes you feel in a measure dependent upon each other like fellow knights errant in a world peopled with monsters in the shape of all the other competitors. Usually a man is generous enough to feel that, if he does not himself win, he would prefer the victory of his partner to that of any other; and when his own fortunes have become desperate, he will lend that partner all the comfort of his sympathy and moral support. This is less the result of the prospect of any little reflected glory than of a genuine fellow-feeling for one passing through the same vale of bunkers as oneself.

Nevertheless you cannot expect your partner's grief for your unmerited misfortunes to be as poignant as your own. This would be pushing altruism to an excess incompatible with that degree of egoism which Mr. Herbert Spencer assures us to be indispensable in this world in its present state of imperfection. But there may after all, lurk in this altruism, so far as it goes, a certain measure of intelligent egoism; for our partner may reasonably expect sympathy from us, when he falls into misfortune, in just the proportion in which he has shown sympathy for us. It is a casting of bread upon the waters which will not fail to bear fruit in return.

You may, without suspicion of your kind motives, weep with a weeping partner on a medal round a measure of tears which, if shed over the sorrows of an antagonist in a match, would inevitably suggest the tears attributed to the crocodile. Nobody ever believes that you are genuinely sorry for the ill-luck of a man you are trying to beat. It is very seldom that you will be able to appreciate that any bad luck at all falls to his share. Nevertheless it is expected of you to make some half-hearted expressions of sympathy. The antagonist will have no real faith in them, but for the time being, and failing other sympathy, he will be fain to find some solace to his woes in what he knows to be the fool's paradise of your consolations; and a certain show of this fictitious sorrow is imperatively demanded by all the kindly rules of etiquette.

It is no less necessary that you should put the utmost curb on yourself to restrain too loud and childish accusations of your own ill-luck. If you can but realise the fact noted above, that your adversary is not at all likely to be able, though with the best heart in the world, to appreciate the fact that your misfortunes are due to any other cause than lack of skill, your own self-respect will help you to restrain yourself. He cannot look upon your lamentations as otherwise than puerile, if he believes them causeless; and you will become both a better golfer, and a pleasanter, if you bring yourself to regard your unkind treatment at fortune's hands with equanimity; for not only is irritation an annoyance to all who come within its sphere, but re-acts disastrously upon the *morale* and game of its unhappy subject.

Truth is great; but it is sometimes indispensable to be petty and untruthful, and no man can possibly expect to bring a foursome to a happy issue who conducts his relations with his partner on perfectly truthful principles. Etiquette is here at one with the most elementary principles of good policy. You must always, during the match, try to give your partner in a foursome an impression that you are more than pleased with him. This impression is usually a very false one. It is scarcely possible not to give a partner credit for more than his fair share of the misfortunes of the joint firm. It is seldom that we can fairly realise the extent of our own contributions to them. Nevertheless good form and good policy compel us to convey an impression the very opposite of this to our partner. We must lead him to think that we are enchanted with him, and he will then play with all the confidence of one enchanted with himself. One might as well try to make love as to play a foursome on perfectly truthful principles.

The laws of etiquette prescribe for us a certain line of conduct not only to our partner in a foursome, and to our antagonist in a single, but also to our other neighbours on the golf links. One of the first things that the young golfer has to learn is that the prime requisitions for good golf generally are silence and immobility. If he be not careful to preserve these conditions, he will render good golf an impossibility not only within the circle of his own match, but also for the moment with any other of the matches which his own may chance to meet. He who rushes noisily up to a match, demanding with loud geniality 'how you stand,' irrespective of whether anyone is playing a stroke at the moment, is a nuisance who ought to be abolished from the golf links. At least there is no law of etiquette which should restrain the terms in which such an one should be answered. It seems scarcely necessary to state so universally observed a maxim as that it is your duty to stand perfectly motionless and silent while another member of your match is playing. Any breach of this first law of golfing etiquette is, happily, of rare occurrence. Offenders are of that class with which we determine 'never to play again.' But scarcely less obnoxious than the talker or the walker is he who rushes on wildly after his own ball immediately he has struck it, partially obstructing our line of aim, and obviously only coming to a halt, at the moment at which we deliver our stroke, out of compulsory respect to the barest exigencies of golfing courtesy.

The proper course of proceeding is this: to drive off first, if it be your honour, and then to stand clear of the teeing ground, behind your adversary's back. Do not stand close enough to him to annoy him, wherever you stand, and do not stand 'behind his eye,' as it is called—that is, in a line which would be a prolongation, backward, of the line of flight of the ball he is about to drive. Find out where he prefers you to stand, if he be a nervous player; but it is a safe rule to stand, motionless, behind his back. There are men in the golfing world—gentlemen, in some respects—who appear to be not above taking the petty advantage which annoyance to an opponent, caused by neglect of these little points, brings. It is not much use writing on points of etiquette for such as these; but there are also a very large number of golfers who, blessed with prosaic nervous systems themselves, thoughtlessly do not appreciate that others can be affected by the trifles of their surroundings. It is to these that one may say a word which may be gratefully received. They should bear in mind that to be forced to make a complaint upon any one of these trifling conditions is no less trying to a man of finely strung nerves than is the very circumstance of which he complains. Seek, then, to avoid giving him reason for making the complaint.

If it be your opponent's honour, it is far better that you should allow him to drive off from the tee before you think of teeing your own ball. Most teeing places are rather circumscribed, and even if you do not absolutely put down your ball upon its little eminence before your opponent has played, you are very apt to bother him as you crawl about the ground looking for the most likely spot. Let him have his shot in peace, and you may fairly expect him to show you equal courtesy in the happy event of your regaining the honour.

After all, what is courtesy but unselfishness and consideration of others? How grossly then does not he offend against every dictate of courtesy who scalps up the turf with his heavy iron, and leaves the 'divot' lying, an unsightly clod of earth, upon the sward! What shall we do to such as he, as, playing after him, our ball finds its way into the poor dumb mouth of a wound which he has thus left gaping, to call down upon him the vengeance of gods and men? In vain we print upon our rules that 'it is the first duty of every golfer to replace, or see replaced, turf cut out in the act of playing'—in vain we post up the ever-forgotten truism that 'golf is not agriculture,' with or without the addendum suggested by some cynical landlord—'though both are games of chance.' No—in spite of all our efforts, the scalps and divots still lie unsightly on the links, and 'nobody seems one penny the worse,' though we curse with bell and book and niblick the sacrilegious villain who left the raw, gaping wound on the sacred soil. No golfer is worthy of the name who does not put back his divot. It is no trouble, and is indeed rather amusing, as we watch how, like a piece of a Chinese puzzle, the divot fits back accurately into the chasm from which it was carved. A divot well replaced is, in most conditions of the ground, as a divot that has never been cut.

There is a rule forbidding players to drive off their tee-shot before the parties in front shall have played off their second—containing the obvious corollary that they are permitted to do so as soon as ever those in front shall have played. But if this corollary be acted upon without the necessary limitations placed upon it by customary etiquette, the rates of life insurance for the short driving, obese school of golfers would be high indeed. Two slashing youngsters coming behind them would imperil the valuable lives of old gentlemen off every tee. In a crowded state of the green, where the parties in front, however slow they be, are well up with the players in front of them again, all etiquette and custom requires that those in front should be allowed to travel well out of range before the legitimate privilege of the players behind, to drive after them, be exercised. We say in a crowded state of the green, and when the parties in front are well up with those again in front of them; for when this is not the case, when a certain slow-going match has a free space of a hole's length, or more, before them, when they are retarding the progress of all behind, then etiquette does not prescribe any such forbearance. The requirements of etiquette then fall upon the slowcoaches—that they shall allow the faster-going singles or foursomes to pass them by. Otherwise they have no just ground for complaint if they find the tee-shots of those behind them whizzing past their ears, after they have played their seconds, in such wise that they will probably deem it the part of prudence, no less than of courtesy, to let their swifter pursuers go before them. Yet the pursuers should in this case reflect that this concession is an act of courtesy, and accept it with due thanks.

In no case and under no circumstances save where a ball is lost, and permission obtained, is it excusable to drive into a party along the green, on the putting-green, or before they have played their seconds. Where the parties behind have infringed this great commandment more than once during a round, any means combining an insistence upon your rights with adequate courtesy to the offenders is beyond our ingenuity to suggest; but it may perhaps be urged that players thus offending have forfeited all claim to courteous dealing.

There is a certain point in regard to match play which has been the cause of considerable exasperation, upon occasions. It occurs more often, perhaps, than elsewhere upon the links of St. Andrews, where caddies, greens, and winds are keen. There the canny caddie upon a windy day will station himself at the hole in such manner as to shield the wind off the ball of the master for whom he carries. Not content with that, he will shuffle after it as it is propelled by the wind and with feet close together coax it, so far as possible, to travel in the way it should go, with all the art of a curler. Should the ball be over-strongly putted, and the wind be opposed to its course, he will jump aside to allow the full current to blow against it. This can, of course, be only done by the caddie who is standing at the hole. There occurs often, therefore, some competition between the rival caddies as to which shall have this post. There results discussion, and some unpleasantness. Now the proper etiquette is that the caddie of him whose turn it is not to play should stand at the hole; for it is in the interest of the non-player that the caddie, who can move aside, stands at the hole in lieu of the flag-stick, which the player might gain an advantage by striking. If this rule then be adhered to, there can be no opportunity for the caddie thus 'favouring' the ball; for even the least scrupulous of them do not go the length of attempting to turn the wind to the disadvantage of the ball of their master's antagonist. And as for this shielding of the wind off the ball, we would say that it is altogether opposed to the true spirit of the game, which consists in the combining of skill of hand with calculation of just such conditions of wind, &c, as this virtually unfair conspiracy between master and caddie tends to modify. In the abstract we believe that all gentlemen condemn the practice, though in actual course of play partly from a dislike to check the zeal shown by the caddie in their interests, they often permit it without rebuke.

The relations between partners in foursomes are governed entirely by a tacit code of etiquette. The better player should be on his guard against any show of patronage in his advice; the inferior partner should show proper contrition for his misdoings, but should not be in a continual state of apology as if a mistake was with him an exception. The amount of conversation between partners should be determined by the inclination of him who wishes to talk least. The prior claim is that of the negative blessing of silence; and this is true no less in your partnership with another in a foursome than in regard to your relations with an opponent in a match.

More especially is it incumbent upon spectators to preserve silence and immobility, and it is in the worst taste for them to come forward and offer unsolicited and probably unwelcome conversation with any of the players in the intervals of the strokes. Spectators should always remember what is due to those who are affording the spectacle; but it is no less true that a duty of courtesy is owed by the players to those who pay them the compliment of being interested in their performance. Moreover, golf links are commonly public places. The spectator has as good a right there as the most finished golfer, and the latter should not forget that if the former defer to the delicate requirements of his nervous system, it is but an act of courtesy, and should be received with the courteous acknowledgment due to such.

Modesty is a virtue, but the mock modesty, the pride which apes humility, was an occasion of much mirth to Satan; and it is a breach, rather than an observance, of etiquette, and even of honesty, to so underrate your game as to gain an unfair advantage in arranging the conditions of a match. Do not tell a player whom you have defeated that he would be sure to beat you next time. He may think so, but he will not believe that you do, and the remark partakes of the nature of an insult to his understanding.

Finally, there are certain points of etiquette, such as those connected with dress, which differ, locally, and you should ever endeavour to conform yourself to the etiquette of the links on which you may be playing. Thus, on some links it is especially requested, as a means of warning the public of the approach of danger, that the golfers should wear red coats. It is but fair towards the local members of the club whose guest or visiting member you temporarily are that you should avail yourself for the nonce in the uniform of the danger-signal. Otherwise, any damage inflicted on the unwary passer-by by your approach unheralded save by the hard flying golf-ball will be laid at the innocent door of the club, to the injury, in the opinion of the vulgar, of its local *habitués*.

GOLF FOR DUFFERS

SIR HENRY RIDER HAGGARD

'Oh! well with thee, my brother,
Who hast not known the game,
When early gleams of gladness
Aye set in after sadness;
And still the end is other,
Far other, than the aim
Oh! well with thee my brother
Who hast not known the game.

So, if memory does not deceive, runs the inspired lay of the bard of
the *Saturday Review*. It is of Golf that he sings, not of Nap or Poker,
or Pitch-farthing, or any other exciting, but deceitful and deleterious
sport. Many have sung and written of it of late, and soon the searcher
of bibliographies will find the titles of a multitude of works under the
heading "Golf". "What," said a friend to this writer the other day, as he
took up Mr Horace Hutchinson's contribution to the Badminton Library,
"what, all that great book about hitting a little ball with a stick!" But this

and other learned works are written by "golfers of degree", past masters in the art of "hitting the little ball". It yet remains for the subject to be treated from the other side, from the point of view, and for the comfort of, the Duffer. This, the present writer considers himself qualified to do, and for the best of reasons, he wots of none who can play worse than he.

Now as all men know, or ought to know, the game of golf consists in striking a small ball of some hard material into a series of holes—generally eighteen in number—with a variety of wooden and iron-headed clubs, which experience has proved to be the best adapted to the purpose. At first sight this looks easy enough. Indeed, strange as it may seem, the beginner does sometimes find it fairly easy—for the first time or two. He takes the driver with that beautiful confidence which is born of ignorance; hits at the ball somehow; and it goes—somehow; not a full drive of 180 yards or so, indeed, but still a very respectable distance. Arrived safely in the neighbourhood of the first green, he is told that he must putt the ball into a hole about the size of a jam pot. Perhaps he does it at the first attempt, and from a distance whence an experienced player would be quite content to lay his ball near the hole. Then he remarks that "it seems pretty easy". Probably his adversary will assent with a sardonic smile, and wait for the revenge that time will surely bring. He need not wait long; it may be today or tomorrow; but an hour will come when he will see the triumphant tyro scarcely able to hit the ball, much less to send it flying through the air, or wriggling sinuously into the putting-hole, perhaps from a dozen yards away. He will see him cutting up huge lumps of turf behind it—this diversion is called "agriculture"—or smiting it on the head with such force as to drive it into the ground, or "topping" it, so that it rolls meekly into the nearest bush, or "pulling" it into the dyke on the left, or "toeing" it into the sand-bunker on the right; doing everything in short, that he should not do, and leaving undone all those things he should do. For days and weeks he will see him thus employed, and then, if he is a revengeful person, he will take some particularly suitable occasion, when the ball has been totally missed three or four times on the tee, say, to ask, if he, the tyro, "really thinks golf so very easy".

Let none be deceived—as golf is the most delightful game in the world, so it is also the most difficult. It is easier even for a person who has never handled a gun to learn to become a really good shot than for him in who has not lifted cleek or driver to bloom into a golfer of the first water. To the young, indeed, all things are possible, but to few of those who begin after thirty will it ever be given to excel. By dint of hard practice and care, in the course of years they may become second- or third-rate players, but for the most part their names will never appear as competitors in the great matches of the world of golf. To begin with, but a small proportion will ever acquire the correct "swing", that is the motion of the arms and club necessary to drive the ball far and sure. We have all heard of and seen the "St Andrews Swing", but how many can practise it with the results common at St Andrews and elsewhere among first-class players? When success attends in the swing, then the ball is topped or heeled, and when the ball goes off well, then the less said about the swing the better. It is instructive to watch any gathering of golfers made up for the most part of players who have not been bred to the game. The majority of them are content with the half-swing; they do not lift the club over the shoulder. If asked their reasons, they will say with truth, that there is only some thirty yards difference between a drive from a half and a drive from a full swing, and that the former is far easier and more certain than the latter. Quite so, but it is not the game; and he who aspires to learn to play the game will prefer to swing full and fail gloriously rather than to attain a moderate success in this fashion. But the swing is only one of a hundred arts that have to be learned before a man can pretend to play golf. Till he has mastered these, or a goodly proportion of them, he does not play, he only knocks a ball along, a humble amusement with which alas! most of us must needs be content for the term of our natural lives. Golf, like Art, is a goddess whom we must woo from early youth if we would win her; we must even be born to her worship. No other skill will avail us here, the most brilliant cricketer does not necessarily make a first-class golfer; on the contrary he must begin by forgetting his cricket; he must not lift himself on his toes and *hit* like a batsman making a drive. Doubtless, the eye which helps a man to excel in shooting, at tennis, or cricket, will advantage him here to some extent, but, on the other hand, he will have much to forget, much to unlearn. He must clear his mind of all superstitions; he must humble his pride in the sand, and begin with a new heart and a meek spirit, well knowing that failure is his goal. For he will never, never learn to play—it is folly to expect otherwise. Each evening he will see his mistakes and avow amendment to himself and to his partner, and yet, when the morrow is done, will come home murmuring:

It was last night I swore to thee
That fond impossibility.

Impossibility! For the middle-aged duffer this word sums it all.

It may be said, Then why have anything to do with such a hopeless sport? Let him who asks play golf once, and he will understand why. He will go on playing because he must. Drink, opium, gambling—from the clutches of all these it is possible to escape, but from, golf, never! Has anybody ever seen a man who gave up golf? Certainly dead donkeys are more common than these. Be once beguiled to the investment of five shillings in a driver, and abandon hope. Your fate is sure. The driver will be broken in a week, but what will you be? You are doomed for life, or till limbs and eyesight fail you—doomed to strive continually to conquer an unconquerable game. Undoubtedly golf is not so innocent as it seems, it has dangerous possibilities. Can we not easily conceive a man middle-aged, happy, prosperous, regular in his attendance at business, and well satisfied with an annual outing at the seaside? And can we not picture him again after golf has laid its hold upon him? He is no longer happy, for he plays not better and better, but worse and worse. Prosperity has gone, for the time that he should give to work he devotes to the pernicious sport. He has quarrelled with his wife, for has he not broken all the drawing-room china in the course of practising his "swing" on Sundays, and estranged all his friends, who can no longer endure to be bored with his eternal talk of golf? As for the annual outing, it does not satisfy him at all; cost what it will, he needs be on the links five days out of every seven. There is no need to follow him further, or we might dwell on the scene, as yet far off, for this poison is slow, when battered, broken, bankrupt, his very clubs in pawn for a few shillings, he perambulates some third-rate links, no longer as a player, but in the capacity of a superannuated caddie. Here is matter of romance indeed: the motive is generously presented to any novelist weary of portraying the effects of drink and cards. "The Golfers End; or The Demon Driver", should prove an effective title.

And yet even for those who will never really master it, the game is worth the caddie. To begin with, it has this startling merit, the worse you play the more sport you get. If the fisherman slacks his line, and lets off the salmon, or the shooter misses the only woodcock clean, or the batsman is bowled first ball off a lob, there is an end to those particular delights. But when the golfer tops his ball, or trickles it into a furze-bush, or lands it in a sand-bunker, it is but the beginning of joy, for there it lies patiently awaiting a renewal of his maltreatment. His sport is only limited by the endurance of his muscle, or, perchance, of his clubs, and at the end of the round, whereas the accomplished player will have enjoyed but eighty or a hundred strokes, the duffer can proudly point to a total of twice that number. Moreover he has hurt no one, unless it be the caddie, or the feelings of his partner in a foursome. By the way, the wise duffer should make a point of playing alone, or search out an opponent of equal incapacity; he should not be led into foursomes with members of the golfing aristocracy, that is if he has a proper sense of pride, and a desire not to look ridiculous. He should even avoid the company of members of his own family on these occasions, lest it chance that they lose respect for a man and a father who repeatedly tries to hit a small ball with a stick with the most abject results, and is even betrayed by his failure into the use of language foreign to the domestic hearth. Here is advice for him who has been bitten of this mania. Let him select a little-frequented island links, and practise on them studiously about two hundred days a year for three years or so, either alone, or in the company of others of his own kidney. By this time, unless he is even less gifted than the majority of beginners, he will probably be able to play after a modest and uncertain fashion. Then let him resort to some more fashionable green, and having invested in an entirely new set of clubs, pose before the world as a novice to the game, for thus he will escape the scorn of men. But let him not reverse the process. Thus he who, in his ignorance or pride, takes the train to Wimbledon, and in the presence of forty or fifty masters of the art, solemnly misses the ball three times on the first tee, may perchance never recover from the shock.

Nor will all those years of effort and failure be without their own reward. He will have tramped his gorsey common till every bush and sod is eloquent to him of some past adventure. This is the short green, that by some marvellous accident he once did in one, driving his ball from the tee even into the little far-away putting-hole. Here is a spot which he can never pass without a shudder, where he nearly killed his opponent's caddie, that scornful boy who, for many days accustomed to see him topping and putting his ball along from green to green, remained unmoved by his warning shouts of "fore", till one unlucky hour, when by some strange chance he drove full and fair. Crack! went the ball from his brassie. Crack! it came full on the youthful head thirty yards away and then a yell of agony, and a sickening vision of heels kicking wildly in the air, and presently a sound of clinking silver coin. There, too is the exact place, when for the first (and perchance the last) time he drove over the beetling cliff, and out of the great bunker, the long way too, not the ladies' way—a feat not often accomplished by the skilful. A hundred and ninety-one yards that drive measured, though it is true an envious and long-legged friend who had forced his own ball an inch deep into the sand of the cliff, stepped it at a hundred and eighty-four. He can never forget that supreme moment, it will be with him till his dying hour. Our first large salmon safely brought to bank, a boy's first rocketing pheasant, clean and coolly killed, these afford memories that draw as near to perfect happiness as anything in this imperfect world, but it may be doubted if they can compare to the sense of utter triumph, of ecstatic exhilaration with which, for the first time, we watch the ball, propelled by our unaided skill, soar swiftly out of the horrid depths of an hitherto unconquered bunker. There is a tale—a true one, or it would not be produced here—that, being true, shall be told as an example of noble patience fitly crowned and celebrated.

A wanderer musing in a rugged place was, of a sudden, astonished to see and hear an old gentleman, bearing a curiously shaped stick, walking up and down and chanting the *Nunc Dimittis* as he walked. Moved by curiosity, he came to the aged singer and asked,

"Why do you chant the *Nunc Dimittis* on the edge of this gulf?"

"For this reason, sir," he answered, pointing to the golf-ball that lay upon the turf. "For seventeen years and more I have attempted almost daily to drive a ball across that bunker, and now I have succeeded for the first time. The object of my life is attained, and I am ready to die. That, sir, is why I sing."

Then the wanderer took off his hat, and went away, marvelling at the infatuation of golfers.

It need scarcely be said that the foregoing remarks apply to and are intended for, the consideration of male duffers. It would have been agreeable to extend them to the other sex, but space demands brevity. Golf is a man's game, but here, too, women assert their rights. Not that they are all fond of it; by no means. On the contrary a young lady has been heard, and recently, to express her decided opinion that a law should be passed against its practice during the summer months. This was a lawn-tennis young lady. And another informed this writer that she held golf to be a "horrid game, where everybody goes off like mad, glaring at a little ball, without a word for anybody." Others, it is true, attack the question in a different spirit—they play, and play well. It is curious to observe their style; that they do everything wrong is obvious even to the male incompetent. They stand in front of the ball, they swing their club wildly in preparation, and finally bring it down with an action that suggests reminiscences of a cook jointing veal; but the ball goes, for these young ladies have a good eye and a strong arm. Perhaps no woman player could ever attain to a really first-rate standard, for however vigorous she may be she cannot drive like a man. But with practice there seems to be no reason why she should not approach and putt as well as any man; and certainly she can talk golfing-shop with equal persistency.

And now this duffer will conclude with a word of advice to the world at large—that they should forthwith enter the noble fraternity of duffers, of those who try to play golf and cannot. They will never succeed—at least, not ten per cent of them will succeed. They will knock balls from green to green, and reverence Mr Horace Hutchinson more truly and deeply than the great ones of the earth are generally reverenced; that is all. But they will gain health and strength in the pursuit of a game which has all the advantages of a sport without its expense and cruelty; they will note many a changing light on land and sea; and last, but not least, for several hours a week they will altogether forget their worries, together with Law, Art, Literature or whatever wretched occupation the Fates have given it to them to follow in the pursuit of their daily bread. For soon—alas! too soon—the votary of golf—that great gift of Scotland to the world—will own but one ambition but rarely to be attained. Thus, he will sing with the poet:

> *Who list may grasp at greatness,*
> *Who list may woo and wive;*
> *Wealth, wisdom, power, position—*
> *These make not my ambition.*
> *Nay but I pray for straightness,*
> *And do desire to drive.*
> *Who list may grasp at greatness,*
> *Who list may woo and wive.'*

GENTLEMEN, YOU CAN'T GO THROUGH!

CHARLES E. VAN LOAN

I

There has been considerable argument about it—even a mention of ethics—though where ethics figures in this case is more than I know. I'd like to take a flat-footed stance as claiming that the end justified the means. Saint George killed the Dragon, and Hercules mopped up the Augean stables, but little Wally Wallace—one hundred and forty-two pounds in his summer underwear—did a bigger job and a better job when the betting was odds-on-and-write-your-own-ticket that it couldn't be done. I wouldn't mind heading a subscription to present him with a gold medal about the size of a soup plate, inscribed as follows, to wit and viz.:

W. W. Wallace—He Put the Fore in Foursome.

Every golfer who ever conceded himself a two-foot putt because he was afraid he might miss it has sweated and suffered and blasphemed in the wake of a slow foursome. All the clubs that I have ever seen—and I've travelled a bit—are cursed with at least one of these Creeping Pestilences which you observe mostly from the rear.

You're a golfer, of course, and you know the make-up of a slow foursome as well as I do: Four nice old gentlemen, prominent in business circles, church members, who remember it even when they top a tee shot, pillars of society, rich enough to be carried over the course in palanquins, but too proud to ride, too dignified to hurry, too meek to argue except among themselves, and too infernally selfish to stand aside and let the younger men go through. They take nine practice swings before hitting a shot, and then flub it disgracefully; they hold a prayer meeting on every putting green and a *post-mortem* on every tee, and a rheumatic snail could give them a flying start and beat them out in a fifty-yard dash. Know 'em? What golfer doesn't?

But nobody knows why it is that the four slowest players in every club always manage to hook up in a sort of permanent alliance. Nobody knows why they never stage their creeping contests on the off days when the course is clear. Nobody knows why they always pick the sunniest afternoons, when the locker room is full of young men dressing in a hurry. Nobody knows why they bolt their luncheons and scuttle out to the first tee, nor where that speed goes as soon as they drive and start down the course. Nobody knows why they refuse to walk any faster than a bogged mooley cow. Nobody knows why they never look behind them. Nobody knows why they never hear any one yell "Fore!" Nobody knows why they are so dead set against letting any one through.

Everybody knows the fatal effect of standing too long over the ball, all dressed up with nowhere to go. Everybody knows of the tee shots that are slopped and sliced and hooked; of the indecision caused by the long wait before playing the second; of the change of clubs when the first choice was the correct one; of the inevitable penalty exacted by loss of temper and mental pose. Everybody knows that a slow foursome gives the Recording Angel a busy afternoon, and leaves a sulphurous haze over an entire course. But the aged reprobates who are responsible for all this trouble—do they care how much grief and rage and bitterness simmers in their wake? You think they do? Think again. Golf and Business are the only games they have ever had time to learn, and one set of rules does for both. The rest of the world may go hang! Golf is a serious matter with these hoary offenders, and they manage to make it serious for everybody behind them—the fast-walking, quick-swinging fellows who are out for a sweat and a good time and lose both because the slow foursome blocks the way.

Yes, you recognize the thumb-nail sketch—it is the slow foursome which infests your course; the one which you find in front of you when you go visiting. You think that four men who are inconsiderate enough to ruin your day's sport and ruffle your temper ought to be disciplined, called up on the carpet, taken in hand by the Greens Committee. You think they are the worst ever—but wait! You are about to hear of the golfing renegades known as the Big Four, who used to sew us up twice a week as regularly as the days came round; you are about to hear of Elsberry J. Watlington, and Colonel Jim Peck, and Samuel Alexander Peebles, and W. Cotton Hamilton—world's champions in the Snail Stakes, undisputed holders of the Challenge Belt for Practice Swinging, and undefeated catch-as-catch-can loiterers on the Putting Green.

Six months ago we would have backed Watlington, Peck, Peebles and Hamilton against the wide world, bet dollars against your dimes and allowed you to select your own stakeholders, timekeepers and judges. That's how much confidence we had in the Big Four. They were without doubt and beyond argument the slowest and most exasperating quartette of obstructionists that ever laid their middle-aged stomachs behind the line of a putt.

Do I hear a faint murmur of dissent? Going a little strong, am I? All right, glad you mentioned it, because we may as well settle this question of supremacy here and now.

To save time, I will admit that your foursome is slower than Congress and more irritating than the Senate. Permit me to ask you one question: Going back over the years, can you recall a single instance when your slow foursome allowed you to play through? . . . A lost ball, was it? . . . Well, anyway, you got through them. . . .Thank you, and your answer puts you against the ropes. I will now knock you clear out of the ring with one well-directed statement of fact. Tie on your bonnet good and tight and listen to this: The Big Four held up our course for seven long and painful years, and during that period of time they never allowed any one to pass them, lost ball or no lost ball.

That stops you, eh? I rather thought it would. It stopped us twice a week.

II

Visitors used to play our course on Wednesdays and Saturdays—our big days—and then sit in the lounging room and try hard to remember that they were our guests. There were two questions which they never failed to ask:

"Don't they ever let anybody through?"

And then:

"How long has this been going on?"

When we answered them truthfully they shook their heads, looked out of the windows, and told us how much better their clubs were handled. Our course was all right—they had to say that much in fairness. It was well trapped and bunkered, and laid out with an eye to the average player; the fair greens were the best in the state; the putting greens were like velvet; the holes were sporty enough to suit anybody; but—And then they looked out of the window again.

You see, the trouble was that the Big Four practically ran the club as they liked. They had financed it in its early days, and as a reward had been elected to almost everything in sight. We used to say that they shook dice to see who should be president and so forth, and probably they did. They might as well have settled it that way as any other, for the annual election and open meeting was a joke.

It usually took place in the lounging room on a wet Saturday afternoon. Somebody would get up and begin to drone through a report of the year's activities. Then somebody else would make a motion and everybody would say "Ay!" After that the result of the annual election of officers would be announced. The voting members always handed in the printed slips which they found on the tables, and the ticket was never scratched—it would be Watlington, Peck, Peebles and Hamilton all the way. The only real question would be whether or not the incoming president of the club would buy a drink for all hands. If it was Peck's turn the motion was lost.

As a natural result of this sort of thing the Big Four never left the saddle for an instant. Talk about perpetuation in office—they had it down to a fine point. They were always on the Board of Directors; they saw to it that control of the Greens Committee never slipped out of their hands; they had two of the three votes on the House Committee, and no outsider was even considered for treasurer. They were dictators with a large D, and nobody could do a thing about it.

If a mild kick was ever made or new blood suggested, the kicker was made to feel like an ingrate. Who started the club anyway? Who dug up the money? Who swung the deal that put the property in our hands? Why, Watlington, Peck, Peebles and Hamilton, to be sure! Could any one blame them for wanting to keep an eye on the organisation? Cer-tain-ly not. The Big Four had us bluffed, bulldozed, buffaloed, licked to a whisper.

Peck, Peebles and Hamilton were the active heads of the Midland Manufacturing Company, and it was pretty well known that the bulk of Watlington's fortune was invested in the same enterprise. Those who knew said they were just as ruthless in business as they were in golf—quite a strong statement.

They seemed to regard the Sundown Golf and Country Club as their private property and we were welcome to pay dues and amuse ourselves five days a week, but on Wednesdays and Saturdays we were not to infringe on the sovereign rights of the Big Four.

They never entered any of the club tournaments, for that would have necessitated breaking up their foursome. They always turned up in a body, on the tick of noon, and there was an immediate scramble to beat them to Number One tee. Those who lost out stampeded over to Number Ten and played the second nine first. Nobody wanted to follow them; but a blind man, playing without a caddie, couldn't have helped but catch up with them somewhere on the course.

If you wonder why the club held together, you have only to recall the story of the cow-puncher whose friend beckoned him away from the faro layout to inform him that the game was crooked.

"Hell!" said the cow-puncher. "I know that; but—it's the only game in town, ain't it?"

The S. G. & C. C. was the only golf club within fifty miles.

III

When Wally Wallace came home from college he blossomed out as a regular member of the club. He had been a junior member before, one of the tennis squad.

Wally is the son of old Hardpan Wallace, of the Trans-Pacific outfit—you may have heard of him—and the sole heir to more millions than he will ever be able to spend; but we didn't hold this against the boy. He isn't the sort that money can spoil, with nothing about him to remind you of old Hardpan, unless it might be a little more chin than he really needs.

Wally's first act as a full-fledged member of the club was to qualify for the James Peck Annual Trophy—a pretty fair sort of cup, considering the donor.

He turned in a nice snappy eighty-one, which showed us that a college education had not been wasted on him, and also caused several of the Class-A men to sit up a bit and take notice.

He came booming through to the semi-finals with his head up and his tail over the dashboard. It was there that he ran into me. Now I am no Jerry Travers, but there are times when I play to my handicap, which is ten, and I had been going fairly well. I had won four matches—one of them by default. Wally had also won four matches, but the best showing made against him was five down and four to go. His handicap was six, so he would have to start me two up; but I had seen enough of his game to know that I was up against the real thing, and would need a lot of luck to give the boy anything like a close battle. He was a strong, heady match player, and if he had a weakness the men whom he had defeated hadn't been able to spot it. Altogether it wasn't a very brilliant outlook for me; but, as a matter of fact, I suppose no ten-handicap man ever ought to have a brilliant outlook. It isn't coming to him. If he has one it is because the handicapper has been careless.

Under our rules a competitor in a club tournament has a week in which to play his man, and it so happened that we agreed on Wednesday for our meeting. Wally called for me in his new runabout, and we had lunch together—I shook him and stuck him for it, and he grinned and remarked that a man couldn't be lucky at everything. While we were dressing he chattered like a magpie, talking about everything in the world but golf, which was a sign that he wasn't worrying much. He expected easy picking, and under normal conditions he would have had it.

We left the first tee promptly at one-forty-five P. M., our caddies carrying the little red flags which demand the right of way over everything. I might have suggested starting at Number Ten if I had thought of it, but to tell the truth I was a wee mite nervous and was wondering whether I had my drive with me or not. You know how the confounded thing comes and goes. So we started at Number One, and my troubles began. Wally opened up on me with a four-four-three, making the third hole in a stroke under par, and when we reached the fourth tee we were all square and my handicap was gone.

It was on the fourth tee that we first began to notice signs of congestion ahead of us. One foursome had just driven off and beckoned us to come through, another was waiting to go, and the fair green on the way to the fifth looked like the advance of the Mexican standing army.

"Somebody has lost the transmission out of his wheel chair," said Wally. "Well, we should worry—we've got the red flags and the right of way. Fore!" And he proceeded to smack a perfect screamer down the middle of the course—two hundred and fifty yards if it was an inch. I staggered into one and laid my ball some distance behind his, but on the direct line to the pin. Then we had to wait a bit while another foursome putted out.

"There oughtn't to be any congestion on a day like this," said Wally. "Must be a bunch of old men ahead."

"It's the Big Four,"said I. "Watlington, Peck, Peebles and Hamilton. They always take their time."

From where we were we could see the seventh and eighth fair greens. There wasn't a player in sight on either one.

"Good Lord!" said Wally. "They've got the whole United States wide open ahead of 'em. They're not holding their place on the course."

"They never do," said I, and just then the foursome moved off the putting green.

"Give her a ride, old top!" said Wally.

I claim that my second shot wasn't half bad—for a ten-handicap man. I used a brassy and reached the green about thirty feet from the pin, but the demon Wally pulled a mid-iron out of his bag, waggled it once or twice, and then made my brassy look sick. When we reached the top of the hill, there was his ball ten feet from the cup. I ran up, playing it safe for a par four, but Wally studied the roll of the green for about ten seconds—and dropped a very fat three. He was decent enough to apologise.

"I'm playing over my head," said he.

I couldn't dispute it—two threes on par fours might well be over anybody's head. One down and fourteen to go; it had all the earmarks of a massacre.

We had quite an audience at the fifth tee—two foursomes were piled up there, cursing. "What's the matter, gentlemen?" asked Wally. "Can't you get through?"

"Nobody can get through," said Billy Williams. "It's the Big Four."

"But they'll respect the red flags, won't they?"

It was a perfectly natural question for a stranger to ask—and Wally was practically a stranger, though most of the men knew who he was. It brought all sorts of answers.

"You think they will? I'll bet you a little two to one, no limit, that they're all colour-blind!"

"Oh, yes, they'll let you through!"

"They'll ask you to come through—won't they, Billy? They'll insist on it, what?"

"They're full of such tricks!"

Wally was puzzled. He didn't quite know what to make of it. "But a red flag," said he, "gives you the right of way."

"Everywhere but here," said Billy Williams.

"But in this case it's a rule!" argued Wally.

"Those fellows in front make their own rules."

"But the Greens Committee—" And this was where everybody laughed. Wally stooped and teed his ball.

"Look here," said he, "I'll bet you anything you like that they let us through. Why, they can't help themselves!"

"You bet that they'll let you through of their own accord?" asked Ben Ashley who never has been known to pass up a plain cinch.

"On our request to be allowed to pass," said Wally.

"If you drive into 'em without their permission you lose," stipulated Ben.

"Right!" said Wally.

"Got you for a dozen balls!" said Ben.

"Anybody else want some of it?" asked Wally.

Before he got off the tee he stood to lose six dozen balls; but his nerve was unshaken and he slammed out another tremendous drive. I sliced into a ditch and away we went, leaving a great deal of promiscuous kidding behind us. It took me two shots to get out at all, and Wally picked up another hole on me.

Two down—murder!

On the sixth tee we ran into another mass meeting of malcontents. Old Man Martin, our prize grouch, grumbled a bit when we called attention to our red flags.

"What's the use?" said he. "You're on your way but you ain't going anywhere. Might just as well sit down and take it easy. Watlington has got a lost ball, and the others have gone on to the green so's nobody can get through. Won't do you a bit of good to drive, Wally. There's two four-somes hung up over the hill now, and they'll be right there till Watlington finds that ball. Sit down and be sociable."

"What'll you bet that we don't get through?" demanded Wally, who was beginning to show signs of irritation.

"Whatever you got the most of, sonny—provided you make the bet this way: they got to let you through. Of course you might drive into 'em or walk through 'em, but that ain't being done—much."

"Right! The bet is that they let us through. One hundred fish."

Old Martin cackled and turned his cigar round and round in the cor-ner of his mouth—a wolf when it comes to a cinch bet.

"Gosh! Listen to our banty rooster crow! Want another hundred, son-ny?"

"Yes—grandpa!" said Wally, and sent another perfect drive soaring up over the hill.

Number Six is a long hole, and the ordinary player never attempts to carry the cross-bunker on his second. I followed with a middling-to-good shot, and we bade the congregation farewell.

"It's ridiculous!" said Wally as we climbed the hill. "I never saw a foursome yet that wouldn't yield to a red flag, or one that wouldn't let a twosome through—if properly approached. And we have the right of way over everything on the course. The Greens Committee—"

"Is composed," said I, "of Watlington, Peck and Peebles—three mem-bers of the Big Four. They built the club, they run the club, and they have never been known to let anybody through. I'm sorry, Wally but I'm afraid you're up against it."

The boy stopped and looked at me.

"Then those fellows behind us," said he, "were betting on a cinch, eh?"

"It was your proposition," I reminded him.

"So it was," and he grinned like the good game kid he is. "The Greens Committee, eh? 'Hast thou appealed unto Caesar? unto Caesar shalt thou go.' I'm a firm believer in the right method of approach. They wouldn't have the nerve—"

"They have nerve enough for anything," said I, and dropped the subject. I didn't want him to get the idea that I was trying to argue with him and upset his game. One foursome was lying down just over the hill; the other was piled up short of the bunker. Watlington had finally found his ball and played onto the green. The others, of course, had been standing round the pin and holding things up for him.

I took an iron on my second and played short, intending to pitch over the bunker on my third. Wally used a spoon and got tremendous height and distance. His ball carried the bunker, kicked to the right and stopped behind a sand-trap. It was a phenomenal shot, and with luck on the kick would have gone straight to the pin.

I thought the Big Four would surely be off the green by the time I got up to my ball, but no, Peck was preparing to hole a three-foot putt. Any ordinary dub would have walked up to that pill and tapped it in, but that wasn't Peck's style. He got down on all fours and sighted along the line to the hole. Then he rose, took out his handkerchief, wiped his hands carefully, called for his putter and took an experimental stance, tramping about like a cat "making bread" on a woollen rug.

"Look at him!" grunted Wally. "You don't mind if I go ahead to my ball? It won't bother you?"

"Not in the least," said I.

"I want to play as soon as they get out of the way," he explained.

The Colonel's first stance did not suit him, so he had to go all through the tramping process again. When he was finally satisfied, he began swinging his putter back and forth over the ball, like the pendulum of a grandfather's clock—ten swings, neither more nor less. Could any one blame Wally for boiling inside?

After the three-footer dropped—he didn't miss it, for a wonder—they all gathered round the hole and pulled out their cards. Knowing each other as well as they did, nobody was trusted to keep the score.

"Fore!" called Wally.

They paid not the slightest attention to him, and it was fully half a minute before they ambled leisurely away in the direction of the seventh tee.

I played my pitch shot, with plenty of back-spin on it, and stopped ten or twelve feet short of the hole. Wally played an instant later, a mashie shot intended to clear the trap, but he had been waiting too long and was burning up with impatience. He topped the ball, hit the far edge of the sand trap and bounced back into a bad lie. Of course I knew why he had been in such a hurry—he wanted to catch the Big Four on the seventh tee. His niblick shot was too strong, but he laid his fifth dead to the hole, giving me two for a win. Just as a matter of record, let me state that I canned a nice rainbow putt for a four. A four on Number Six is rare.

"Nice work!" said Wally. "You're only one down now. Come on, let's get through these miserable old men!"

Watlington was just addressing his ball, the others had already driven. He fussed and he fooled and he waggled his old dreadnaught for fifteen or twenty seconds, and then shot straight into the bunker—a wretchedly topped ball.

"Bless my heart!" said he. "Now why—why do I always miss my drive on this hole?"

Peck started to tell him, being his partner, but Wally interrupted, politely but firmly.

"Gentlemen," said he, "if you have no objection we will go through. We are playing a tournament match. Mr. Curtiss, your honour, I believe."

Well, sir, for all the notice they took of him he might have been speaking to four graven images. Not one of them so much as turned his head. Colonel Peck had the floor.

"I'll tell you, Wat," said he, "I think it's your stance. You're playing the ball too much off your right foot—coming down on it too much. Now if you want it to rise more—" They were moving away now; but very slowly.

"*Fore!*"

This time they had to notice the boy. He was mad clear through, and his voice showed it. They all turned, took one good look at him, and then toddled away, keeping well in the middle of the course. Peck was still explaining the theory of the perfect drive. Wally yelled again; this time they did not even look at him. "Well!" said he. "Of all the damned swine! I—I believe we should drive anyway!"

"You'll lose a lot of bets if you do." Perhaps I shouldn't have said that. Goodness knows I didn't want to see his game go to pieces behind the Big Four—I didn't want to play behind them myself. I tried to explain. The kid came over and patted me on the back.

"You're perfectly right," said he. "I forgot all about those fool bets, but I'd gladly lose all of 'em if I thought I could hit that long-nosed stiff in the back of the neck!" He meant the Colonel. "And so that's the Greens Committee, eh? Holy jumping Jemima! What a club!"

I couldn't think of much of anything to say, so we sat still and watched Watlington dig his way out of the bunker. Peck offering advice after each failure. When Watlington disagreed with Peck's point of view he took issue with him, and all hands joined in the argument. Wally was simply sizzling with pent-up emotion, and after Watlington's fifth shot he began to lift the safety-valve a bit. The language which he used was wonderful, and a great tribute to higher education. Old Hardpan himself couldn't have beaten it, even in his mule-skinning days.

At last the foursome was out of range and I got off a pretty fair tee shot. Wally was still telling me what he thought of the Greens Committee when he swung at the ball, and never have I seen a wider hook. It was still hooking when it disappeared in the woods, out of bounds. His next ball took a slice and rolled into long grass.

"Serves me right for losing my temper," said he with a grin. "I can play this game all right, old top, but when I'm riled it sort of unsettles me.

Something tells me that I'm going to be riled for the next half hour or so. Don't mind what I say. It's all meant for those hogs ahead of us."

I helped him find his ball, and even then we had to wait on Peebles and Hamilton, who were churning along down the middle of the course in easy range. I lighted a cigarette and thought about something else— my income tax, I think it was. I had found this a good system when sewed up behind the Big Four. I don't know what poor Wally was thinking about—man's inhumanity to man, I suppose—for when it came time to shoot he failed to get down to his ball and hammered it still deeper into the grass.

"If it wasn't for the bets," said he, "I'd pick up and we'd go over to Number Eight. I'm afraid that on a strict interpretation of the terms of agreement Martin could spear me for two hundred fish if we skipped a hole."

"He could," said I, "and what's more to the point, he would. They were to let us through—on request."

Wally sighed.

"I've tried one method of approach," said he, "and now I'll try another one. I might tell 'em that I bet two hundred dollars on the suspicion that they were gentlemen, but likely they'd want me to split the winnings. They look like that sort."

Number Seven was a gift on a golden platter. I won it with a frightful eight, getting into all sorts of grief along the way, but Wally was entirely up in the air and blew the short putt which should have given him a half.

"All square!" said he. "Fair enough! Now we shall see what we shall see!"

His chin was very much in evidence as he hiked to Number Eight tee, and he lost no time getting into action. Colonel Peck was preparing to drive as Wally hove alongside. The Colonel is very fussy about his drive. He has been known to send a caddie to the clubhouse for whispering on the bench. Wally walked up behind him.

"Stand still, young man! Can't you see I'm driving?"

It was in the nature of a royal command.

"Oh!" said Wally. "Meaning me, I presume. Do you know, it strikes me that for a golfer with absolutely no consideration for others, you're quite considerate—of yourself!"

Now I had always sized up the Colonel for a bluffer. He proved himself one by turning a rich maroon colour and trying to swallow his Adam's apple. Not a word came from him.

"Quiet," murmured old Peebles, who looks exactly like a sheep. "Absolute quiet, please."

Wally rounded on him like a flash.

"Another considerate golfer, eh?" he snapped. "Now, gentlemen, under the rules governing tournament play I demand for my opponent and myself the right to go through. There are open holes ahead; you are not holding your place on the course—"

"Drive, Jim," interposed Watlington in that quiet way of his. "Don't pay any attention to him. Drive."

"But how can I drive while he's hopping up and down behind me? He puts me all off my swing!"

"I'm glad my protest has some effect on you," said Wally. "Now I understand that some of you are members of the Greens Committee of this club. As a member of the said club, I wish to make a formal request that we be allowed to pass."

"Denied," said Watlington. "Drive, Jim."

"Do you mean to say that you refuse us our rights—that you won't let us through?"

"Absolutely," murmured old Peebles. "Absolutely."

"But why—why? On what grounds?"

"On the grounds that you're too fresh," said Colonel Peck. "On the grounds that we don't want you to go through. Sit down and cool off."

"Drive, Jim," said Watlington. "You talk too much, young man."

"Wait a second," said Wally. "I want to get you all on record. I have made a courteous request—"

"And it has been refused," said old Peebles, blinking at both of us. "Gentlemen, you can't go through!"

"Is that final?"

"It is—absolutely."

And Watlington and Peck nodded.

"Drive, Jim!"

This time it was Hamilton who spoke.

"Pardon me," said Wally. He skipped out in front of the tee, lifted his cap and made a low bow. "Members of the Greens Committee," said he, "and one other hog as yet unclassified, you are witnesses that I default my match to Mr. Curtiss. I do this rather than be forced to play behind four such pitiable dubs as you are. Golf is a gentleman's game, which doubtless accounts for your playing it so poorly. They tell me that you never let any one through. God giving me strength, the day will come when you will not only allow people to pass you, but you will *beg* them to do it. Make a note of that. Come along, Curtiss. We'll play the last nine—for the fun of the thing."

"Oh, Curtiss!" It was Watlington speaking. "How many did you have him down when he quit?"

The insult would have made a saint angry, but no saint on the calendar could have summoned the vocabulary with which Wally replied. It was a wonderful exhibition of blistering invective. Watlington's thick hide stood him in good stead. He did not turn a hair or bat an eye, but waited for Wally to run out of breath. Then:

"Drive, Jim," said he.

Now I did not care to win that match by default, and I did everything in my power to arrange the matter otherwise. I offered to play the remaining holes later in the day or skip the eighth and begin all square on the ninth tee.

"Nothing doing," said Wally "You're a good sport, but there are other men still in the tournament, and we're not allowed to concede anything. The defaults goes, but tell me one thing—why didn't you back me up on that kick?"

I was afraid he had noticed that I had been pretty much in the background throughout, so when he asked me I told him the truth.

"Just a matter of bread and butter," said I. "My uncle's law firm handles all the Midland's business. I'm only the junior member, but I can't afford—"

"The Midland?" asked Wally.

"Yes, the Midland Manufacturing Company—Peck, Peebles and Hamilton. Watlington's money is invested in the concern too."

"Why," said Wally, "that's the entire gang, isn't it—Greens Committee and all?"

"The Big Four," said I. "You can see how it is. They're rather important—as clients. There has been no end of litigation over the site for that new plant of theirs down on Third Avenue, and we've handled all of it."

But Wally hadn't been listening to me.

"So all the eggs are in one basket!" he exclaimed. "That simplifies matters. Now, if one of 'em had been a doctor and one of 'em a lawyer and one of 'em—"

"What are you talking about?" I demanded.

"Blest if I know!" said Wally.

So far as I could learn no official action was taken by the Big Four because of conduct and language unbecoming a gentleman and a golfer. Before I left the clubhouse I had a word or two with Peebles. He was sitting at a table in the corner of the lounging room, nibbling at a piece of cheese and looking as meek as Moses.

"We—ah—considered the source," said he. "The boy is young and—rash, quite rash. His father was a mule-skinner—it's in the blood—can't help it possibly. Yes, we considered the source. Absolutely!"

I didn't see very much of Wally after that, but I understood that he played the course in the mornings and gave the club a wide berth on Wednesdays and Saturdays. His default didn't help me any. I was handsomely licked in the finals—four and three, I believe it was. About that time something happened which knocked golf completely out of my mind.

IV

I was sitting in my office one morning when Atkinson, of the C. G. & N., called me on the phone. The railroad offices are in the same building, on the floor above ours.

"That you, Curtiss? I'll be right down. I want to see you."

Now, our firm handles the legal end for the C. G. & N., and it struck me that Atkinson's voice had a nervous worried ring to it. I was wondering what could be the matter, when he came breezing in all out of breath.

"You told me," said he, "that there wouldn't be any trouble about that spur track along Third Avenue."

"For the Midland people, you mean? Oh, that's arranged for. All we have to do is appear before the City Council and make the request for a permit. To-morrow morning it comes off. What are you so excited about?"

"This," said Atkinson. He pulled a big red handbill out of his pocket and unfolded it. "Possibly I'm no judge, Curtiss, but this seems to be enough to excite anybody."

I spread the thing out on my desk and took a look at it. Across the top was one of those headlines that hit you right between the eyes:

SHALL THE CITY COUNCIL LICENSE CHILD MURDER?

Well, that was a fair start, you'll admit, but it went on from there. I don't remember ever reading anything quite so vitriolic. It was a bitter attack on the proposed spur track along Third Avenue, which is the habitat of the down-trodden workingman and the playground of his children. Judging solely by the handbill, any one would have thought that the main idea of the C. G. & N. was to kill and maim as many toddling infants as possible. The Council was made an accessory before the fact, and the thing wound up with an appeal to class prejudice and a ringing call to arms.

"Men of Third Avenue, shall the City Council give to the bloated bond-holders of an impudent monopoly the right to torture and murder your innocent babes? Shall your street be turned into a speedway for a modern car of Juggernaut? Let your answer be heard in the Council Chamber tomorrow morning—'No, a thousand times, no!'"

I read it through to the end. Then I whistled.

"This," said I, "is hot stuff—very hot stuff! Where did it come from?"

"The whole south end of town is plastered with bills like it," said Atkinson glumly. "What have we done now, that they should be picking on us? When have we killed any children, I would like to know? What started this? Who started it? Why?"

"That isn't the big question," said I. "The big question is: Will the City Council stand hitched in the face of this attack?"

The door opened and the answer to that question appeared—Barney MacShane, officially of the rank and file of the City Council of our fair city, in reality the guiding spirit of that body of petty pirates. Barney was moist and nervous, and he held one of the bills in his right hand. His first words were not reassuring.

"All hell is loose—loose for fair!" said he. "Take a look at this thing."

"We have already been looking at it," said I with a laugh intended to be light and care-free. "What of it? You don't mean to tell me that you are going to let a mere scrap of paper bother you?"

Barney mopped his forehead and sat down heavily.

"You can laugh," said he, "but there is more than paper behind this. The whole west end of town is up in arms overnight, and I don't know why. Nobody ever kicked up such a rumpus about a spur track before. That's my ward, you know, and I just made my escape from a deputation of women and children. They treed me at the City Hall—before all the newspaper men—and they held their babies up in their arms and they dared me—yes, dared me—to let this thing go through. And the election coming on and all. It's hell, that's what it is!"

"But, Barney," I argued, "we are not asking for anything which the city should not be glad to grant. Think what it means to your ward to have this fine big manufacturing plant in it! Think of the men who will have work—"

"I'm thinking of them," said Barney sorrowfully. "They're coming to the Council meeting to-morrow morning, and if this thing goes through I may as well clean out my desk. Yes, they're coming, and so are their wives and their children, and they'll bring transparencies and banners and God knows what all—"

"But listen, Barney! This plant means prosperity to every one of your people—"

"They're saying they'll make it an issue in the next campaign," mumbled MacShane. "They say that if that spur track goes down on Third Avenue it's me out of public life—and they mean it too. God knows what's got into them all at once—they're like a nest of hornets. And the women voting now too. That makes it bad—awful bad! You know as well as I do that any agitation with children mixed up in it is the toughest thing in the world to meet." He struck at the poster with a sudden spiteful gesture. "From beginning to end," he snarled, "it's just an appeal not to let the railroad kill the kids!"

"But that's nonsense—bunk!" said Atkinson. "Every precaution will be taken to prevent accidents. You've got to think of the capital invested."

Barney rolled a troubled eye in his direction.

"You go down on Third Avenue," said he, "and begin talking to them people about capital! Try it once. What the hell do they care about capital? They was brought up to hate the sound of the word! You know and I know that capital ain't near as black as it's painted, but can you tell them that? Huh! And a railroad ain't ever got any friends in a gang standing round on the street corners!"

"But," said I, "this isn't a question of friends—it's a straight proposition of right and wrong. The Midland people have gone ahead and put up this big plant. They were given to understand that there would be no opposition to the spur track going down. They've got to have it! The success of their business depends on it! Surely you don't mean to tell me that the Council will refuse this permit?"

"Well," said Barney slowly, "I've talked with the boys—Carter and Garvey and Dillon. They're all figuring on running again, and they're scared to death of it. Garvey says we'd be damned fools to go against an agitation like this—so close to election, anyhow."

I argued the matter from every angle—the good of the city; the benefit to Barney's ward—but I couldn't budge him.

"They say that the voice of the people is the voice of God," said he, "but we know that most of the time it's only noise. Sometimes the noise kind of dies out, and then's the time to step in and cut the melon. But any kind of noise so close to election? Huh! Safety first!"

Before the meeting adjourned it was augmented by the appearance of the president and vice-president of the Midland Manufacturing Company, Colonel Jim Peck and old Peebles, and never had I seen those stiff-necked gentlemen so humanly agitated.

"This is terrible!" stormed the Colonel. "Terrible! This is unheard of. It is an outrage—a crime—a crying shame to the city! Think of our investment! Other manufacturing plants got their spur tracks for the asking.

There was no talk of killing children. Why—why have we been singled out for attack—for—for blackmail?"

"You can cut out that kind of talk right now!" said Barney sternly. "There ain't a nickel in granting this permit, and you know it as well as I do. Nobody ain't trying to blackmail you! All the dough in town won't swing the boys into line behind this proposition while this rumpus is going on. And since you're taking that slant at it, here's the last word—sit tight and wait till after election!"

"But the pl-plant!" bleated Peebles, tearing a blotter to shreds with shaking fingers. "The plant! Think of the loss of time—and we—we expected to open up next month!"

"Go ahead and open up," said Barney "You can truck your stuff to the depots, can't you? Yes, yes—I get you about the loss! Us boys in the Council—we got something to lose too. Now here it is, straight from the shoulder, and you can bet on it." Barney spoke slowly, wagging his forefinger at each word. "If that application comes up to-morrow morning, with the Council chamber jammed with folks from the south end of the town—good-a-by, John! Fare thee well! It ain't in human nature to commit political suicide when a second term is making eyes at you. Look at our end of it for a while. We got futures to think of, too, and Garvey—Garvey wants to run for mayor some day. You can't afford to have that application turned down, can you? Of course not. Have a little sense. Keep your shirts on. Get out and see who's behind this thing. Chances are somebody wants something. Find out what it is—rig up a compromise—get him to call off the dogs. Then talk to me again, and I'll promise you it'll go through as slick as a greased pig!"

"I believe there's something in that," said I. "We've never run into such a hornets' nest as this before. There must be a reason. Atkinson, you've got a lot of gumshoe men on your staff. Why don't you turn 'em loose to locate this opposition?"

"You're about two hours late with that suggestion," said the railroad representative. "Our sleuths are on the job now. If they find out anything I'll communicate with you P. D. Q."

"Good!" ejaculated Colonel Peck. "And if it's money—"

"Aw, you make me sick!" snapped Barney MacShane. "You think money can do everything, don't you? Well, it can't! For one thing, it couldn't get me to shake hands with a stiff like you!"

I was called away from the dinner table on the following Friday evening. Watlington was on the telephone.

"That you, Curtiss? Well, we think we've got in touch with the bug under the chip. Can you arrange to meet us in Room 85 at the Hotel Brookmore at nine to-night? . . . No, I can't tell you a thing about it. We're asked to be there—you're asked to be there—and that's as far as my information goes. Don't be late."

When I entered Room 85 four men were seated at a long table. They were Elsberry J. Watlington, Colonel Jim Peck, Samuel Alexander Peebles and W. Cotton Hamilton. They greeted me with a certain amount of nervous irritability. The Big Four had been through a cruel week and showed the marks of strain.

"Where's Atkinson?" I asked.

"It was stipulated, expressly stipulated," said old Peebles, "that only the five of us should be present. The whole thing is most mysterious. I—I don't like the looks of it."

"Probably a hold-up!" grunted Colonel Peck.

Watlington didn't say anything. He had aged ten years, his heavy smooth-shaven face was set in stern lines and his mouth looked as if it might have been made with a single slash of a razor.

Hamilton mumbled to himself and kept trying to light the end of his thumb instead of his cigar. Peck had his watch in his hand. Peebles played a tattoo on his chin with his fingers.

"Good thing we didn't make that application at the Council meeting," said Hamilton. "I never saw such a gang of thugs!"

"Male and female!" added Colonel Peck. "Well, time's up! Whoever he is, I hope he won't keep us waiting!"

"Ah!" said a cheerful voice. "You don't like to be held up on the tee, do you, Colonel?"

There in the doorway stood Wally Wallace, beaming upon the Big Four. Not even on the stage have I ever seen anything to match the expressions on the faces round that table. Old Peebles' mouth kept opening and shutting, like the mouth of a fresh caught carp. The others were frozen, petrified. Wally glanced at me as he advanced into the room, and there was a faint trembling of his left eyelid.

"Well," said Wally briskly, "shall we proceed with the business of the meeting?"

"Business!" Colonel Peck exploded like a firecracker.

"With—you?" It was all Watlington could do to tear the two words out of his throat. He croaked like a big bullfrog.

"With me," said Wally, bowing and taking his place at the head of the table. "Unless," he added, "you would prefer to discuss the situation with the rank and file of the Third Avenue Country Club."

The silence which followed that remark was impressive. I could hear somebody's heart beating. It may have been my own. As usual Colonel Peck was first to recover the power of speech, and again as usual he made poor use of it.

"You—you young whelp!" he gurgled. "So it was—"

"Shut up, Jim!" growled Watlington, whose eyes had never left Wally's face. Hamilton carefully placed his cigar in the ashtray and tried to put a match into his mouth. Then he turned on me, sputtering.

"Are you in on this?" he demanded.

"Be perfectly calm," said Wally. "Mr. Curtiss is not in on it, as you so elegantly express it. I am the only one who is in on it. Me, myself, W. W. Wallace, at your service. If you will favour me with your attention, I will explain—"

"You'd better!" ripped out the Colonel.

"Ah," said the youngster, grinning at Peck, "always a little nervous on the tee, aren't you?"

"Drive, young man!" said Watlington.

A sudden light flickered in Wally's eyes. He turned to Elsberry J. with an expression that was almost friendly.

"Do you know," said he, "I'm beginning to think there may be human qualities in you after all."

Watlington grunted and nodded his head.

"Take the honour!" said he.

Wally rose and laid the tips of his fingers on the table.

"Members of the Greens Committee and one other"—and here he looked at Hamilton, whose face showed that he had not forgotten the unclassified hog—"we are here this evening to arrange an exchange of courtesies. You think you represent the Midland Manufacturing Company at this meeting. You do not. You represent the Sundown Golf and Country Club. I represent the Third Avenue Country Club—an organisation lately formed. You may have heard something of it, though not under that name."

He paused to let this sink in.

"Gentlemen," he continued, "you may recall that I once made a courteous request of you for something which was entirely within my rights. You made an arbitrary ruling on that request. You refused to let me through. You told me I was too fresh, and advised me to sit down and cool off. I see by your faces that you recall the occasion.

"You may also recall that I promised to devote myself to the task of teaching you to be more considerate of others. Gentlemen, I am the opposition to your playing through on Third Avenue. I am the Man Behind. I am the Voice of the People. I am a singleton on the course, holding you up while I sink a putt. If you ask me why I will give you your own words in your teeth: You can't go through because I don't want you to go through."

Here he stopped long enough to light a cigarette, and again his left eyelid flickered, though he did not look at me. I think if he had I should have erupted.

"You see," said he, flipping the match into the air, "it has been necessary to teach you a lesson—the lesson, gentlemen, of courtesy on the course, consideration for others. I realised that this could never be done on a course where you have power to make the rules—or break them. So I selected another course. Members of the Greens Committee and one other, you do not make the rules on Third Avenue. You are perfectly within your rights in asking to go through; but I have blocked you. I have made you sit down on the bench and cool off. Gentlemen, how do you like being held up when you want to play through? How does it feel?"

I do not regret my inability to quote Colonel Peck's reply to this question.

"Quit it, Jim!" snapped Watlington. "Your bark was always worse than your bite, and it's not much of a bark at that—'Sound and fury, signifying nothing.' Young man, I take it you are the chairman of the Greens Committee of this Third Avenue Country Club, empowered to act. May I ask what are our chances of getting through?"

"I *know* I'm going to like you—in time!" exclaimed Wally. "I feel it coming on. Let's see, tomorrow is Saturday, isn't it?"

"What's that got to do with it?" mumbled Hamilton.

"Much," answered Wally. "Oh, much, I assure you! I expect to be at the Sundown Club to-morrow." His chin shot out and his voice carried the sting of a lash. "I expect to see you gentlemen there, playing your usual crawling foursome. I expect to see you allowing your fellow members to pass you on the course. You might even invite them to come through— you might insist on it, courteously, you understand, and with such grace as you may be able to muster. I want to see every member of that club play through you—every member!"

"All d-damned nonsense!" bleated Peebles, sucking his fingers.

"Shut up!" ordered Watlington savagely. "And, young man, if we do this—what then?"

"Ah, then!" said Wally. "Then the reward of merit. If you show me that you can learn to be considerate of others—if you show me that you can be courteous on the course where you make the rules—I feel safe in promising that you will be treated with consideration on this other course which has been mentioned. Yes, quite safe. In fact, gentlemen, you may even be *asked* to play through on Third Avenue!"

"But this agitation!" began Hamilton.

"Was paid for by the day," smiled the brazen rascal, with a graceful inclination of his head. "People may be hired to do anything—even to annoy prominent citizens and frighten a City Council." Hamilton stirred uneasily but Wally read his thought and froze him with a single keen glance. "Of course," said he, "you understand that what has been done once may be done again. Sentiment crystallises—when helped out with a few more red handbills—a few more speeches on the street corners—"

"The point is well taken!" interrupted Watlington hurriedly. "Damn well taken! Young man, talk to me. *I'm* the head of this outfit. Pay no attention to Jim Peck. He's nothing but a bag of wind. Hamilton doesn't count. His nerves are no good. Peebles—he's an old goat. *I'm* the one with power to act. Talk to me. Is there anything else you want?"

"Nothing," said Wally. "I think your streak of consideration is likely to prove a lasting one. If not—well, I may have to spread this story round town a bit—"

"Oh, my Lord!" groaned Colonel Peck.

It was a noble and inspiring sight to see the Big Four, caps in hand, inviting the common people to play through. The entire club marched through them—too full of amazement to demand explanations. Even Purdue McCormick, trudging along with a putter in one hand and a mid-iron in the other, without a bag, without a caddie, without a vestige of right in the wide world, even Purdue was coerced into passing them. At dusk he was found wandering aimlessly about on the seventeenth fairway, babbling to himself. We fear that he will never be the same again.

I have received word from Barney MacShane that the City Council will be pleased to grant a permit to lay a spur track on Third Avenue. The voice of the people, he says, has died away to a faint murmuring. Some day I think I will tell Barney the truth. He does not play golf, but he has a sense of humour.

ABERDOVEY

BERNARD DARWIN

The golfer is often said to be a selfish person. He deserts his wife for days together; he objects to the presence of bank-holiday makers upon the common, where he desires to play his game; he commits various other crimes. He is almost certainly selfish about the festival of Christmas, in that the kind of Christmas which other people want is to him hateful beyond words. For the Christmas which English people are at any rate supposed to enjoy there are necessary, besides mistletoe and plum pudding, which do no one any harm, a fall of snow and a good hard frost—two things which, it is superfluous to observe, are wholly inimical to golf. The golfer likes to read of the typical "old-fashioned" Christmas, such as Caldecott drew, or Dickens described, but in reading he likes to translate it, as it were, into his own terms.

For instance, one of the most delightful pieces of literature in the world, and the one most redolent of Christmas, is the account of the Pickwickians' journey by the Muggleton coach, on their way to Dingley Dell. There is Mr. Pickwick watching the "implacable" codfish squeezed into the boot: Mr. Pickwick begging the guard to drink his health in a glass of hot brandy and water: the horses cantering, and the wheels skimming over the hard and frosty ground: the meeting with the fat boy who had been asleep "right in front of the tap-room fire." All these things are perfectly heavenly, but it is one of the disadvantages of having a mind warped by golf that one cannot help remembering that this journey was a prelude to Mr. Winkle's skating and Mr. Pickwick's sliding, and where there is ice, there is no golf worthy of the name. So I have to translate this glorious journey to myself into my own language. It may sound lamentably prosaic; there will be no cracking of whips and tooting of horns, but this journey of mine is good to look forward to, nevertheless.

Before the journey comes the packing, a thing usually loathsome, but on this occasion positively delicious, more especially the packing of clubs. All the clubs are taken out one by one, looked at with a gloating eye, and then stowed triumphantly into the bag. Of course, I shall take more than I really want, just for the fun of packing them. There are one or two wooden clubs from my reserve which must certainly go. There is one brassy that only wants just a drop of lead let into the head to make it an enchanter's wand. There is an iron that I have not used for some time that will be just the thing for carrying the mighty sandhill, crowned with ominous sleepers, that guards the fourth green; and then, of course, one must take a spare putter or two, against the almost unthinkable event of going off one's putting. Also there is a large umbrella, though it can never be that the fates will be so unkind as to make one use it.

So much for the packing, and now for the journey, which will begin, not in a coach, but in a cab, which will take me to Euston, most dear and romantic of stations. I shall instruct a porter as to the label to be affixed to my bag, adding quite unnecessarily, but with an additional thrill of joy, "On the Cambrian Railway, you know." I shall not ask him to drink my health in brandy and water, but in the enthusiasm of the moment I shall probably give him sixpence. I shall take my seat in the carriage and that almost certainly a corner seat, because in my excitement I shall have reached the station absurdly early. Then I shall start. I shall not read the paper that I have bought, because I shall be looking out of the window at the golf courses that I pass on my way and thinking, without any dis-respect to them, how far pleasanter is the course to which I am bound.

The stations will whirl past. Bletchley, Rugby, Stafford, Wellington, and at last beloved Shrewsbury. So far I shall have been alone, but at Shrews-bury will be encountered my two kind hosts and other golfers bound for the same paradise. We shall greet each other uproariously, behaving in an abominably hearty and Christmas-like way, and then we shall pack our-selves into another carriage, for the second half of our journey. Our talk, surprising as it may appear, will be about the game of golf—whether there is casual water in the Crater green, and how many of the new bunkers have been made. I should not be surprised if we even attempted to waggle each other's clubs in the extremely confined space at our disposal.

More stations will go by us. They will not whirl this time, for the trains from Shrewsbury to Wales are not given to whirling; they will pass in lei-surely order. Hanwood, Westbury, and now the Welsh border is crossed; Buttington, Welshpool, Abermule, Montgomery, Newtown—I forget their order, but love to write down their names. The train comes into a country of mountains and jolly, foaming, mountain streams; it pants up a steep hill to a solitary little station called Talerddig. Near Talerddig there is a certain mysterious natural arch in the rock, and it is a point of honour with us to look for it out of the window. However, since we never can remember exactly where it is, and the twilight is deepening, we never see it. Now the train has reached the end of its painful climb, and dashes down the hill into the valley and by this time we feel as if we could almost smell the sea. There is a pause at Machynlleth (let any Saxon try to pronounce that!), and we have tea and listen to the people talking Welsh upon the platform. Then on again through the darkness, till we stop once more. There is a wild rush of small boys outside our carriage window, fighting and clam-ouring for the privilege of carrying our clubs. *Nunc dimittis*—we have arrived at Aberdovey.

Escaping with difficulty from this rabble of boys, we clamber up a steep and rocky road to where our house stands, perched upon the hill-side, looking out over the estuary and at the lights of Borth that twinkle across the water. We have our annual argument with an old retainer of Scottish ancestry and pedantically exact mind, who points out to us that it is clearly impossible that we should all be called at precisely eight o'clock in the morning. We suggest as a compromise that one should be called at two minutes to eight, and another at two minutes past, and to this course, though still unconvinced, he grudgingly assents. Then next day when the hour of calling has come, we wake, if all is well, to one of the most seraphic of imaginable winter days, for be it known that Aberdovey is called by the local guidebook the Madeira of North Wales, and that one hardy schoolmaster played there on two successive New Year's days in his shirt sleeves. Warm, still and grey, with no dancing shadows to distract the more fanciful of our party—that is how I like it best, and that is how, in a good hour be it spoken, it generally is. Yet there are exceptions, and I remember almost painfully well one Christmas, when it was indeed a "fine time for them as is well wropped up." This, it will be remembered, was the soliloquy of the polar bear when he was practising his skating, and we who were practising our golfing heartily endorsed the reflections of that arctic philosopher. Yet even so we played our two rounds a day like men, and that says something both for us and for Aberdovey.

The ground was iron hard with frost, the east wind blew remorselessly and we were certainly very well wrapped up indeed. Spartan persons who had never yielded before were glad to nestle inside Shetland waistcoats, while at the same time reluctantly admitting that mittens did restore some vestige of feeling to the fingers. It is indeed dreadful to contemplate life in winter-time without that blessed invention the mitten, or, to give it its technical name, the muffetee. A mitten proper has a hole for one's thumb, and so comes too far over the palm of the hand to allow a comfortable grip of the club. The muffetee, which is made of silk, if one is extravagant, and of wool, if one is economical, only encircles the wrist with a delicious warmth that in a surprisingly short space of time permeates the wearer's entire frame.

There are still a good many people who will not believe that this is so. I have come across this wilful blindness among my own relations,

who are of a highly scientific and sceptical turn of mind. They allege the most futile and irrebuttable reasons why the warmth of the wrist should have no connection with the warmth of the hand, but there is a measure of consolation in the fact that they suffer agonies from cold fingers, and, better still, top their mashie shots in consequence. Of course, when they have once tried the experiment they have to give in and own churlishly enough that there seems to be something in it. Even the most distinguished of golfers are sometimes to be caught without mittens. I have twice played the part of Sir Philip Sidney and lent mine to eminent professionals when they were playing quite important matches on the most bitterly cold days.

Those that I lent to Taylor were, needless to say, returned to me permanently enlarged, and ever afterwards hung loosely upon my puny and attenuated wrists. If, however, they are no longer very useful as mittens, they are as precious to me as were the three cherry stones to Calverley's young lady from having "once dallied with the teeth of royalty itself."

I believe that there is a Brobdingnagian kind of mitten to be bought which reaches from the wrist to the elbow. I have never yet had a pair, but some day I shall certainly try to afford one. Meanwhile, the ordinary woollen mitten is within the reach of all, since a pair costs, if I remember rightly, no more than sevenpence halfpenny. They will do more towards winning you your winter half-crowns than all the curly-necked clubs in the world, or even, I suspect, than the patent putter for which the advertisement used to claim that it "made every stroke practically a certainty."

This rhapsody on mittens has carried me far away from Aberdovey, where we were left battling with the elements. It is a curious game, that golf on frozen ground and in an easterly gale, for one reason because, after a few days of it, it is hard to remain entirely level-headed about our driving powers. The ball goes such portentous distances that we really cannot believe that it is entirely attributable to the weather. In our heart of hearts we half believe that some subtle change has come over us, and that we shall drive just a little farther ever afterwards. Thus, when we came in to lunch after our morning round—and oh! how good lunch was—we each had our little boast of some green reached, some bunker passed. We fully appreciated that the shots of others were mere accidents due to the ball falling upon a particularly frozen spot; but as to our own, there must have been just a little extra sting behind those—we thought we detected a new and wonderful use of our wrists that accounted for it.

Needless to say, at that Christmas time of bitter memory the obdurate wind took a rest on Sunday, as did the golfers. There was a cloudless day, without a breath of wind; we could have kept quite warm, and our approach shots would not have skipped like young rams upon the green, ere they buried themselves in a bunker fifty yards beyond it. All we could do was to bemoan our luck, and look at the view, a very beautiful one truly, for the Dovey estuary on a fine winter's day can show hills and woods and bracken as lovely as may be. Then one round in the thaw on Monday morning, just to rub it in that we were going to leave the course at its best, and so home to a singularly depressing London of slush and drizzle.

I have written of Aberdovey in winter because it is then, I think, that it is at its best, perhaps because I love it so much that I selfishly like to have it to myself. It is good in summer-time too; good even in August when the rain too often comes pitilessly down, when the hand of the great midland towns lies heavy on the course and a pitched battle rages daily between the outgoing and incoming battalions in the narrow space that lies between the Pulpit and the Crater hole. September is a divine month there, when there are but few people left, and so is June, when there are none at all. It was in June that I paid my last summer visit there, and that on a somewhat sacrilegious errand, for I was to aid in the altering of old holes and the making of new bunkers. The committee had decided to call in a highly distinguished golfing architect to set their house in order, and I was asked to attend him as *amicus curiæ* or bottle-holder, or clerk of the works—in short, in a menial capacity of an indefinite character. This task I undertook with alacrity, but after the first day's work I was a physical and mental wreck and felt a positive loathing for my architectural friend. Yet this I must say for him; like Rogue Riderhood, he does "Earn his living by the sweat of his brow." I never saw any one work harder. Save for a wholly insufficient interval for lunch, we were on our legs from 9.15 in the morning to 7.30 at night. As a warning to others who may lightly undertake this kind of work, even at the risk of too wide a digression, I will shortly describe our day.

We started out first of all with two caddies. One of them carried our two waterproofs and a large plan of the course nailed on to a board. The other carried my clubs. The architect himself did not take any clubs, but stated that I should hit balls for him when required. My sensations rather resembled, as I should imagine, those of one who accompanies a water diviner. The architect behaved in the same mysterious and interesting manner. Sometimes he would come to a full stop and remain buried in thought for no ostensible reason. Then he would suddenly turn round and retrace his steps to the tee. Then he would pace a certain distance, counting his paces aloud in a solemn manner. Finally he would give a cry of joy, make a dash up to the top of a little sandhill, and declare with triumph that it would make the most perfect plateau green in the world, and that why in the world those who had originally laid out the course had not discovered it he for one could not conceive.

By slow stages the first two holes, which the members had always considered rather good in a humble way, were completely transmogrified. The greens were moved in the architect's mind's eye from their then reasonably open and easy-going positions to the most devilish little narrow gullies surrounded by sandhills and bents, where only a ball that flies as straight as did an arrow from the bow of Robin Hood might hope to reach the green. Beautiful holes they were, both of them, and would make a magnificent beginning to the course, but I could not but feel an uneasy doubt as to whether all the long-handicap members of the club would appreciate them at quite their true value. Nothing much happened at the third hole, and then we approached the fourth, over which I personally felt rather nervous. The club is proud of this fourth hole, which consists of a rather terrifying iron shot, perfectly blind, over a vast and formidable hill shored up with black railway sleepers, on to a little green oasis amid a desert of sand. Now, the hole is really a sacred institution (it is one of the few holes on the course that is known by a name and not a number), but it is also one of the type of hole for which I knew my architect to feel a most utter contempt. I wondered uneasily whether he would want to do some horribly revolutionary thing, and I reflected that if he did I should certainly be lynched by the committee for his sins. However, he merely cast a withering look at a grass bank behind the green, commanded that "that back wall" should be taken away and passed on, deeming the hole unworthy of any further notice. I will not enter into further details of this our first progress round the course. At intervals I was ordered to drive a ball from a specified place, and my efforts were commended as being admirably adapted for showing where the normal, short, bad driver would get to against the wind: this when I was driving with a fairly strong breeze behind me. To cut a long story short, we finally got round in something over three hours, and fell ravenously on our lunch.

I had faintly hoped that in the afternoon we might relax our labours so far as to play a friendly round, but as a matter of fact, what I had undergone in the morning was the merest child's play to the afternoon. After lunch we started out again with a large cart driven by a sleepy boy, and pulled by a sleepy horse. In the cart were about 200 stakes, commandeered from a neighbouring sawmill, for the purpose of marking the sites of proposed new bunkers. We started about 2.30, and we stopped about 6.30, and I cannot help thinking that those two small caddies who hammered in stakes with violent blows and a heavy mallet, must have been very stiff after their labours. Personally I grew infinitely more faint and weary than I have ever done even at a picture gallery, which is generally believed to be the most exhausting thing in the world. To give the devil his due, my architect was wonderful, and filled me with admiration. Like a comet, he left a shining tail behind him—of white stakes gleaming in the sunlight. The speed with which he would decide on the position of a bunker was really astounding. While I was feebly wondering what a certain stake was for, he had decided that the right policy was to make people play at the green from the right-hand side: to make a series of bunkers all along the left of the fairway so as to drive them towards the rushes: to dig out that hollow close to the green, and so on, and so on. He is really a wonderful person, but it is a fearful thing to do a day's work with him, even though it be in the service of the course one loves best in the world.

WINTER DREAMS

F. SCOTT FITZGERALD

I

S ome of the caddies were poor as sin and lived in one-room houses with a neurasthenic cow in the front yard, but Dexter Green's father owned the second best grocery store in Black Bear—the best one was "The Hub," patronized by the wealthy people from Sherry Island—and Dexter caddied only for pocket money.

In the fall when the days became crisp and gray and the long Minnesota winter shut down like the white lid of a box, Dexter's skis moved over the snow that hid the fairways of the golf course. At these times the country gave him a feeling of profound melancholy—it offended him that the links should lie in enforced fallowness, haunted by ragged sparrows for the long season. It was dreary, too, that on the tees where the gay colors fluttered in summer there were now only the desolate sandboxes knee-deep in crusted ice. When he crossed the hills the wind blew cold as misery and if the sun was out he tramped with his eyes squinted up against the hard dimensionless glare.

In April the winter ceased abruptly. The snow ran down into Black Bear Lake scarcely tarrying for the early golfers to brave the season with red and black balls. Without elation, without an interval of moist glory, the cold was gone.

Dexter knew that there was something dismal about this Northern spring, just as he knew there was something gorgeous about the fall. Fall made him clinch his hands and tremble and repeat idiotic sentences to himself, and make brisk abrupt gestures of command to imaginary audiences and armies. October filled him with hope which November raised to a sort of ecstatic triumph, and in this mood the fleeting brilliant impressions of the summer at Sherry Island were ready grist to his mill. He became a golf champion and defeated Mr. T. A. Hedrick in a marvelous match played a hundred times over the fairways of his imagination, a match each detail of which he changed about untiringly—sometimes he won with almost laughable ease, sometimes he came up magnificently from behind. Again, stepping from a Pierce-Arrow automobile, like Mr. Mortimer Jones, he strolled frigidly into the lounge of the Sherry Island Golf Club—or perhaps, surrounded by an admiring crowd, he gave an exhibition of fancy diving from the springboard of the club raft. . . . Among those who watched him in open-mouthed wonder was Mr. Mortimer Jones.

And one day it came to pass that Mr. Jones—himself and not his ghost—came up to Dexter with tears in his eyes and said that Dexter was the damned best caddy in the club, and wouldn't he decide not to quit if Mr. Jones made it worth his while, because every other damn caddy in the club lost one ball a hole for him—regularly—

"No, sir," said Dexter decisively. "I don't want to caddie any more." Then, after a pause: "I'm too old."

"You're not more than fourteen. Why the devil did you decide just this morning that you wanted to quit? You promised that next week you'd go over to the state tournament with me."

"I decided I was too old."

Dexter handed in his "A Class" badge, collected what money was due him from the caddy master, and walked home to Black Bear Village.

"The best damned caddy I ever saw," shouted Mr. Mortimer Jones over a drink that afternoon. "Never lost a ball! Willing! Intelligent! Quiet! Honest! Grateful!"

The little girl who had done this was eleven—beautifully ugly as little girls are apt to be who are destined after a few years to be inexpressibly lovely and bring no end of misery to a great number of men. The spark, however, was perceptible. There was a general ungodliness in the way her lips twisted down at the corners when she smiled, and in the—Heaven help us!—in the almost passionate quality of her eyes. Vitality is born in such women. It was utterly in evidence now, shining through her thin frame in a sort of glow.

She had come eagerly out on to the course at nine o'clock with a white linen nurse and five small new golf-clubs in a white canvas bag which the nurse was carrying. When Dexter first saw her she was standing by the caddy house, rather ill at ease and trying to conceal the fact by engaging her nurse in an obviously unnatural conversation graced by startling and irrelevant grimaces from herself.

"Well, it's certainly a nice day, Hilda," Dexter heard her say. She drew down the corners of her mouth, smiled, and glanced furtively around, her eyes in transit falling for an instant on Dexter.

Then to the nurse:

"Well, I guess there aren't very many people out here this morning, are there?"

The smile again—radiant, blatantly artificial—convincing.

"I don't know what we're supposed to do now," said the nurse, looking nowhere in particular.

"Oh, that's all right. I'll fix it up."

Dexter stood perfectly still, his mouth slightly ajar. He knew that if he moved forward a step his stare would be in her line of vision—if he moved backward he would lose his full view of her face. For a moment he had not realized how young she was. Now he remembered having seen her several times the year before—in bloomers.

Suddenly, involuntarily, he laughed, a short abrupt laugh—then, startled by himself, he turned and began to walk quickly away.

"Boy!"

Dexter stopped.

"Boy—"

Beyond question he was addressed. Not only that, but he was treated to that absurd smile, that preposterous smile—the memory of which at least a dozen men were to carry into middle age.

"Boy, do you know where the golf teacher is?"

"He's giving a lesson."

"Well, do you know where the caddy master is?"

"He isn't here yet this morning."

"Oh." For a moment this baffled her. She stood alternately on her right and left foot.

"We'd like to get a caddy," said the nurse. "Mrs. Mortimer Jones sent us out to play golf, and we don't know how without we get a caddy."

Here she was stopped by an ominous glance from Miss Jones, followed immediately by the smile.

"There aren't any caddies here except me," said Dexter to the nurse, "and I got to stay here in charge until the caddy master gets here."

"Oh."

Miss Jones and her retinue now withdrew, and at a proper distance from Dexter became involved in a heated conversation, which was concluded by Miss Jones taking one of the clubs and hitting it on the ground with violence. For further emphasis she raised it again and was about to bring it down smartly upon the nurse's bosom, when the nurse seized the club and twisted it from her hands.

"You damn little mean old thing!" cried Miss Jones wildly.

Another argument ensued. Realizing that the elements of the comedy were implied in the scene, Dexter several times began to laugh, but each time restrained the laugh before it reached audibility. He could not resist the monstrous conviction that the little girl was justified in beating the nurse.

The situation was resolved by the fortuitous appearance of the caddy master, who was appealed to immediately by the nurse.

"Miss Jones is to have a little caddy, and this one says he can't go."

"Mr. McKenna said I was to wait here till you came," said Dexter quickly.

"Well, he's here now." Miss Jones smiled cheerfully at the caddy master. Then she dropped her bag and set off at a haughty mince toward the first tee.

"Well?" The caddy master turned to Dexter. "What you standing there like a dummy for? Go pick up the young lady's clubs."

"I don't think I'll go out today," said Dexter.

"You don't—"

"I think I'll quit."

The enormity of his decision frightened him. He was a favorite caddy, and the thirty dollars a month he earned through the summer were not to be made elsewhere around the lake. But he had received a strong emotional shock, and his perturbation required a violent and immediate outlet.

It is not so simple as that, either. As so frequently would be the case in the future, Dexter was unconsciously dictated to by his winter dreams.

II

Now, of course, the quality and the seasonability of these winter dreams varied, but the stuff of them remained. They persuaded Dexter several years later to pass up a business course at the state university—his father, prospering now, would have paid his way—for the precarious advantage of attending an older and more famous university in the East, where he was bothered by his scanty funds. But do not get the impression, because his winter dreams happened to be concerned at first with musings on the rich, that there was anything merely snobbish in the boy. He wanted not association with glittering things and glittering people—he wanted the glittering things themselves. Often he reached out for the best without knowing why he wanted it—and sometimes he ran up against the mysterious denials and prohibitions in which life indulges. It is with one of those denials and not with his career as a whole that this story deals.

He made money. It was rather amazing. After college he went to the city from which Black Bear Lake draws its wealthy patrons. When he was only twenty-three and had been there not quite two years, there were already people who liked to say: "Now *there's* a boy—"All about him rich men's sons were peddling bonds precariously or investing patrimonies precariously, or plodding through the two dozen volumes of the "George Washington Commercial Course," but Dexter borrowed a thousand dollars on his college degree and his confident mouth, and bought a partnership in a laundry.

It was a small laundry when he went into it, but Dexter made a specialty of learning how the English washed fine woolen golf stockings without shrinking them, and within a year he was catering to the trade that wore knickerbockers. Men were insisting that their Shetland hose and sweaters go to his laundry, just as they had insisted on a caddy who could find golf balls. A little later he was doing then-wives' lingerie as well—and running five branches in different parts of the city. Before he was twenty-seven he owned the largest string of laundries in his section of the country. It was then that he sold out and went to New York. But the part of his story that concerns us goes back to the days when he was making his first big success.

When he was twenty-three Mr. Hart—one of the gray-haired men who like to say, "Now there's a boy"—gave him a guest card to the Sherry Island Golf Club for a weekend. So he signed his name one day on the register, and that afternoon played golf in a foursome with Mr. Hart and Mr. Sandwood and Mr. T. A. Hedrick. He did not consider it necessary to remark that he had once carried Mr. Hart's bag over this same links, and that he knew every trap and gully with his eyes shut—but he found himself glancing at the four caddies who trailed them, trying to catch a gleam or gesture that would remind him of himself, that would lessen the gap which lay between his present and his past.

It was a curious day slashed abruptly with fleeting, familiar impressions. One minute he had the sense of being a trespasser—in the next he was impressed by the tremendous superiority he felt toward Mr. T. A. Hedrick, who was a bore and not even a good golfer any more.

Then, because of a ball Mr. Hart lost near the fifteenth green, an enormous thing happened. While they were searching the stiff grasses of the rough there was a clear call of "Fore!" from behind a hill in their rear. And as they all turned abruptly from their search a bright new ball sliced abruptly over the hill and caught Mr. T. A. Hedrick in the abdomen.

"By Gad!" cried Mr. T. A. Hedrick, "they ought to put some of these crazy women off the course. It's getting to be outrageous."

A head and a voice came up together over the hill:

"Do you mind if we go through?"

"You hit me in the stomach!" declared Mr. Hedrick wildly.

"Did I?" The girl approached the group of men. "I'm sorry. I yelled, 'Fore!' "

Her glance fell casually on each of the men—then scanned the fairway for her ball.

"Did I bounce into the rough?"

It was impossible to determine whether this question was ingenuous or malicious. In a moment, however, she left no doubt, for as her partner came up over the hill she called cheerfully:

"Here I am! I'd have gone on the green except that I hit something."

As she took her stance for a short mashie shot, Dexter looked at her closely. She wore a blue gingham dress, rimmed at throat and shoulders with a white edging that accentuated her tan. The quality of exaggeration, of thinness, which had made her passionate eyes and down-turning mouth absurd at eleven, was gone now She was arrestingly beautiful. The color in her cheeks was centered like the color in a picture—it was not a "high" color, but a sort of fluctuating and feverish warmth, so shaded that it seemed at any moment it would recede and disappear. This color and the mobility of her mouth gave a continual impression of flux, of intense life, of passionate vitality—balanced only partially by the sad luxury of her eyes.

She swung her mashie impatiently and without interest, pitching the ball into a sand pit on the other side of the green. With a quick, insincere smile and a careless "Thank you!" she went on after it.

"That Judy Jones!" remarked Mr. Hedrick on the next tee, as they waited—some moments—for her to play on ahead. "All she needs is to be turned up and spanked for six months and then to be married off to an old-fashioned cavalry captain."

"My God, she's good-looking!" said Mr. Sandwood, who was just over thirty.

"Good-looking!" cried Mr. Hedrick contemptuously. "She always looks as if she wanted to be kissed! Turning those big cow eyes on every calf in town!"

It was doubtful if Mr. Hedrick intended a reference to the maternal instinct.

"She'd play pretty good golf if she'd try," said Mr. Sandwood.

"She has no form," said Mr. Hedrick solemnly.

"She has a nice figure," said Mr. Sandwood.

"Better thank the Lord she doesn't drive a swifter ball," said Mr. Hart, winking at Dexter.

Later in the afternoon the sun went down with a swirl of gold and varying blues and scarlets, and left the dry, rustling night of Western summer. Dexter watched from the veranda of the golf club, watched the even overlap of the waters in the little wind, silver molasses under the harvest moon. Then the moon held a finger to her lips and the lake became a clear pool, pale and quiet. Dexter put on his bathing suit and swam out to the farthest raft, where he stretched dripping on the wet canvas of the springboard.

There was a fish jumping and a star shining and the lights around the lake were gleaming. Over on a dark peninsula a piano was playing the songs of last summer and of summers before that—songs from "Chin-Chin" and "The Count of Luxembourg" and "The Chocolate Soldier"*—

---

* Popular Broadway musicals of the day.

and because the sound of a piano over a stretch of water had always seemed beautiful to Dexter he lay perfectly quiet and listened.

The tune the piano was playing at that moment had been gay and new five years before when Dexter was a sophomore at college. They had played it at a prom once when he could not afford the luxury of proms, and he had stood outside the gymnasium and listened. The sound of the tune precipitated in him a sort of ecstasy and it was with that ecstasy he viewed what happened to him now. It was a mood of intense appreciation, a sense that, for once, he was magnificently attuned to life and that everything about him was radiating brightness and a glamor he might never know again.

A low, pale oblong detached itself suddenly from the darkness of the island, spitting forth the reverberate sound of a racing motorboat. Two white streamers of cleft water rolled themselves out behind it and almost immediately the boat was beside him, drowning out the hot tinkle of the piano in the drone of its spray. Dexter raising himself on his arms was aware of a figure standing at the wheel, of two dark eyes regarding him over the lengthening space of water—then the boat had gone by and was sweeping in an immense and purposeless circle of spray round and round in the middle of the lake. With equal eccentricity one of the circles flattened out and headed back toward the raft.

"Who's that?" she called, shutting off her motor. She was so near now that Dexter could see her bathing suit, which consisted apparently of pink rompers.

The nose of the boat bumped the raft, and as the latter tilted rakishly he was precipitated toward her. With different degrees of interest they recognized each other.

"Aren't you one of those men we played through this afternoon?" she demanded.

He was.

"Well, do you know how to drive a motorboat? Because if you do I wish you'd drive this one so I can ride on the surfboard behind. My name is Judy Jones"—she favored him with an absurd smirk—rather, what tried to be a smirk, for, twist her mouth as she might, it was not grotesque, it was merely beautiful—"and I live in a house over there on the island, and in that house there is a man waiting for me. When he drove up at the door I drove out of the dock because he says I'm his ideal."

There was a fish jumping and a star shining and the lights around the lake were gleaming. Dexter sat beside Judy Jones and she explained how her boat was driven. Then she was in the water, swimming to the floating surfboard with a sinuous crawl. Watching her was without effort to the eye, watching a branch waving or a sea gull flying. Her arms, burned to butternut, moved sinuously among the dull platinum ripples, elbow appearing first, casting the forearm back with a cadence of falling water, then reaching out and down, stabbing a path ahead.

They moved out into the lake: turning, Dexter saw that she was kneeling on the low rear of the now uptilted surfboard.

"Go faster," she called, "fast as it'll go."

Obediently he jammed the lever forward and the white spray mounted at the bow. When he looked around again the girl was standing up on the rushing board, her arms spread wide, her eyes lifted toward the moon.

"It's awful cold," she shouted. "What's your name?"

He told her.

"Well, why don't you come to dinner tomorrow night?"

His heart turned over like the flywheel of the boat, and, for the second time, her casual whim gave a new direction to his life.

III

Next evening while he waited for her to come downstairs, Dexter peopled the soft deep summer room and the sun porch that opened from it with the men who had already loved Judy Jones. He knew the sort of men they were—the men who when he first went to college had entered from the great prep schools with graceful clothes and the deep tan of healthy summers. He had seen that, in one sense, he was better than these men. He was newer and stronger. Yet in acknowledging to himself that he wished his children to be like them he was admitting that he was but the rough, strong stuff from which they eternally sprang.

When the time had come for him to wear good clothes, he had known who were the best tailors in America, and the best tailors in America had made him the suit he wore this evening. He had acquired that particular reserve peculiar to his university that set it off from other universities. He recognized the value to him of such a mannerism and he had adopted it; he knew that to be careless in dress and manner required more confidence than to be careful. But carelessness was for his children. His mother's name had been Krimplich. She was a Bohemian of the peasant class and she had talked broken English to the end of her days. Her son must keep to the set patterns.

At a little after seven Judy Jones came downstairs. She wore a blue silk afternoon dress, and he was disappointed at first that she had not put on something more elaborate. This feeling was accentuated when, after a brief greeting, she went to the door of a butler's pantry and pushing it open called: "You can serve dinner, Martha." He had rather expected that a butler would announce dinner, that there would be a cocktail. Then he put these thoughts behind him as they sat down side by side on a lounge and looked at each other.

"Father and mother won't be here," she said thoughtfully.

He remembered the last time he had seen her father, and he was glad the parents were not to be here tonight—they might wonder who he was. He had been born in Keeble, a Minnesota village fifty miles farther north, and he always gave Keeble as his home instead of Black Bear Village. Country towns were well enough to come from if they weren't inconveniently in sight and used as footstools by fashionable lakes.

They talked of his university, which she had visited frequently during the past two years, and of the nearby city which supplied Sherry Island with its patrons, and whither Dexter would return next day to his prospering laundries.

During dinner she slipped into a moody depression which gave Dexter a feeling of uneasiness. Whatever petulance she uttered in her throaty voice worried him. Whatever she smiled at—at him, at a chicken liver, at nothing—it disturbed him that her smile could have no root in mirth, or even in amusement. When the scarlet corners of her lips curved down, it was less a smile than an invitation to a kiss.

Then, after dinner, she led him out on the dark sun porch and deliberately changed the atmosphere.

"Do you mind if I weep a little?" she said.

"I'm afraid I'm boring you," he responded quickly.

"You're not. I like you. But I've just had a terrible afternoon. There was a man I cared about, and this afternoon he told me out of a clear sky that he was poor as a churchmouse. He'd never even hinted it before. Does this sound horribly mundane?"

"Perhaps he was afraid to tell you."

"Suppose he was," she answered. "He didn't start right. You see, if I'd thought of him as poor—well, I've been mad about loads of poor men, and fully intended to marry them all. But in this case, I hadn't thought of him that way, and my interest in him wasn't strong enough to survive the shock. As if a girl calmly informed her fiancée that she was a widow. He might not object to widows, but—

"Let's start right," she interrupted herself suddenly. "Who are you, anyhow?"

For a moment Dexter hesitated. Then: "I'm nobody," he announced. "My career is largely a matter of futures."

"Are you poor?"

"No," he said frankly. "I'm probably making more money than any man my age in the Northwest. I know that's an obnoxious remark, but you advised me to start right."

There was a pause. Then she smiled and the corners of her mouth drooped and an almost imperceptible sway brought her closer to him, looking up into his eyes. A lump rose in Dexter's throat, and he waited breathless for the experiment, facing the unpredictable compound that would form mysteriously from the elements of their lips. Then he saw—she communicated her excitement to him, lavishly, deeply, with kisses that

were not a promise but a fulfilment. They aroused in him not hunger demanding renewal but surfeit that would demand more surfeit . . . kisses that were like charity creating want by holding back nothing at all.

It did not take him many hours to decide that he had wanted Judy Jones ever since he was a proud, desirous little boy.

IV

It began like that—and continued, with varying shades of intensity on such a note right up to the denouement. Dexter surrendered a part of himself to the most direct and unprincipled personality with which he had ever come in contact. Whatever Judy wanted, she went after with the full pressure of her charm. There was no divergence of method, no jockeying for position or premeditation of effects—there was a very little mental side to any of her affairs. She simply made men conscious to the highest degree of her physical loveliness. Dexter had no desire to change her. Her deficiencies were knit up with a passionate energy that transcended and justified them.

When, as Judy's head lay against his shoulder that first night, she whispered, "I don't know what's the matter with me. Last night I thought I was in love with a man and tonight I think I'm in love with you—" It seemed to him a beautiful and romantic thing to say. It was the exquisite excitability that for the moment he controlled and owned. But a week later he was compelled to view this same quality in a different light. She took him in her roadster to a picnic supper, and after supper she disappeared, likewise in her roadster, with another man. Dexter became enormously upset and was scarcely able to be decently civil to the other people present. When she assured him that she had not kissed the other man, he knew she was lying—yet he was glad that she had taken the trouble to lie to him.

He was, as he found before the summer ended, one of a varying dozen who circulated about her. Each of them had at one time been favored above all others—about half of them still basked in the solace of occasional sentimental revivals. Whenever one showed signs of dropping out through long neglect, she granted him a brief honeyed hour, which encouraged him to tag along for a year or so longer. Judy made these forays upon the helpless and defeated without malice, indeed half unconscious that there was anything mischievous in what she did.

When a new man came to town every one dropped out—dates were automatically canceled.

The helpless part of trying to do anything about it was that she did it all herself. She was not a girl who could be "won" in the kinetic sense—she was proof against cleverness, she was proof against charm: if any of these assailed her too strongly she would immediately resolve the affair to a physical basis, and under the magic of her physical splendor the strong as well as the brilliant played her game and not their own. She was entertained only by the gratification of her desires and by the direct exercise of her own charm. Perhaps from so much youthful love, so many youthful lovers, she had come, in self-defense, to nourish herself wholly from within.

Succeeding Dexter's first exhilaration came restlessness and dissatisfaction. The helpless ecstasy of losing himself in her was opiate rather than tonic. It was fortunate for his work during the winter that those moments of ecstasy came infrequently. Early in their acquaintance it had seemed for a while that there was a deep and spontaneous mutual attraction—that first August, for example—three days of long evenings on her dusky veranda, of strange wan kisses through the late afternoon, in shadowy alcoves or behind the protecting trellises of the garden arbors, of mornings when she was fresh as a dream and almost shy at meeting him in the clarity of the rising day. There was all the ecstasy of an engagement about it, sharpened by his realization that there was no engagement. It was during those three days that, for the first time, he had asked her to marry him. She said, "Maybe someday." She said, "Kiss me." She said, "I'd like to marry you." She said, "I love you"—she said—nothing.

The three days were interrupted by the arrival of a New York man who visited at her house for half September. To Dexter's agony rumor engaged them. The man was the son of the president of a great trust company. But at the end of a month it was reported that Judy was yawning. At a dance one night she sat all evening in a motorboat with a local beau, while the New Yorker searched the club for her frantically. She told the local beau that she was bored with her visitor, and two days later he left. She was seen with him at the station, and it was reported that he looked very mournful indeed.

On this note the summer ended. Dexter was twenty-four, and he found himself increasingly in a position to do as he wished. He joined two clubs in the city and lived at one of them. Though he was by no means an integral part of the stag lines at these clubs, he managed to be on hand at dances where Judy Jones was likely to appear. He could have gone out socially as much as he liked—he was an eligible young man, now, and popular with downtown fathers. His confessed devotion to Judy Jones had rather solidified his position. But he had no social aspirations and rather despised the dancing men who were always on tap for the Thursday or Saturday parties and who filled in at dinners with the younger married set. Already he was playing with the idea of going East to New York. He wanted to take Judy Jones with him. No disillusion as to the world in which she had grown up could cure his illusion as to her desirability.

Remember that—for only in the light of it can what he did for her be understood.

Eighteen months after he first met Judy Jones he became engaged to another girl. Her name was Irene Scheerer, and her father was one of the men who had always believed in Dexter. Irene was light-haired and sweet and honorable, and a little stout, and she had two suitors whom she pleasantly relinquished when Dexter formally asked her to marry him.

Summer, fall, winter, spring, another summer, another fall—so much he had given of his active life to the incorrigible lips of Judy Jones. She had treated him with interest, with encouragement, with malice, with indifference, with contempt. She had inflicted on him the innumerable little slights and indignities possible in such a case—as if in revenge for having ever cared for him at all. She had beckoned him and yawned at him and beckoned him again and he had responded often with bitterness and narrowed eyes. She had brought him ecstatic happiness and intolerable agony of spirit. She had caused him untold inconvenience and not a little trouble. She had insulted him, and she had ridden over him, and she had played his interest in her against his interest in his work—for fun. She had done everything to him except to criticize him—this she had not done—it seemed to him only because it might have sullied the utter indifference she manifested and sincerely felt toward him.

When autumn had come and gone again it occurred to him that he could not have Judy Jones. He had to beat this into his mind but he convinced himself at last. He lay awake at night for a while and argued it over. He told himself the trouble and the pain she had caused him, he enumerated her glaring deficiencies as a wife. Then he said to himself that he loved her, and after a while he fell asleep. For a week, lest he imagined her husky voice over the telephone or her eyes opposite him at lunch, he worked hard and late, and at night he went to his office and plotted out his years.

At the end of a week he went to a dance and cut in on her once. For almost the first time since they had met he did not ask her to sit out with him or tell her that she was lovely. It hurt him that she did not miss these things—that was all. He was not jealous when he saw that there was a new man tonight. He had been hardened against jealousy long before.

He stayed late at the dance. He sat for an hour with Irene Scheerer and talked about books and about music. He knew very little about either. But he was beginning to be master of his own time now, and he had a rather priggish notion that he—the young and already fabulously successful Dexter Green—should know more about such things.

That was in October, when he was twenty-five. In January, Dexter and Irene became engaged. It was to be announced in June, and they were to be married three months later.

The Minnesota winter prolonged itself interminably, and it was almost May when the winds came soft and the snow ran down into Black Bear Lake at last. For the first time in over a year Dexter was enjoying a certain tranquillity of spirit. Judy Jones had been in Florida, and afterward in Hot Springs, and somewhere she had been engaged, and somewhere she had broken it off. At first, when Dexter had definitely given her up, it had made him sad that people still linked them together and asked for news of her, but when he began to be placed at dinner next to Irene Scheerer people didn't ask him about her any more—they told him about her. He ceased to be an authority on her.

May at last. Dexter walked the streets at night when the darkness was damp as rain, wondering that so soon, with so little done, so much of ecstasy had gone from him. May one year back had been marked by Judy's poignant, unforgivable, yet forgiven turbulence—it had been one of those rare times when he fancied she had grown to care for him. That old penny's worth of happiness he had spent for this bushel of content. He knew that Irene would be no more than a curtain spread behind him, a hand moving among gleaming teacups, a voice calling to children . . . fire and loveliness were gone, the magic of nights and the wonder of the varying hours and seasons . . . slender lips, down-turning, dropping to his lips and bearing him up into a heaven of eyes. . . . The thing was deep in him. He was too strong and alive for it to die lightly.

In the middle of May when the weather balanced for a few days on the thin bridge that led to deep summer he turned in one night at Irene's house. Their engagement was to be announced in a week now—no one would be surprised at it. And tonight they would sit together on the lounge at the University Club and look on for an hour at the dancers. It gave him a sense of solidity to go with her—she was so sturdily popular, so intensely "great."

He mounted the steps of the brownstone house and stepped inside.

"Irene," he called.

Mrs. Scheerer came out of the living room to meet him.

"Dexter," she said. "Irene's gone upstairs with a splitting headache. She wanted to go with you, but I made her go to bed."

"Nothing serious, I—"

"Oh, no. She's going to play golf with you in the morning. You can spare her for just one night, can't you, Dexter?"

Her smile was kind. She and Dexter liked each other. In the living room he talked for a moment before he said good night.

Returning to the University Club, where he had rooms, he stood in the doorway for a moment and watched the dancers. He leaned against the door post, nodded at a man or two—yawned.

"Hello, darling."

The familiar voice at his elbow startled him. Judy Jones had left a man and crossed the room to him—Judy Jones, a slender enameled doll in cloth of gold: gold in a band at her head, gold in two slipper points at her dress's hem. The fragile glow of her face seemed to blossom as she smiled, at him. A breeze of warmth and light blew through the room.

His hands in the pockets of his dinner jacket tightened spasmodically. He was filled with a sudden excitement.

"When did you get back?" he asked casually.

"Come here and I'll tell you about it."

She turned and he followed her. She had been away—he could have wept at the wonder of her return. She had passed through enchanted streets, doing things that were like provocative music. All mysterious happenings, all fresh and quickening hopes, had gone away with her, come back with her now.

She turned in the doorway.

"Have you a car here? If you haven't, I have."

"I have a coupé."

In then, with a rustle of golden cloth. He slammed the door. Into so many cars she had stepped—like this—like that—her back against the leather, so—her elbow resting on the door—waiting. She would have been soiled long since had there been anything to soil her—except herself—but this was her own self outpouring.

With an effort he forced himself to start the car and back into the street. This was nothing, he must remember. She had done this before, and he had put her behind him, as he would have crossed a bad account from his books.

He drove slowly downtown and, affecting abstraction, traversed the deserted streets of the business section, peopled here and there where a movie was giving out its crowd or where consumptive or pugilistic youth lounged in front of pool halls. The clink of glasses and the slap of hands on the bars issued from saloons, cloisters of glazed glass and dirty yellow light.

She was watching him closely and the silence was embarrassing, yet in this crisis he could find no casual word with which to profane the hour. At a convenient turning he began to zigzag back toward the University Club.

"Have you missed me?" she asked suddenly.

"Everybody missed you."

He wondered if she knew of Irene Scheerer. She had been back only a day—her absence had been almost contemporaneous with his engagement.

"What a remark!" Judy laughed sadly—without sadness. She looked at him searchingly. He became absorbed in the dashboard.

"You're handsomer than you used to be," she said thoughtfully. "Dexter, you have the most rememberable eyes."

He could have laughed at this, but he did not laugh. It was the sort of thing that was said to sophomores. Yet it stabbed at him.

"I'm awfully tired of everything, darling." She called everyone darling, endowing the endearment with careless, individual camaraderie. "I wish you'd marry me."

The directness of this confused him. He should have told her now that he was going to marry another girl, but he could not tell her. He could as easily have sworn that he had never loved her.

"I think we'd get along," she continued on the same note, "unless probably you've forgotten me and fallen in love with another girl."

Her confidence was obviously enormous. She had said, in effect, that she found such a thing impossible to believe, that if it were true he had merely committed a childish indiscretion—and probably to show off. She would forgive him, because it was not a matter of any moment but rather something to be brushed aside lightly.

"Of course you could never love anybody but me," she continued. "I like the way you love me. Oh, Dexter, have you forgotten last year?"

"No, I haven't forgotten."

"Neither have I!"

Was she sincerely moved—or was she carried along by the wave of her own acting?

"I wish we could be like that again," she said, and he forced himself to answer:

"I don't think we can."

"I suppose not. . . . I hear you're giving Irene Scheerer a violent rush."

There was not the faintest emphasis on the name, yet Dexter was suddenly ashamed.

"Oh, take me home," cried Judy suddenly: "I don't want to go back to that idiotic dance—with those children."

Then, as he turned up the street that led to the residence district, Judy began to cry quietly to herself. He had never seen her cry before.

The dark street lightened, the dwellings of the rich loomed up around them, he stopped his coupé in front of the great white bulk of the Mortimer Joneses' house, somnolent, gorgeous, drenched with the splendor of the damp moonlight. Its solidity startled him. The strong walls, the steel of the girders, the breadth and beam and pomp of it were there only to bring out the contrast with the young beauty beside him. It was sturdy to accentuate her slightness—as if to show what a breeze could be generated by a butterfly's wing.

He sat perfectly quiet, his nerves in wild clamor, afraid that if he moved he would find her irresistibly in his arms. Two tears had rolled down her wet face and trembled on her upper lip.

"I'm more beautiful than anybody else," she said brokenly. "Why can't I be happy?" Her moist eyes tore at his stability—her mouth turned slowly downward with an exquisite sadness: "I'd like to marry you if you'll have me, Dexter. I suppose you think I'm not worth having, but I'll be so beautiful for you, Dexter."

A million phrases of anger, pride, passion, hatred, tenderness fought on his lips. Then a perfect wave of emotion washed over him, carrying off with it a sediment of wisdom, of convention, of doubt, of honor. This was his girl who was speaking, his own, his beautiful, his pride.

"Won't you come in?" He heard her draw in her breath sharply.

Waiting.

"All right," his voice was trembling. "I'll come in."

V

It was strange that neither when it was over nor a long time afterward did he regret that night. Looking at it from the perspective of ten years, the fact that Judy's flare for him endured just one month seemed of little importance. Nor did it matter that by his yielding he subjected himself to a deeper agony in the end and gave serious hurt to Irene Scheerer and to

Irene's parents, who had befriended him. There was nothing sufficiently pictorial about Irene's grief to stamp itself on his mind.

Dexter was at bottom hard-minded. The attitude of the city on his action was of no importance to him, not because he was going to leave the city but because any outside attitude on the situation seemed superficial. He was completely indifferent to popular opinion. Nor, when he had seen that it was no use, that he did not possess in himself the power to move fundamentally or to hold Judy Jones, did he bear any malice toward her. He loved her, and he would love her until the day he was too old for loving but he could not have her. So he tasted the deep pain that is reserved only for the strong, just as he had tasted for a little while the deep happiness.

Even the ultimate falsity of the grounds upon which Judy terminated the engagement that she did not want to "take him away" from Irene— Judy who had wanted nothing else—did not revolt him. He was beyond any revulsion or any amusement.

He went East in February with the intention of selling out his laundries and settling in New York—but the war came to America in March and changed his plans. He returned to the West, handed over the management of the business to his partner, and went into the first officers' training camp in late April. He was one of those young thousands who greeted the war with a certain amount of relief, welcoming the liberation from webs of tangled emotion.

VI

This story is not his biography, remember, although things creep into it which have nothing to do with those dreams he had when he was young. We are almost done with them and with him now. There is only one more incident to be related here, and it happens seven years farther on.

It took place in New York, where he had done well—so well that there were no barriers too high for him. He was thirty-two years old, and, except for one flying trip immediately after the war, he had not been West

in seven years. A man named Devlin from Detroit came into his office to see him in a business way, and then and there this incident occurred, and closed out, so to speak, this particular side of his life.

"So you're from the Middle West," said the man Devlin with careless curiosity. "That's funny—I thought men like you were probably born and

raised on Wall Street. You know—wife of one of my best friends in Detroit came from your city. I was an usher at the wedding."

Dexter waited with no apprehension of what was coming.

"Judy Simms," said Devlin with no particular interest: "Judy Jones she was once."

"Yes, I knew her." A dull impatience spread over him. He had heard, of course, that she was married—perhaps deliberately he had heard no more.

"Awfully nice girl," brooded Devlin meaninglessly, "I'm sort of sorry for her."

"Why?" Something in Dexter was alert, receptive, at once.

"Oh, Lud Simms has gone to pieces in a way. I don't mean he ill-uses her, but he drinks and runs around—"

"Doesn't she run around?"

"No. Stays at home with her kids."

"Oh."

"She's a little too old for him," said Devlin.

"Too old!" cried Dexter. "Why, man, she's only twenty-seven."

He was possessed with a wild notion of rushing out into the streets and taking a train to Detroit. He rose to his feet spasmodically.

"I guess you're busy," Devlin apologized quickly. "I didn't realize—"

"No, I'm not busy," said Dexter, steadying his voice. "I'm not busy at all. Not busy at all. Did you say she was—twenty-seven? No, I said she was twenty-seven."

"Yes, you did," agreed Devlin dryly.

"Go on, then. Go on."

"What do you mean?"

"About Judy Jones."

Devlin looked at him helplessly.

"Well, that's—I told you all there is to it. He treats her like the devil. Oh, they're not going to get divorced or anything. When he's particularly outrageous she forgives him. In fact, I'm inclined to think she loves him. She was a pretty girl when she first came to Detroit."

A pretty girl! The phrase struck Dexter as ludicrous.

"Isn't she—a pretty girl, any more?"

"Oh, she's all right."

"Look here," said Dexter, sitting down suddenly. "I don't understand. You say she was a 'pretty girl' and now you say she's 'all right.' I don't understand what you mean—Judy Jones wasn't a pretty girl, at all. She was a great beauty. Why, I knew her. I knew her. She was—"

Devlin laughed pleasantly.

"I'm not trying to start a row," he said. "I think Judy's a nice girl and I like her. I can't understand how a man like Lud Simms could fall madly in love with her, but he did." Then he added: "Most of the women like her."

Dexter looked closely at Devlin, thinking wildly that there must be a reason for this, some insensitivity in the man or some private malice.

"Lots of women fade just like *that*," Devlin snapped his fingers. "You must have seen it happen. Perhaps I've forgotten how pretty she was at her wedding. I've seen her so much since then, you see. She has nice eyes."

A sort of dullness settled down upon Dexter. For the first time in his life he felt like getting very drunk. He knew that he was laughing loudly at something Devlin had said, but he did not know what it was or why it was funny. When, in a few minutes, Devlin went he lay down on his lounge and looked out the window at the New York skyline into which the sun was sinking in dull lovely shades of pink and gold.

He had thought that having nothing else to lose he was invulnerable at last—but he knew that he had just lost something more, as surely as if he had married Judy Jones and seen her fade away before his eyes.

The dream was gone. Something had been taken from him. In a sort of panic he pushed the palms of his hands into his eyes and tried to bring up a picture of the waters lapping on Sherry Island and the moonlit veranda, and gingham on the golf links and the dry sun and the gold color of her neck's soft down. And her mouth damp to his kisses and her eyes plaintive with melancholy and her freshness like new fine linen in the morning. Why, these things were no longer in the world! They had existed and they existed no longer.

For the first time in years the tears were streaming down his face. But they were for himself now. He did not care about mouth and eyes and moving hands. He wanted to care, and he could not care. For he had gone away and he could never go back any more. The gates were closed, the sun was gone down, and there was no beauty but the gray beauty of steel that withstands all time. Even the grief he could have borne was left behind in the country of illusion, of youth, of the richness of life, where his winter dreams had flourished.

"Long ago," he said, "long ago, there was something in me, but now that thing is gone. Now that thing is gone, that thing is gone. I cannot cry I cannot care. That thing will come back no more."

ABOUT THE EDITOR

J eff Silverman, a former columnist for *The Los Angeles Herald Examiner*, has written for *The New York Times*, *The Los Angeles Times*, *Sports Illustrated*, *Travel & Leisure Golf*, and *Golf World*. The editor of several anthologies, he teaches at Villanova University and lives with his family in Chadds Ford, Pennsylvania.

SOURCES

Excerpt from "Verses on Games" by Rudyard Kipling, 1898.

"The Praise and Origin of Golf" by W. G. Simpson. From *The Art of Golf*, 1887.

"The Mystery of Golf" by Arnold Haultain. From "The Mystery of Golf," 1908.

"The Chicken" by S. F. Outwood. From *The Poetry of Sport* (Badminton Library), 1896.

"Miss Carrington's Professional" by M. Gertrude Cundill. From *Outing Magazine*, 1898.

"An Inland Voyage" by A. A. Milne. From *The Holiday Round*, 1912.

"A Method of Play" by J. H. Taylor. From *Taylor on Golf*, 1902.

"Even Threes" by Owen Johnson. From *The Century Magazine*, 1912.

"Good Resolutions" by Bernard Darwin. From *Tee Shots and Others*, 1911.

"The Humorous Side of Golf" by A. W. Tillinghast. From *Country Club Life*, 1914.

"A Novel Golfing Match" by "A. Niblick." From *Fore's Sporting Sketches*, 1890.

"A One-Ball Match" by Gerald Batchelor. From *Golf Stories*, 1914.

"Dormie One" by Holworthy Hall. From *Dormie One and Other Stories*, 1917.

"Mathematics for Golfers" by Stephen Leacock, 1921.

"The Science of Golf" by Anonymous. From *Mr. Punch's Golf Stories*, 1910.

"Hit the Ball" by Eddie Loos. From *American Golfer*, 1922.

"A Lesson in Golf" by Anonymous. From *Mr. Punch's Golf Stories*, 1910.

"A Mixed Threesome" by P. G. Wodehouse. From "Golf Without Tears," 1919.

"Mr. Dooley on Golf" by Finley Peter Dunne, circa 1910.

"A Caddy's Diary" by Ring Lardner. From *The Saturday Evening Post*, 1922.

"How I Began to Play Golf" by Francis Ouimet. From *The Children's Hour*, 1916.

"Shush!!!" by Ring Lardner. From *American Golfer*, 1921.

"Etiquette and Behaviour" by Horace Hutchinson. From *Golf* (Badminton Library), 1890.

"Golf for Duffers" by H. Rider Haggard, circa 1890.

"Gentlemen, You Can't Go Through!" by Charles E. Van Loan. From *Fore!*, 1919.

"Aberdovey" by Bernard Darwin. From *Tee Shots and Others*, 1911.

"Winter Dreams" by F. Scott Fitzgerald. From *All the Sad Young Men*, 1922.

ACKNOWLEDGEMENTS

S pecial thanks to Dawn Setzer and Gil Hanse, two peerless pals, for letting me pillage their libraries, to the crew at Skyhorse, for making these excursions possible; and, as ever, to Abby Van Pelt, simply for staying the course.